Reward Management
A critical text
Edited by Geoff White and Janet Druker

Working for McDonald's in Europe
The unequal struggle
Tony Royle

Working for McDonald's in Europe

The McDonald's Corporation is the most famous brand and the largest food-service system in the world. It is a phenomenon in its own right, uniquely representing the opportunities and dangers associated with the process of globalisation.

This volume provides a detailed analysis of the extent to which the McDonald's Corporation adapts or imposes its labour relations policies in Europe. It is based on more than 6 years of empirical research and examines the interaction between this global corporation and both national- and European-level systems of industrial relations. The author exposes the conflict that arises in these differing regulatory systems, particularly that between the trade unions and the corporation. He argues that this conflict is an inevitable outcome of the struggle to protect workers' rights in an increasingly internationalised global economy. In the current climate it is a struggle which is unequally blanaced in favour of the ideology of economic liberalism and the interests of the multinational. In this analysis, even in the countries of mainland Europe, which are often seen as the last bastion of collectivism, the multinational corporation is increasingly seen as a threat to workers' statutory and democratic rights.

Key features include:

- an overview of the McDonald's Corporation's history, development and structure;
- an analysis of the corporation's franchising system, work organisation and corporate culture;
- an analysis of the problems of unionisation and establishing collective agreements;
- an examination of the realities of workplace representation and co-determination, including national systems of statutory works councils and union representation rights;
- a chapter dealing specifically with European legislation, in particular the McDonald's European Works Council.

Tony Royle is Senior Lecturer in the Department of Human Resource Management, Nottingham Trent University. He has published widely in the area of labour relations in multinational corporations and his principal interest is in comparative and European industrial relations.

Routledge Studies in Employment Relations
Series editors: Rick Delbridge and Edmund Heery
Cardiff Business School

Aspects of the employment relationship are central to numerous courses at both undergraduate and postgraduate level. Drawing from insights from industrial relations, human resource management and industrial sociology, this series provides an alternative source of research-based materials and texts, reviewing key developments in employment research.

Books published in this series are works of high academic merit, drawn from a wide range of academic studies in the social sciences.

Rethinking Industrial Relations
Mobilization, collectivism and long waves
John Kelly

Social Partnership at Work
Workplace relations in post-unification Germany
Carola M. Frege

Employee Relations in the Public Services
Themes and issues
Edited by Susan Corby and Geoff White

The Insecure Workforce
Edited by Edmund Heery and John Salmon

Public Service Employment Relations in Europe
Transformation, modernization or inertia?
Edited by Stephen Bach, Lorenzo Bordogna, Giuseppe Della Rocca and David Winchester

Human Resource Management in the Hotel Industry
Strategy, innovation and performance
Kim Hoque

Working for McDonald's in Europe

The unequal struggle

Tony Royle

London and New York

First published 2000
by Routledge
11 New Fetter Lane, London EC4P 4EE

Simultaneously published in the USA and Canada
by Routledge
29 West 35th Street, New York, NY 10001

Routledge is an imprint of the Taylor & Francis Group

© 2000 Tony Royle

Typeset in Baskerville by
Prepress Projects Ltd, Perth, Scotland
Printed and bound in Great Britain by
MPG Books Ltd, Bodmin

British Library Cataloguing in Publication Data
A catalogue record for this book is available
from the British Library

Library of Congress Cataloging in Publication Data
A catalog record for this book has been applied for

ISBN 0-415-20786-X (hbk)
ISBN 0-415-20787-8 (pbk)

Contents

Figures and tables

Figures

Tables

1 Liberalism, collectivism and the multinational corporation

> The men who run global corporations are the first in history with the organization, technology, money and ideology to make a credible try at managing the world as an integrated economic unit.
>
> (Barnet and Mueller, 1974, quoted in Clarke, 1996: 26)

> The self-destructive tendency of modern capitalism begins with the large corporation.
>
> (Galbraith, 1992: 53)

This book is concerned with the protection of democratic rights in the workplace and raises a number of important questions about the regulation of multinational corporations in modern society. Multinationals have come in for a great deal of criticism; some of their detractors suggest that they are the means by which exploitative practices are dispersed world-wide (Van der Pijl, 1989; Sklair, 1995). Indeed, Pilger (1998) in his critique of the global capitalist system has described them as the 'shock troops of the imperial powers'. Other commentators have been more sanguine and have suggested that multinationals are subject to the constraints of the global competitive economy (Gray, 1992) and that they are mostly interested in promoting the common good, being a benign source of investment, technology transfer and a means of upgrading labour forces (Dunning, 1993).

The round of negotiations at the World Trade Organisation (WTO) in Seattle at the end of 1999 and the role of the multinational were the focus of a good deal of organised protest from groups concerned about Third World development, environmental and health issues and labour standards. No fewer than 1,200 non-governmental organisations (NGOs) had formed a coalition criticising the activities of multinationals and calling for a halt to the WTO's drive to cut trade tariffs and open up markets. They suggest that the WTO itself is too strongly influenced by the big corporations and that its powerful disputes system, which allows for punishing sanctions if trade rules are broken, undermines international agreements on the environment and affects the sovereignty of countries on issues as diverse as food safety and labour standards (Goldsmith, 1996; Nader and Wallach, 1996; *The Guardian*, 1999).

Clarke (1996) argues that the current free trade regimes such as GATT and NAFTA[1] have created global conditions in which multinationals and banks can move their capital, goods and services freely throughout the world, unfettered by the regulations of nation-states. In other words, the constant demands to 'open up' countries for 'competitiveness' and the rhetoric of 'free trade' that the multinationals and the WTO espouse are just euphemisms for 'plunder' (Pilger, 1998). Other commentators are more positive about the role of the WTO, which they suggest is at least a move in the right direction, because it provides a system which can agree on trade rules and can put pressure on the rich countries to open their markets. It could also be argued that freer trade has contributed to the well-being of most economies in the post-war period (Marr, 1999). However, this rather upbeat assessment may be called into question by the experience of several Latin American countries since the dismantling of protectionist import-substituting regimes (Dussel Peters, 1997).

Whether one sees multinationals as a force for good or evil, there seems little doubt that they do have some influence on national governments and institutions such as the WTO and that this influence has been increasing. Over 10 years ago, Dunning (1993) estimated that there were 20,000 multinationals with foreign assets amounting to $1.1 trillion or 8% of gross world product and total assets of over $4 trillion. At that time, they accounted for 25–30% of combined gross domestic product (GDP) in all market economies, 75% of international commodity trade and 80% of international exchanges of technology and managerial skills. Over 5 years ago, UNCTAD (1994) reported that multinationals employed around one-fifth of the world's workers outside the agricultural sector in the industrialised countries. The report also stated that the total number of workers employed by multinationals across the globe was around 70 million, with some 29 million working for foreign subsidiaries. More recently, Gorringe (1999) suggests that the ten largest transnational corporations control assets that represent three times the total income of the world's thirty-eight poorest countries, which have populations amounting to over 1 billion people. The leading 350 multinational corporations employ only a small fraction of the world's population, but they control 40% of global trade. These are staggering statistics, perhaps even more so when one considers that through increased merger activity the corporations are getting even bigger. Indeed, some corporations are so large that they control more assets than do some nation-states. If one compares national economies and corporations in this way, fifty of the world's 100 largest economies are in fact multinational corporations (Gorringe, 1999).

This book focuses on the activities of one very large multinational and deals in simplistic terms with the practical outcomes of an ideological confrontation. One might use the analogy of a boxing match between two powerful opponents trying to win points or a knock-out blow. In the 'blue corner', we have what might be described as 'the new Right', the multinationals and big corporations, a fair swathe of neo-classical economists, right-wing think-tanks and many governments who are mostly interested in making the world economy safer and more efficient for business. Those in the blue corner represent the continuing demand for more 'free trade' and less regulation. In the 'red corner', on the other hand, we have 'the new Left', a large number of NGOs of all sorts, those claiming to represent 'civil society', the trade unions and those European institutions and national governments that still engender some socialist principles.[2] In most mainland European countries, the social market economy still prevails. In these countries, trade unions and employees still enjoy considerable rights supported by national legislation that were by and large carved out during the post-war era.

We examine the 'contest' between one 'heavyweight' multinational, the American McDonald's Corporation, and the trade unions and national systems of industrial relations in over twelve European countries. However, it is questionable whether this is a fair contest or an equal struggle. Despite the increase in the protests by NGOs, those in the 'red corner' arguably have the odds stacked against them. The collapse of Eastern bloc-style socialism gave a great fillip to those supporting the liberal economic agenda, and probably more than at any time in the past multinationals enjoy a favoured position in the world economy. In this context, the 'contest' begins to look more like a bout between a heavyweight and a middleweight, and those in the 'red corner' appear to be on the ropes. There have been some attempts to equalise the struggle in the European Union (EU) through social legislation, but there is a powerful lobby against such efforts. One need look no further than the failed Vredling directive, which proposed to establish European Works Councils on a similar model to that found in Germany. The proposal was quashed by opposition from the European employer's federation Union of Industrial Employers' Confederations of Europe (UNICE) and the UK government (Hall, 1992). Nevertheless, compared with the US-centred trade bloc North American Free Trade Agreement (NAFTA), the EU has an obvious detailed approach and a greater capacity to regulate multinationals, whereas NAFTA arguably has no real desire to regulate at all and as a result has very minimal labour and environmental standards. In our study of the McDonald's Corporation, the early 'rounds' have already been slugged out over the last 30 years since the corporation first entered the European market. We provide an analysis of the points and the issues that appear to have been 'won' and 'lost' by the two sides and we attempt to see if one side has the upper hand. Of course, the 'contest' between these contenders is not by any means over and, as we shall argue in the following chapters, it is a contest which has considerable implications for employment rights, both now and in the future. In particular, this is because those in the 'blue corner' are bent on removing the state intervention that those in the 'red corner' argue is essential if workers interests are to be fully protected. Indeed, those in the 'red corner' are likely to argue for additional national or supranational intervention to take account of the new scenarios created by the growing power of multinationals and the increasing internationalisation of trade; something to which those in the 'blue corner' are fundamentally opposed. The next section examines the principal ideas that have driven and continue to drive the two contenders, placing them on 'opposite sides of the ring': for those in the 'red corner' the concept of 'collectivism', and for those in the 'blue corner' the concept of 'liberalism'.

In the ring: liberalism versus collectivism

The concept of collectivism is based on the conviction that society as a whole may have rights and interests. Collectivism ran contrary to the individualism which had been strongly emphasised after the Renaissance and the Protestant Reformation (Davies, 1997), but it was explicit in Rousseau's [1712–78] essay the 'Social Contract'. In responding to Hobbes's [1588–1679] concept of the autocratic dictator in 'Leviathan', Rousseau argued that man can be forced to be free within the law through the 'general will', an abstract expression of what is best for all, i.e. liberty and equality. Collectivism is also implicit in the idea of the modern state, which establishes certain common goals or purposes that a society governed and guided by the state should strive to achieve. Cockett (1995) suggests that before anyone had formulated a coherent intellectual case for collectivism in Britain, the British government had started to intervene in such matters as industrial relations and national education. For example, in the nineteenth century the British State was gradually extended through the introduction of legislation on matters such as factory and public health reforms that were intended to promote 'social justice'. These early changes in society may have been based on pragmatism rather than ideology. However, the Fabian Society, established in 1884 by Beatrice and Sidney Webb and George Bernard Shaw, was the first British organisation to promote successfully a coherent intellectual justification for the extension of the State. One way or another, it sought to replace the scramble for private gain with the conscious pursuit of 'collective welfare'. Collectivism is also associated with 'socialism', initially a philosophical and ethical impulse taking its name from the idea of fellowship or the modern idiom of 'solidarity'. According to Davies (1997), nineteenth-century socialism is generally considered to have drawn its strength from four separate sources: Christian socialism, the trade union movement, the co-operative movement and the 'utopian' socialist theorists such as Fourrier and Saint-Simon. It was Karl Marx who first elaborated socialism as a comprehensive economic theory. Giddens (1998) suggests that socialism seeks to confront the limitations of capitalism to humanise it or to overthrow it altogether. Although the communist interpretation of socialism and collectivism may appear to be dead, in the West it lives on in a more moderate form: social democracy. However, where collectivism and socialism encourage the state as arbiter and prime mover of compassionate measures, liberalism opposes it.

Davies (1997) suggests that liberalism developed along two parallel tracks, the political and the economic. Much of political liberalism's early history was indistinguishable from the growth of limited government. Its first lasting success may have been the American Revolution, which focused on the concept of government by consent. The intellectual roots of political liberalism can be traced back to John Locke and his two treatises on government published in 1689 and 1690. Much of the emphasis was placed on the ownership of property, which was seen as the principal source of responsible judgement and solid citizenship. Although political liberals laid the foundations for modern democracy, *they were not prepared to envisage universal suffrage or egalitarianism*. Economic liberalism focused on free trade and the associated doctrine of *laissez-faire*, which opposed the habit of governments to regulate economic life. It stressed the right of (White) men of property to engage in commercial and industrial activities without undue restraint and railed against all forms of collectivist organisation, *especially trade unions*. Economic liberalism is not, of course, necessarily tied to its political counterpart – whereas some states made advances in liberalising their economies through the removal of tariffs, they may have been slow to liberalise their polities.[3]

Hayek and his work *The Road to Serfdom* (1944) was probably the most influential of modern exponents of economic liberalism. He is largely credited as a key figure in reviving its fortunes and its eventual triumph over collectivism in the UK from the mid-1970s onwards. Indeed, Cockett (1995) argues that it was the determined work of several individuals such as Hayek and various 'think-tanks' and other organisations which they established[4] that brought about an ideological counter-revolution in political and economic thinking. In fact, he suggests that the history of the last two centuries has been characterised by cycles of liberalism and collectivism. The first cycle saw the victory of liberalism around 1760, Davies (1997) suggests that liberalism shattered the protectionist philosophy of mercantilism that had reigned supreme in economic thought for some 200 years before then. Economic liberalism then dominated in various forms until 1880. The second cycle covers the period from 1880 to the mid-1970s. Cockett (1995) suggests that the first part of this period, between 1880 and 1930, was when the ideological battle against liberalism was fought and won. The latter period from the 1940s to the mid-1970s was when collectivism based on Fabianism and Keynesianism became the ruling orthodoxy. The third cycle is said to have begun in the 1930s and is continuing, with the period from the 1930s to the 1970s being the period when the battle for the return of liberalism was fought and won.

This intellectual battle is sometimes referred to as the 'economic calculation' debate, and it was arguably one of the most crucial intellectual debates of the twentieth century. From the 1920s onwards, the 'Keynesians', as they became known, began to argue for a large programme of economic works, and by implication planning, to solve the country's economic problems. Keynes had already outlined his approach in 1924 in a short piece entitled *The End of Laissez-Faire*, in which he proposed a mixed economy. Keynes suggested that it was time to move out of the nineteenth-century *'laissez-*

faire' state and into an era of liberal socialism in which economic and social justice would be promoted. At the same time, Keynes argued that it would be possible to respect and protect the individual's mind and expression, faith, enterprise and property. On the other hand, the economic liberals headed by Lionel Robbins argued for the opposite. They wanted measures to increase the level of workers' output and measures to reduce the level of wages and the removal of other 'rigidities', such as unemployment insurance, restrictive work practices and trade union influence.

What really decided the success of the collectivist ideal were the political deliberations that surrounded the depression of the 1920s and 1930s. By the time of the general strike in 1926, the British government was well aware that it could not afford to offend the trade unions by removing restrictive practices and reducing wages. Indeed, British politicians were concerned that the whole British government system and capitalist economy might collapse if they pursued this policy in a depressed industry. Keynes saw this as a problem of insufficient demand that could be remedied by expertise and contended that the capitalist system could survive if the government intervened to protect workers wages. When the economists and politicians accepted Keynes's alternative, i.e. it was better to have mild inflation than class war, then organised labour had effectively won the argument. Cockett (1995: 45) states:

> Keynes was, in fact, running up the white flag on behalf of capitalism and negotiating an honourable withdrawal. It was a very English revolution – virtually unnoticed at the time, and presided over by an old Etonian.[5]

Keynes was swimming with the tide of collectivism; his 'middle-way' of liberal socialism offered politicians a way to avoid the two extremes of communist-style planning and *laissez-faire* individualism and also provided the basis for the Butskellite post-war consensus. By the late 1930s, the liberal economic agenda was at a low ebb. Hubert Henderson, a staunch critic of Keynes, complained in 1936 about how exasperated he was

> ...by the assumption that prevails in certain circles that those who do not accept its [Keynesian] general doctrines are to be regarded as intellectually inferior beings.

(Cockett, 1995: 49)

As we have already suggested, the fortunes of the economic liberals were slowly but surely revived by the work of Hayek and other like-minded individuals and by the work of various think-tanks over a period of over 30 years. By the late 1970s, the situation had turned full circle. Reagan, in the USA, and Thatcher, in the UK, had returned to the liberal economic agenda with a vengeance. Just as it had seemed unthinkable between the 1930s and the 1960s to question the collectivist agenda, by the early 1980s the liberal economic agenda had become dominant and few dared to criticise it. At the same time, there was the emergence of the World Bank and the International Monetary Fund and their influence on domestic policy formulation, particularly in less developed countries. Indeed, Galbraith (1992: 82) argues that in what he terms the 'age of contentment' the liberal economic agenda was strong. Any case made against it must be strongly proved because government regulation is seen as unnecessary and normally damaging to the beneficent processes of nature. Indeed, Galbraith (1992: 82) suggests that the case for the liberal economic agenda

> ... rests not on empirical demonstration, but ... on deeper theological grounds. As you must have faith in God you must have faith in the system; to some extent the two are identical.

In similar terms, Fukuyama's (1992) *The End of History* triumphantly proclaims the victory of economic liberalism and the victory of capitalism over socialism. However, some years earlier, Daniel Bell (1962), in his work *The End of Ideology*, sang the praises of collectivism and suggested that the dominant force behind 'globalisation' was the collectivist agenda and the economic policies of John Maynard Keynes. Both authors assumed that the dominant ideologies of their age were the final words in world development. The notion of revolution and counter-revolution in economic thinking also has Hegelian undertones, i.e. Hegel's principle of dialectical progress, consisting of evolutionary conflict of ideas (thesis and antithesis) and resulting in an eventual synthesis. Nevertheless, although economic liberalism has become more predominant in the UK, Australia, Latin America, the USA, parts of Asia and some other countries, it has made less of an impact on the countries of mainland Europe, where more collectivist principles are still evident and where the focus of this book will take us. However, before we examine the various national systems of labour regulation in Europe in more detail, we need to review the attempts that have so far been made at a supranational level to regulate the activities of multinationals in terms of employment rights.

Regulating employment rights in multinationals

Historically, the regulation of employment rights has largely been seen as a matter for regulation by nation-states, but it has become increasingly clear that the growth and significance of the multinationals only highlights the inability of nation-states to deal with them. There are already a plethora of examples in which multinationals have successfully played off one nation-state against another with the threat of reducing employment or the promise of new investment to get what they want.

If nation-states cannot cope with multinationals then, argue those in the 'red corner', some other mechanism at another level has to be found to regulate their activities. However, as we shall see in the following sections, those in the 'blue corner' have largely dominated the agenda in this area. Where 'regulation' does exist, it is predominantly through their preferred liberal economic sphere: voluntary codes of conduct. Ironically, even Adam Smith, the darling of those in the 'blue corner' who first described free trade and the 'invisible hand' of the free-market economy, admitted that business had to be 'watched'. In his book *An Inquiry into the Nature and Causes of the Wealth of Nations*, written in 1776, he states that, left to themselves, business people are natural monopolists, who will want to dominate their markets and sources of supply, eliminate the competition and reduce labour costs towards zero. Indeed, he was particularly critical of joint-stock companies or what we now think of as modern corporations. The protagonists for free market economics may well find the regulation of corporate activities undesirable. However, legislation designed to provide free collective bargaining, minimum wages and other labour standards is arguably essential in halting the exploitation of workers and the worst excesses of the market system. As Tony Benn pointed out in a recent commons debate, 'Corporations can move quite easily but people cannot'. There is also another side to the issue of regulation. Although some may argue in Darwin-like terms that regulation only interferes with the efficiency of the market mechanism, it is also suggested that stringent systems of employment rights help to foster more co-operative, more productive and ultimately more efficient organisations (Hutton, 1996). The question that remains is not whether multinationals should be regulated, but to what extent, by what means and at what level.

The International Labour Organisation (ILO), which for many years has been attempting to improve the lot of workers around the globe, has so far only been able to insist that multinationals adopt voluntary codes of conduct. Nearly 30 years ago, Levinson (1972) was arguing that the organisational structures and global mobility of multinationals allowed them to pursue their interests with little regard for labour standards imposed through national regulation. Given the limitations of national and international trade union organisation at that time (Northrup and Rowan, 1979), much reliance was placed upon 'public codes' of conduct, such as OECD[6] guidelines acting directly upon multinationals or indirectly through encouraging national regulation of corporate behaviour via ILO conventions. More recently, the ILO (1998) has put more emphasis on what it calls 'core standards'[7] as part of its *Declaration on Fundamental Principles and Rights at Work and its Follow-up*.

In addition to public codes, there have been a number of attempts to establish 'private codes', including the Sullivan Principles in relation to trade with South Africa under apartheid and the UK's Ethical Trading Initiative. Recently, there has also been substantial growth in corporate codes of conduct in multinationals, such as those at Nike, Reebok, C&A and Levi's. In the USA, all of the Fortune 500 companies now have codes of conduct. However, the reasons for this increasing interest in such codes appear to be much more to do with protecting corporate reputations and attracting customers and better recruits than they are to do with the pay and conditions of workers (Maitland, 1999). Many of the codes developed by businesses that are widely considered to be pioneers in social responsibility (for example Levi's) make no reference to international standards, liveable wages or other ILO instruments. Indeed, Diller (1999) states that Reebok's code contains only a general reference to international human rights standards and that many codes differ from and even contradict international labour principles. For example, whereas some affirm the right to collective bargaining, some (for example Toyota) only allude to respect between labour and management and others (for example Caterpillar and Sara Lee Knit Products) actually favour the elimination of trade union activities. It is no wonder that these codes have been increasingly attracting the largely negative attention of trade unions and NGOs.

Attempts at international regulation of the employment relationship through public codes to encourage a 'race to the top' (i.e. the highest level of standards) have, according to Hepple (1999), two main weaknesses. First, there are no instruments to enforce compliance with even the minimal list of 'core' labour standards let alone 'core plus' standards regulating minimum pay, health and safety at work and employment benefits. Second, the codes specifically exclude interference with national employment laws at a time when 'globalisation' is severely limiting the regulatory influence of national governments. A third possible weakness is that the existence of weak international agencies with responsibility for labour standards, such as the ILO, allows the powerful international economic agencies (i.e. the IMF, World Bank and WTO) to sideline the problems of social regulation.

In fact, it is not very surprising that the ILO has not as yet been able to impose much more than codes of conduct on multinationals. The OECD's own *Labour Standards Index* is tailor-made for countries such as the USA because it is premised on the notion that successful economies have less regulated labour markets. It seeks to measure the strength of the legislation governing five different aspects of labour markets: working time, fixed-term contracts, employment protection, minimum wages and workers' representation rights. It suggests that more legislation means more rigidity and its policy conclusion is simplistic: countries with high levels of workers' rights should change their systems by reducing the rights of the workers to create more jobs (Larsson, 1998).

It can be argued that regulation is more effective in regional organisations such as the EU, with treaty provisions binding on member states and enforceable through supranational institutions (Hepple, 1999). However, this also requires a minimum level of political cohesion, effective institutions for resolving differences and not radically unequal levels of economic development among member countries. The EU can readily point to the availability of legally binding directives in important areas such as discrimination, health and safety, working time and parental leave. For example, in recent years there has been the European Works Council directive providing for information and consultation rights in multinationals and the legally based EU-wide framework agreement processes of the Social Dialogue.[8]

However, there are many inherent weaknesses within EU regional arrangements. First, the development of maximum competition within the single market is not conditional upon the parallel development of employment rights. Second, EU directives are not intended to impose detailed supranational regulation on national systems. Indeed, if one examines the development of some of the legislation at the European level, it is what Streeck (1991) describes as 'menu' driven; in other words, it allows employers to choose from a menu of options to suit themselves. Third, the number of directives arising from the Social Dialogue have been disappointing (Keller and Sörries, 1999). The Social Dialogue is in any case designed to seek compromises over conflicts of interests rather than advancing *social* rights *per se*. Fourth, the legal scope of EU directives, under the treaties, excludes them from the regulation of most core and core plus rights such as freedom of association, access to collective bargaining and the right to strike and minimum pay and benefits. The only places where we will find 'core plus rights' are in national arrangements. However, even within mainland EU nation-states that are well known for their detailed and stringent national legislative systems, there are considerable weaknesses. Indeed, the following chapters examine the extent to which the McDonald's Corporation has been able to take advantage of such weaknesses in important provisions of national legislation.

Clarifying some concepts

It should be noted that our focus on 'liberalism' and 'collectivism' is both an economic and a political analysis. However, we need some words of caution here. We do not want readers to assume that this is a discussion of 'globalisation'. The concepts may be interrelated, but to assume that globalisation was only an economic and political process would be inaccurate. A more in-depth analysis of the concept of globalisation would take into account three spheres: economics, politics and culture. Even a cursory review of the subject would quickly reveal that there are disagreements about when globalisation began, what form it is taking and even whether it is really taking place at all. It is generally accepted that there are three main streams of thought on the globalisation thesis. Most recent interpretations of globalisation have, to varying extents, all been developed on the three classical theorists Durkheim, Marx and Weber. First is the largely functionalist thesis of Kerr *et al.* (1960), which suggests that in a modernising world each society is likely to converge on a single set of basic principles, on the basis of choices rationally made by its members in relation to individual and collective advancement. Second are those who, developing the work of Marx, suggest that globalisation is a process driven not by choice but by the domination of the capitalist mode of production (Wallerstein, 1974; Friedmann, 1990; Sklair, 1995). Third are those who base their argument on a largely Weberian analysis of globalisation and see it as driven by a common mass culture, e.g. Giddens (1990), Robertson (1992) and the 'McDonaldisation' thesis of Ritzer (1993).[9]

It should also be noted that throughout the text we generally use the term 'multinational' not 'transnational'. Dunning (1993: 6) defines a multinational as:

> ... an enterprise that engages in foreign direct investment (FDI) and organises the production of goods or services in more than one country.

However, this definition does not explain the full range or scope of multinational or transnational activities. Hirst and Thompson (1996: 11) distinguish between the two terms multinational corporation and transnational corporation (MNC and TNC). They argue that genuine TNCs are very rare and that most of the large corporations that exist today are multinationals not transnationals:

> The TNC would be genuine footloose capital, without specific national identification and with an internationalised management, and at least potentially willing to locate and relocate anywhere in the globe to obtain either the most secure or highest returns. ...Thus the TNC, unlike the MNC could no longer be controlled by the particular policies of particular national states.

As we shall see in Chapter 2, the McDonald's Corporation does source, produce and market at a global level, as strategy and opportunities dictate. Although McDonald's trades transnationally, it returns its profits to, is effectively policed by and is strongly identified with the USA. It does not therefore meet the criteria to be a 'true' TNC, as defined by Hirst and Thompson (1996). Hirst and Thompson (1996) argue that for a truly globalised economy to exist MNCs would have to be transformed into TNCs, in this context the use of these terms is therefore important.

Research issues and questions

That the fast-food industry is a *global* industry has now been recognised. Dunning (1993) identifies a series of what he sees as true global industries, those that are dominated by large corporations of diverse national origins, producing and marketing in all of the world's largest economies. Dunning places these industries in order of importance. The first seven are manufacturers: chemicals, cars, consumer electronics, tyres, pharmaceuticals, tobacco and soft drinks. The last three are more service orientated. The fast-food industry is placed eighth, followed by financial consultancies and luxury hotels. The hospitality industry, and particularly the fast-food industry, has until now been somewhat overlooked by industrial relations researchers. Until recently, much of the writing on multinationals focused on manufacturing, and scant attention was paid to the service sector. The hospitality industry, in particular, has tended to be seen as something of a 'Cinderella'. This is hard to understand when one considers that multinationals are increasingly extending beyond manufacturing and into the service sector (Ferner, 1994). Jobs in manufacturing industries in the industrialised economies of the West have been in decline for some years. For example, some jobs are being created in new information technology companies, but these jobs are likely to be for relatively small numbers of workers. It is not Intel, Boeing or Microsoft who are the largest creators of jobs in the USA, but companies such as Wal-Mart and McDonald's. It is therefore time for research to focus more on service industries; although there has been a rise in the popularity of research on such areas as call centres, much work remains to be done and especially in a comparative setting. It is hoped that this book will make a small but significant contribution in this regard.

The research for this book was carried out over a period of 6 years. Some of the research was carried out with the consent of the German and UK subsidiaries of the McDonald's Corporation. However, most of the research was carried out without McDonald's direct support but with the support of the International Organisation for the Restaurant, Hotel, Food and Allied Workers Associations and a large number of national trade union organisations. A full account of how the research was conducted, the methods used and the various problems that were encountered are located at the end of the book in the Appendix .

Multinationals are seen as important agents in the transmission of work organisation and employee relations practices across societal borders (Mueller and Purcell, 1992; Sparrow *et al.*, 1994). As we have already suggested, the increasing internationalisation and growth of multinationals raises questions about the ability of labour to maintain or raise labour standards, and, as we have seen, the current orthodoxy of economic liberalism appears to work against the further regulation of multinationals. With this in mind, the book sets out to examine a number of issues.

1   How has McDonald's actually managed its employee relations in a number of different European countries in practice?

2   How and to what extent has McDonald's been able to operate an essentially American and non-union approach to employee relations in the face of well-organised trade unions and highly regulated industrial relations systems of Europe?

3   How effective are the varying national European systems in protecting employment rights? Are some systems more effective than others and what are the reasons for this?

4   What do the findings tell us about the way in which multinational corporations adapt to or operate independently of the societal frameworks in which they operate?

5   What implications do the findings have for the future of European industrial relations and, on a wider level, for the future of the collectivist and liberal economic agendas?

Outline of the book

In Chapter 2, we begin with an analysis of the McDonald's Corporation itself. The chapter examines the corporation's origins and early development and moves on to provide a broad picture of the modern corporation, its expansion abroad and some of the problems associated with maintaining the uniformity of its operations overseas. We then provide an analysis of the European market and organisation structure. Chapter 3 focuses on the issue of franchising. The majority of McDonald's restaurants are operated as franchise operations, and the corporation frequently argues that the whole system is run as a loose confederation of independent operators. However, Chapter 3 asks if this really is the case. It examines this assertion in detail, arguing that to all intents and purposes franchisees are little more than subsidiaries of the corporation. This is an important point because, as we shall see in later chapters, although franchise operations are economically dependent on the multinational their legal 'independence' allows the majority of the corporation's operations to slip through a variety of regulatory loopholes.

In Chapter 4, we examine 'McDonald's at work'. The chapter begins with a brief overview of the typical restaurant hierarchy and the nature of the work in the restaurants. We then move on to examine the employment relationship at McDonald's, examining how management attempts to gain the control and consent of the workforce and the role that is played by 'corporate culture'. How does McDonald's deal with considerable differences in the availability of different kinds of workers in different labour markets? The chapter also provides an analysis of the characteristics of its workforce in its European operations. McDonald's appears to be able to manage the employment relationship across societal borders in a remarkably similar way through exceptionally rigid and detailed rules and procedures, a paternalistic management style and what we have termed 'recruited acquiescence'. This allows McDonald's to take advantage of weak and marginalised sectors of the labour market, enabling the corporation to 'weed out' many of those who may question managerial prerogative or those who are sympathetic to trade union organisation. However, in many European countries, trade unions enjoy considerable rights, allowing them to enter workplaces and, in some cases, entitling them to automatic recognition. Chapter 5 examines how McDonald's has dealt with the issue of the European trade unions over time. The findings suggest that in most cases McDonald's tried to operate without trade unions and collective bargaining arrangements where this is possible and to use its preferred form of employee relations policies.

In a number of European countries, sectoral level collective agreements were automatically imposed on McDonald's by law. However, these agreements vary considerably and have not always had a large impact on the corporation's mode of operation or the pay and conditions of the workers. In other cases where sectoral-level collective arrangements could not be automatically imposed, the unions had to fight with McDonald's over many years before they were able to bring McDonald's to the table. This has often involved damaging conflict and bad publicity for the corporation. It is suggested that the decision to take part in collective bargaining arrangements in some countries does not represent a fundamental shift in the values and norms of the corporation but a pragmatic response to improve its public image. Trade unions are for the most part still finding it extremely difficult to recruit and retain union members. Some trade unions have been more successful than others in recruiting union members, the reason for which appears to be associated with the stringency of supporting national legislation. However, in every case, average union density at McDonald's is lower than the norm for the country as a whole. A second reason for the larger proportions of union members in some countries appears to be associated with the issue of worker representation and statutory forms of worker participation found in some countries.

To provide a better understanding of this complex issue, Chapter 6 begins with an analysis of 'worker participation' and how this concept relates to the kind of 'McParticipation' favoured by the corporation. The chapter then provides an analysis of the way in which the corporation has responded to statutory mechanisms of worker participation, such as works councils and union delegates. In some countries, such as Germany, works councils enjoy considerable protection in law, and on paper at least they present a serious challenge to large corporations. Nevertheless, the analysis suggests that despite often very supportive legislation McDonald's has been extremely adept at finding legal loopholes in most national systems. In Germany, despite considerable ongoing conflict over this issue, McDonald's has been able to minimise the impact of works councils through what we have termed a number of 'avoidance strategies' (Royle, 1998). In other countries, such as Spain, various legislative loopholes have allowed McDonald's to organise works council election processes that effectively remove all trade union involvement, capturing Spanish works councils for a managerially sponsored agenda. Chapter 7 examines the outcomes that the various national legislative systems and the existence or non-existence of collective bargaining arrangements have had on the pay and conditions of McDonald's workers. It also provides a comparison and an analysis of the relative value of McDonald's starting pay to the average wage in fourteen countries and compares the pay of restaurant workers with that earned by top executives. The overall conclusion is that pay and conditions are low in this industry and that national collective bargaining and legislative arrangements have had varying outcomes in terms of overall pay and conditions. In countries where unions are not recognised or where statutory minimum wages are low, such as the USA, the UK and Ireland, workers tend to do worse than elsewhere. In particular, where collective bargaining arrangements are in place, McDonald's workers do much better in terms of the broader conditions of employment such as holidays, special leave and additional rates for unsociable hours. However, the analysis also suggests that in some countries, such as Germany and Austria, the tightness of labour markets and workforce characteristics tend to have a detrimental effect on the level of pay.

Chapter 8 examines the impact of one piece of EU legislation affecting multinationals, i.e. that of the European Works Council (EWC) directive. This analysis highlights the weaknesses inherent in European-level legislation which are based on a 'menu-driven' approach to social policy development. In this case, McDonald's does not appear to meet either the intent or the spirit of the directive. There are a number of reasons for this. First, the questionable way in which the EWC was established. Second, the way in which trade unions appear, in most cases, to have been kept out of the election process for employee representatives altogether. Third, in most cases, the election process for employee representatives has resulted in the election of restaurant or senior salaried managers and not hourly paid or part-time workers, who make up over 90% of the workforce. Fourth, the corporation has placed a 'ban' on employee pre-meetings on the basis of cost and does not allow the admission of outside experts without management authority. Finally, as it stands at present, the directive does not cover the 65% or so of McDonald's European workers who are employed in franchise restaurants at all. Overall, the analysis suggests that the EWC, as it currently operates, cannot represent the interests of the majority of McDonald's European workers and is little more than a talking shop for a management-sponsored agenda.

The concluding chapter provides a brief review of the findings in each chapter and returns to the theme of multinational regulation. We examine the ways in which McDonald's lobbies national governments and the EU and some of the practical effects of this lobbying activity. The discussion then moves on to consider the implications of the findings for the future of European industrial relations and the concept of 'convergence'. Finally, we discuss the broader implications of the findings in terms of the liberal economic agenda and discuss the prospects for the return to a more collectivist and arguably more co-operative approach to the regulation of employment rights in modern society.

2   Welcome to Big Mac

Every day, we serve more than 40 million people in more than 24,500 restaurants in 116 countries around the world. ...Yet, on any given day, that is less than 1 percent of the world's population.
(The McDonald's Corporation's world-wide web site)

The McDonald's Corporation is the largest food service operation in the world in terms of system-wide sales. At the befinning of 2000 it was operating more than 25,000 restaurants in 116 countries. A modest estimate of its current world-wide workforce would be around 1.5 million people, and 10 million people are estimated to have worked for the corporation since it was formed. More than one in ten Americans are reckoned to have got their first job at McDonald's, and it has now taken over from the US Army as having America's largest job-training programme (Vidal, 1997). It is an incredibly successful multinational and is expanding at a breath-taking rate. It plans to open between 2,500 and 3,200 new restaurants every year, the equivalent of one restaurant every 3 hours. If this rate of expansion is achieved, the corporation will have more than doubled in size to well over 50,000 restaurants by 2010. Part of this rapid expansion may also be aided by developments in technology. Two British companies claim the world record for the construction of a fifty-seat McDonald's restaurant in Peterborough, which was completed in 1 day and was open for business 48 hours after the site work was completed (Brown, 1999).

McDonald's shares are said to be the best-performing consumer stock on Wall Street. According to the McDonald's web site, in 1965 when McDonald's went public, 100 shares cost $2,250. On 31 December 1998, some 33 years later, those same shares adjusted for stock splits were worth more than $2.8 billion. The corporation has apparently now replaced General Motors as the bellwether of how America fares (Heskett et al., 1990) and in 1996 it was rated as the world's top brand by the Interbrand Consultancy, knocking Coca-Cola off its perch (The Economist, 1997). McDonald's has become a modern icon; in a survey of American children, Ronald McDonald came second after Santa Claus as the most famous person that they could think of, ahead of the President of the USA (TICL, 1987; Love, 1995). Indeed, the superlatives go on and on – the Big Mac has allegedly become the 'communion wafer' of the consumer society (Vidal, 1997: 37). The corporation is described as being about the globalising of culture and belief systems and as the most important institution of our time. Appleyard (1994: 17) writes:

> Ronald (McDonald) is a revolutionary beside whom Lenin and Robespierre pale into insignificance. He has utterly changed eating, the most elemental of commercialised activities. ...His formula works everywhere, the style and imagery slipping without the slightest modifications into local streets and alien lives.

The only flexibility in this system seems to be a few alterations in the menu, the addition of McSpaghetti noodles in the Philippines, teriyaki burgers in Japan and McLaks salmon rolls in Norway. The success of the corporation is undisputed, but the results of this success have also brought McDonald's a good deal of criticism from all quarters. Ritzer (1993), in his book *The McDonaldization of Society*, suggests that McDonald's represents the paradigm case for an increasingly 'rational' society. Developing Weber's (1968) concept of 'rationality', Ritzer suggests that McDonald's epitomises the relentless drive towards a less human society, one centred on 'efficiency', 'calculability', 'predictability' and 'control'. The corporation has also become the focus of much direct anger and outrage. According to Vallely (1995), in 1994 there were mass demonstrations of 'healthists', 'green activists' and 'animalists' outside 3,000 McDonald's restaurants in Canada, the USA and Mexico and 400 rioting youths ransacked a restaurant in Copenhagen and set fire to its furniture in the street. In 1995, on the day of its 40th birthday, Vallely (1995: 18) also states that ' "environmentalists"...gathered to denounce it en masse from New Zealand to Finland'. More recently, French farmers wrecked a McDonald's restaurant under construction near Montpelier; the attack appeared to galvanise French public opinion, which sees McDonald's as exemplifying the inexorable march of globalisation and the multinationals. The head of a French think-tank commented (Henley, 1999: 14):

> McDonald's encapsulates it all ... it's economic horror and gastronomic horror in the same bun.

The McLibel trial, the longest running ever civil court case in the UK, raised many of these kinds of issues. Two London Greenpeace activists found themselves in court for distributing leaflets criticising the corporation over the effect of McDonald's food on people's diets, concerns about the rain forests, animal welfare and, of course, the treatment of its employees. After McDonald's spent millions on this libel action against the two defendants, it ended in stalemate with the Judge's verdict apparently exonerating in part the two activists. McDonald's was originally awarded £60,000 in costs, but McDonald's made it clear that it would not be trying to collect this amount from the two unemployed activists. The court case spawned a book and a film and a great deal of rather negative publicity for the corporation (Vidal, 1997). In the UK, the previous Conservative government, in power until 1997, with its avowedly liberal economic agenda, was very enthusiastic about the expansion of this kind of work: profits, jobs and flexible labour. However, there are many others who suggest that work at McDonald's is so systematised, automated and closely monitored that all opportunity for thought, initiative and human contact, let alone self-development, has been removed (Garson, 1988). In this interpretation, 'McJobs' offer nothing more than a dreary existence to a shiftless army of unskilled workers.

Advertising has undoubtedly played a big part in establishing McDonald's as a global product. In 1995, McDonald's announced a global alliance, sharing exclusive marketing rights for everything from films to food for 10 years from January 1997 onwards. It has also signed a sponsorship agreement to give it exclusive rights to the 1998 Winter and 2000 Summer Olympics; this agreement will shut out all other fast-food operators (*The Economist*, 1996a). The amounts spent on advertising in this industry are extremely high, and McDonald's advertises on a massive scale. As Reiter (1996: 52) points out, brand identification is an all-important factor because:

> Blind tastings have proven it's easier to tell a Big Mac apart from a Whopper in television commercials than when you're eating them.

In 1986, McDonald's spent some $789 million on advertising (6.3% of system-wide sales) and in 1989 it spent $1.1 billion, more than all other major chains combined. By 1995, the corporation was spending closer to $1.5 billion. It is the single most advertised brand in the world (*Advertising Age*, 1990). As the UK marketing manager recently stated (Vallely, 1995: 18):

> It is our objective to dominate the communications area…because we are competing for a share of the customer's mind.

During the McLibel trial, McDonald's also came under criticism for the amount of its advertising budget it spends in targeting children and the manner in which it does so. The corporation's own operations manual states (Vallely, 1995: 18):

> Children are often the key decision-makers concerning where a family goes to eat. …Ronald (the McDonald's clown) loves McDonald's and McDonald's food. And so do children, because they love Ronald. Remember, children exert a phenomenal influence when it comes to restaurant selection. This means you should do everything you can to appeal to children's love for Ronald and McDonald's.

Sometimes, McDonald's is picked out merely because it is seen as symbolic of broader issues in society. In May 1999, for example, a petrol bomb was thrown at a McDonald's restaurant in Rome; it followed three similar attacks on McDonald's outlets in March of the same year. McDonald's appears to have been attacked because it is seen as a symbol of American imperialism and the attacks were not so much against McDonald's directly but a protest against American air strikes on Yugoslavia (*Financial Times*, 1999a). It seems that McDonald's is like a number of other multinationals, i.e. 'everybody's favourite monster' (Emmott, 1993). We are quick to see it as being responsible for so many of the problems of modern society; yet, at the same time, some 40 billion people eat at McDonald's around the world every day. As Vallely (1995: 15) puts it:

> McDonald's has become a symbol of the modern globalised economy and of the cheap lowest-common denominator culture it fosters – a system which we all use and yet in which, we all feel entrapped.

There is no doubt that McDonald's is something of a phenomenon in its own right, but what were the roots of its creation and when does the story of McDonald's really begin?

From small acorns...

In 1930, like so many other hopeful Americans, two brothers Maurice (Mac) and Richard (Dick) McDonald left New Hampshire for California in search of new opportunity. To begin with, they pushed sets around in the Hollywood movie industry and then, a little later, they tried and failed in their attempt to run a movie theatre. In 1937, they eventually opened a tiny carhop drive-in restaurant in Pasadena. This was by no means the first carhop drive-in, nor was it a completely original idea. Love (1995) suggests that as early as the 1920s some restaurants in the east of the USA had developed a so-called kerb service, where waitresses would deliver food and drinks to customers parked on the street outside the restaurant. Love (1995) states that the first drive-in was probably opened in 1932 in Hollywood and was called the 'Pig Stand' as it specialised in barbecued pork sandwiches. It was the first of many drive-in chains; in the mid-1930s, Charles and Harry Carpenter opened a drive-in that catered exclusively to customers in cars. By the time the McDonald brothers opened their restaurant, California was full of carhop drive-ins. It was a time of experimentation, not only with products and menus but also with the type and speed of the service itself; at some carhops, customers were served on roller skates. One such 'experiment' was carried out by Bob Wian, who was established years before the McDonald brothers got involved, and resulted in a new and popular product that was quickly copied by others and was arguably the forerunner of the Big Mac. When some of Wian's customers complained about the monotony of his hamburgers, he invented the 'Big Boy' sandwich, which Love states (1995: 11):

...looked more like a meal – two hamburger patties topped with 'the works' and served on a triple-decker bun.

Ten years before fast-food franchising really developed, Wian was selling 'Big Boy' franchises in several US states. The McDonald brothers' decision to get involved in fast-food was undoubtedly made at the right time; they had perhaps unwittingly stumbled onto the cutting edge of the food service business. But there were no burgers sold in their first restaurant; instead, they concentrated on hot dogs and milk shakes and waited on customers, who were seated on stools, while three carhops served customers in the car park. In 1940, they opened a much larger drive-in in San Berdino; this was considerably different from their previous restaurant. It was octagonal and there was no inside seating, just stools placed on the outside of the counter, but the feature that was most unusual was that the whole kitchen area was visible from the outside. The brothers called this building the 'fishbowl' and it proved to be extremely successful; however, after a few years, Love (1995) suggests that the brothers became disgruntled. Drive-ins had become identified with low-cost food and a high-cost labour-intensive format; in addition, there was a high turnover of both carhops and eating utensils. They came close to selling their carhop drive-in and opening a restaurant in a shopping centre, but finally they decided to stick with what they knew best and instead decided to revamp their entire operation. By checking through their sales receipts, they realised that hamburger sales generated 80% of their business. They decided to make speed, low prices and volume the essence of their service by having the customer serve him/herself. In autumn 1948, they closed their business for 3 months. They sacked their twenty carhops and replaced their utensils and chinaware with disposable bags, wrappers and cups. They dropped their hot dogs and other barbecued foods to concentrate on the hamburger. The kitchen was redesigned to facilitate speed and volume production and the menu was reduced from twenty-five to just nine items. There would be no choice of condiments, all hamburgers would be prepared in the same way with ketchup, mustard, onions and two pickles and any order that deviated from that format would be penalised by a delay in service. As the brothers put it, 'If we gave people a choice, there would be chaos' (Love, 1995: 15). The burger size was also reduced in weight and the price was halved to an extremely low 15 cents (Love, 1995; Vidal, 1997).

However, when the restaurant reopened in December 1948, the increased levels of sales that the brothers had hoped to achieve with their 'Speedee Service System' were not forthcoming. Initially, sales dropped off, but within 6 months and with the introduction of French fries sales began to recover. The changes also brought about a change in their clientele. Families were now being attracted to their self-service drive-in. In particular, the new format and the 'fishbowl' with its newly designed kitchen layout was a big attraction for children, who, Love (1995: 16) suggests, 'were fascinated by their first glimpse of a commercial kitchen'. The brothers soon realised that their new format was attracting adults by appealing to the adults' children and they changed their advertising accordingly, focusing on families and promotional give-aways for children.

Nevertheless, it was not until the brothers began to introduce Fordist work practices and a number of other innovations that the big increase in volume materialised. They used a local craftsman to design and build new types of equipment, including the hand-held ketchup and mustard dispenser that is still in use today. They 'Taylorised' jobs for efficiency and developed rigid operating procedures to eliminate, as far as possible, the human element. In addition, they began to cook and prepackage food in anticipation of orders, something that Love (1995) suggests was a major innovation and distinguished them from their competitors. Jobs became so regulated and specialised that the brothers could now employ untrained cooks at a lower wage and with minimal training. By 1949, they had so refined their production techniques that they had effectively developed a unique restaurant format, converting their hamburger stand into a small assembly plant. The McDonald brothers had arguably developed a system that was vastly different from any of its forerunners. The main features were self-service, paper service and quick service; according to Love (1995: 19), '...there was nothing in the food service business that remotely resembled it'. This new system perhaps reflected a faster paced more mobile post-war America, more orientated to conveniences, the replacement of grocery restaurants by supermarkets and the desire for instant gratification.

The new system proved to be extremely successful and popular with customers. In 1951, the first year of operation, turnover reached $277,000; by the mid-1950s, turnover averaged close to $350,000. It was not unusual for 150 customers to crowd around the stand during lunch and dinner hours, with queues of twenty or more people at each of the two windows. Love (1995) suggests that their restaurant had become something of a 'Mecca' for opportunists all around the country. *American Restaurant Magazine* ran a cover story on the brothers' restaurant in July 1952, and the brothers were inundated with letters and telephone enquiries. The brothers had already begun licensing their concept in 1952. It was during this period that the famous golden arches were created. The brothers wanted to make the restaurant of their first licensee in Phoenix a prototype for the chain of restaurants that they wanted to build. Although they had engaged an architect, the golden arches included in the design were actually created by one of the brothers and by a signmaker named George Dexter, who suggested that they be bright yellow and illuminated. Despite this early interest in licensing their concept, the brothers' enthusiasm eventually waned. Part of the problem was that the brothers' franchising scheme involved little more than renting their name. It comprised a one-off payment of $1,000, franchisees were not required to follow their procedures and there was no continuing revenue. In fact, they turned down several opportunities to sell franchises and expand their system. Vidal (1997) suggests that they were simply content with the money that they were making from their San Bernardino restaurant.

Enter the salesman

One of those who had heard about this new phenomenon was the 52-year-old Ray Kroc. Kroc, a high school dropout, was working as a milk-shake-mixer salesman when he first heard about the McDonald brothers. He had already heard about the McDonald's restaurant through the sales reports of his milk shake machines. The sheer number of the machines that the brothers were buying intrigued Kroc. A burger bar on the edge of the Californian desert seemed an unlikely place to turn over $250,000 every year. Kroc's curiosity finally got the better of him in the summer of 1954. Vidal (1997: 30) states:

> He (Kroc) watches the two brothers and their helpers in spiffy white suits and white paper hats bustling around like ants at a picnic and a steady procession of customers lockstepping up to the windows.

Kroc liked what he saw and was impressed with the speed of the operation. According to Love (1995), he had never before seen anything that came close to matching the speed of an operation that filled orders in 15 seconds. Kroc introduced himself to the brothers and, bubbling over with enthusiasm, told the brothers that he 'wanted in' and that he also liked the name (Vidal, 1997: 30):

> I had a feeling it would be one of those promotable names that would catch the public fancy.

Kroc was aware of the growing trend towards convenience foods in the USA and, Love suggests, immediately recognised the importance of the McDonald brothers' system. However, according to Vidal (1997), the brothers were not very enthusiastic about Kroc's involvement, but Kroc was 'tenacious'. Later the same year, he became the brothers' franchise agent. The brothers only allowed Kroc to become their franchise agent on the basis that no changes could be made to restaurants unless by their written authorisation. The brothers held the franchise fee at $950 and required that Kroc charge each franchise a service fee of 1.9% of a restaurant's sales. Of that 1.9%, Kroc got 1.4% to cover his costs and the brothers got 0.5% of the sales. This was clearly an unsatisfactory situation, but desperate to get involved Kroc nevertheless accepted the terms. He set up his franchising company, the McDonald's System Inc., on 2 March 1955. In 1960, the name of the franchising company was changed to the McDonald's Corporation. Kroc wanted to buy all rights, copyrights, formulas, trademarks, the golden arches and the name from the brothers. By this time, the brothers were making a good living from their own restaurant in San Bernardino and from the royalties that they were getting from Kroc's chain of restaurants. Nevertheless, they also wanted to sell because of their growing concerns about tax demands on the increasing royalties. Kroc offered $500,000, but the brothers wanted $1 million each in cash after capital gains tax, i.e. a total of $2.7 million. The brothers knew that they could earn a whole lot more by simply holding onto their rights in their fast-food system, but they saw nothing in great wealth but great worry. As one brother pointed out to the other (Love, 1995: 194):

What the hell can we do with $5 million that we can't do now?

Kroc did not have the $2.7 million, but he knew that it would be worth every cent. Nevertheless, it infuriated Kroc that the brothers insisted on keeping their highly profitable original restaurant in San Bernardino, which they gave to two long-time employees. Kroc believed that he had tolerated their stubborn ways for years, but now they had gone too far. According to Love (1995: 194), he could contain his rage no longer. A few years later, Kroc reflected, 'I closed the door to my office and paced up and down the floor calling them every kind of son of a bitch there was. I hated their guts'.

In 1961, as soon as the finance deal was completed that allowed him to pay off the brothers, Kroc got on a plane to Los Angeles, bought a piece of property just one block away from the brothers' restaurant and ordered the construction of a brand-new McDonald's restaurant. As Love states (1995: 200),

It had only one purpose: to put the McDonald's brothers' unit out of business. The brothers were forced to take down the McDonald's sign – since Kroc's company now owned their trade name.

Kroc stated to his first franchise operator, Art Bender (Love, 1995: 200):

I'm not normally a vindictive man but this time I'm going to get those sons of bitches.

The effect was devastating: the brothers' restaurant, now renamed Big M and operated by the brothers' long-time employees, rapidly began to lose sales. In early 1968, the restaurant was sold to another fast-food chain, but by 1970 it was closed. The building which had been home to what was arguably the birthplace of the world-wide fast-food industry was later reopened as a music shop. It may not have significantly damaged the McDonald brothers as the main victims were the two long-time employees who had been given the restaurant for their loyalty to the brothers. Maurice McDonald died 1 year after their restaurant was closed in 1971 but Richard McDonald outlived Ray Kroc, who died in January 1984. Ten months after Ray Kroc's death, it appeared that Richard McDonald was being welcomed back into the fold when he was invited to what Love (1995) describes as the most widely covered media event ever staged by McDonald's. On 21 November 1984 at the Grand Hyatt Hotel in New York, the surviving brother was served the corporation's 50 billionth hamburger by McDonald's US President Ed Rensi.

In 1965, the McDonald's Corporation went public; common shares were offered at $22.50. By the end of the first day's trading, the share price had risen to $30. The price that Kroc had paid the brothers proved to be a real bargain; by 1986, the corporation's sales had amounted to a total of $77 billion (Love, 1995; IDCH, 1990). Whereas the brothers had standardised their food preparation techniques, Kroc took this a stage further by standardising procedures for book-keeping, purchasing, dealing with customers and workers and virtually every other aspect of the business. Over the years, the menu has expanded somewhat and prices have risen, but the emphasis on strict, detailed standardisation has never varied. Luxenburg (1985: 77) suggests that:

> Kroc introduced an extreme regimentation that had never been attempted in a service business.

By the 1970s, the corporation was a major success in the USA, but would it continue? Competition from other fast-food businesses in the USA had become fierce. Ray Kroc had at first considered diversification as a way to continue growth; there were various schemes which included a theme park (suggested to him by his World War I comrade Walt Disney), real estate, other food chains and even florist shops. Finally, Kroc decided to forget diversification and go for international expansion.

Exporting 'McBurgers'

The first overseas restaurants were opened as franchises in the Caribbean and parts of South America in 1965 and in Canada in 1967. By the mid-1980s, McDonald's was establishing its presence around the globe, becoming the number one food service chain in Japan, Germany, the UK, Canada and Australia. McDonald's International became the fastest growing segment of the McDonald's Corporation. In 1975, the company had already opened restaurants in Europe, Asia and the Americas, but at that time only 8% of sales came from outside the USA. Ten years later, this figure had increased to 20%, McDonald's International was now generating $2.1 billion in food sales outside the USA (Love, 1995). By 1995, the 38% of restaurants outside the USA accounted for 47% of total sales and 54% of profits. For the first time, in 1996 more than half of all McDonald's restaurants were outside the USA. The continuing expansion abroad appears to be the logical answer to an increasingly competitive market in the USA, where McDonald's is no longer trying to expand but is instead trying to increase the sales of existing restaurants.

Opportunities for further international expansion still appear to be considerable; besides the expected increases in numbers of restaurants in the Western and industrialised economies, the corporation has wasted little time moving into the old Eastern bloc. After 20 years of negotiations, McDonald's succeeded in opening its first Moscow restaurant in 1990. It is the largest McDonald's restaurant in the world with 700 seats, 27 cash registers and around 1,200 employees (Kristof, 1992; Utchitelle, 1992; Vikhanski and Puffer, 1993). McDonald's invested some $50 million and had to agree not to remove profits but to reinvest them in a chain of twenty restaurants in Moscow; however, this has paid off, the first Moscow McDonald's sells on average 30,000 hamburgers every day with an average turnover of $1.5 million per month (Frantz, 1993).

McDonald's opened its first restaurant in China in 1990 in the southern city of Shenzhen and its first Beijing restaurant in 1992. Before that time, it was already working with the People's Republic of China to improve its future foreign exchange. The Chinese market is potentially huge. In 1996, McDonald's already had twenty-nine restaurants in Beijing with over seventy restaurants in the rest of China, and it plans to have 600 restaurants in China by 2003. The only limitation on further expansion, besides any political problems, is that the infrastructure cannot be developed quickly enough to meet demand. In December 1993, the corporation opened its first restaurant in Saudi Arabia, with a sheikh as franchisee. This was just the first of a number of new restaurants to be opened in the Middle East. In May 1996, Lithuania became the ninety-fourth country to have a McDonald's restaurant. In 1998, McDonald's opened 199 restaurants in Brazil, bringing its total there to 681 (*The Economist*, 1989a, 1993a, 1996a; *Big Mäc Nachrichten*, 1994; Edgecliffe-Johnson, 1999a).

It is impossible to provide exact figures for the current number of restaurants because of the rapid and continual growth rate. At the time this research began in 1993, McDonald's was active in some seventy countries with around 14,000 restaurants. Some 6 years later, McDonald's opened its 25,000th restaurant and, at the time of writing, was active in 116 countries, serving over 40 billion people per day. In 1990, the corporation reported turnover of $6.8 billion and profits of $800 million; by 1993, turnover had reached $24 billion and by 1995 turnover was $29.9 billion and operating profit was $2.6 billion. In 1998, sales reached $36 billion and operating income was $3 billion. In the same year, McDonald's was valued at $40 billion and moved up from number eighty-six to number seventy-two in the list of the world's largest corporations compiled by the *Financial Times*, ahead of companies such as General Motors, American Express, Texaco, Boeing, Monsanto, Siemens, Sony and Deutsche Bank. In fact, its system-wide sales have increased nearly every year since 1960. McDonald's not only has restaurants in the high street and out-of-town shopping areas but also in airports, aeroplanes, service stations, hospitals, cruise ships and trains. Approximately 70–75% of its restaurants world-wide are franchises, but the corporation owns a large proportion of the sites and most are freehold.

The success and growth rate of the corporation is to some extent reflected by the growth of the fast-food industry in general. In the USA alone, this market was estimated to be worth $200 billion a year in the mid-1990s. It was originally thought that the expansion of fast-food restaurants had already reached saturation level in the 1970s; however, restaurant numbers have increased continually since then. By 1990, it was estimated that there was one fast-food restaurant for every 400 US citizens; indeed, fast-food was already accounting for 40% of all restaurant sales and 10% of food expenditures in the USA (Reiter, 1996). Furthermore, half of the commercial restaurants in Canada now specialise in fast-food, accounting for 12% of all restaurant sales, and most are affiliated to an American chain (Ramirez, 1990; Emerson, 1990; Reiter, 1996).

The history of the international expansion of McDonald's has until recently stuck closely to its old formula of avoiding diversification. However, in February 1998, under the new leadership of Jack Greenberg [Chief Executive Officer (CEO) and President], McDonald's intrigued analysts and investors by buying a minority stake in the Chipotle Mexican Grill, a chain of eighteen fast-food restaurants serving Mexican style food in and around Denver, Colorado. In fact, this was only the first of three purchases that the corporation has made outside its usual hamburger business.

In the UK, McDonald's purchased the coffee bar chain 'Aroma' for an estimated £10 million. Aroma will retain its brand identity and management team, but its managing director was previously group accountant at McDonald's UK. It then purchased a small Midwestern pizza chain. Donatos Pizzas was a family-owned group of 143 restaurants based in and around Ohio. Jack Greenberg describes all three investments as experimental and says that there will be more (Edgecliffe-Johnson, 1999b). McDonald's only added some forty-nine restaurants in the USA in 1998; any further expansion is limited because it may damage burger sales in its own restaurants and damage relationships with its franchisees. The purchase of Donatos will probably allow McDonald's to restore its domestic unit growth without any risk to the existing sales.

Other changes are also being made to try to provide more choice for customers. Competition in the North American market is extremely tough, so the emphasis on opening new restaurants has stopped and now the chains are concentrating instead on trying to increase restaurant sales. After the success of Burger King's 'have it your way' burgers, McDonald's has introduced its 'made for you cooking system'. Every kitchen in the USA and Canada will have been reorganised so that each burger can be assembled to order.

There are apparently no plans to extend this system outside North America at the moment. However, despite the supposedly saturated American market, all three big players have been able to increase their market share, mostly at the expense of small operators (Edgecliffe-Johnson, 1999c). There have of course been some adaptations to the menu over time in different countries. There are more fish-based products on the menus in Norway and Japan, and beer is still sold in some European restaurants such as those in Italy, Denmark and Germany. In India, they have lamb burgers instead of beef and there have been numerous other experiments with various types of chicken, bacon and eggs and a 'Chinese' menu. In the UK, McDonald's recently introduced what they call the 'McChicken Korma Naan', which is supposed to be a taste of Indian cuisine. Although there are more choices on the menu, these alterations do not affect the corporation's basic mode of operation or represent any major change in the principles first developed by the McDonald brothers in 1948.

The problems of international expansion

McDonald's entry into foreign markets was not just about finding suitable locations but also about overcoming a number of significant obstacles in establishing operations in another country. Although, for example, there was very little competition from other American hamburger chains overseas, many countries had no locally based fast-food restaurants and no experience of fast-food. Among other things, the corporation would be attempting to change people's eating habits, imposing the McDonald's system and an American culture on host countries.

Significantly, Love (1995) suggests McDonald's became successful in international markets with more or less the same formula that it had perfected in the USA. Many mistakes were made with its first attempts at expansion abroad; McDonald's moved away from its usual franchise agreement in Canada and the Caribbean; these first overseas franchises were flops and McDonald's lost money. Adaptations were also made to local cultures, including menus, buildings and interiors. For example, large variations were made in the Australian menu, but once again this did not prove successful. Most of these early adaptations were later reverted and the mistakes rectified. It appears that whenever McDonald's left its established system things began to go wrong. As the then president of McDonald's Germany Walter Rettenwender states (Love, 1995: 437):

> It seems that any detour we made from the standard McDonald's didn't work…we realised it was better to stick with the system and, if necessary, wait for the German consumer to accept it.

However, it is perhaps easier to understand the success of the McDonald's system in European or English-speaking countries, where America's dominant cultural roots were not so far removed. What would happen in a totally alien culture such as Japan, where not only the diet but also the cultural values are very different? As Love (1995: 418) states:

> To succeed abroad, McDonald's had to introduce a major cultural change…it was attempting to export something that was now endemic to American life but totally foreign everywhere else. Quick service food was uniquely American. So were drive-ins and self-service restaurants…in Japan and the Far East, McDonald's was faced not only with the task of introducing the hamburger but with an even more fundamental challenge of establishing beef as a common food.

Might a country such as Japan be just too different for the system to work? In this regard, Schneider (1988: 243) quotes Fujisawa, the founder of Honda: 'Japanese and US management is 95 percent alike and differs in all important aspects'. This statement suggests that the kind of standardised approach to employee relations implicit in other commentators' accounts would be difficult or impossible to achieve. After all, Hofstede's (1980) research suggests that even within a large multinational well known for its 'strong' corporate culture, such as IBM, societal culture still plays a major role in differentiating work values. In fact, the opposite appears to be the case; the company's experience in Japan suggested that the McDonald's system could work in any culture (Love, 1995: 425):

> Japan was really the acid test...after that we realised that the American menu could fly abroad and that modifications were not needed or at best would be minor.

It is worth briefly reviewing how the corporation went about its conquest of the Japanese market because it seems to epitomise the success that the corporation has had in overcoming cultural barriers. The first Japanese McDonald's was opened as a fifty–fifty partnership between McDonald's and Den Fujita. Not in the traditional Japanese mould, Den Fujita had started his own company by the age of 25. He was a well-connected graduate of the Tokyo University law school, he was fluent in English and he ran his own business importing whisky, cigarettes and, later, women's accessories and handbags (Martin, 1998). He overruled McDonald's American management for the choice of the first site; instead of choosing a suburban Tokyo drive-in, he chose a high-rent location right in the centre of Tokyo, which he said would give the little known McDonald's brand more prestige. He also argued that in order for McDonald's to succeed in Japan it must appear to be a 100% Japanese operation. In 1971, Den Fujita began selling the hamburger as a 'revolutionary' product. He gave lectures at universities that attracted considerable press coverage by making some outrageous statements to reporters (Love, 1995: 426):

> The reason Japanese people are so short and have yellow skins is because they have eaten nothing but fish and rice for 2000 years. If we eat McDonald's hamburgers and potatoes for a thousand years, we will become taller, our skin will become white, and our hair blonde.

Before the first Japanese restaurant was opened, Den Fujita opened a 'hamburger university' to train restaurant managers. In 4 days, he had opened three restaurants; within 18 months, he had nineteen restaurants. According to Love, the only major change in approach that was allowed was the way in which the products were marketed. For example, the spelling of McDonald's was changed to make it easier for the Japanese to pronounce, so it became

'Makudonarudo'. Being a fifty–fifty operation, Fujita was allowed a bit more freedom in the marketing area. However, McDonald's would not allow deviation from its proven operating principles and they insisted on having the rights to the new name signed over to them for the price of US$1 (Martin, 1998). The then president of the corporation, Fred Turner, concluded that if the corporation were to remain successful it would have to be as heavily involved overseeing its foreign restaurants as it was in its American operations and that this would include determining the management culture in Japan. Although all of Fujita's 1,500 managers are Japanese, his company is not run in typical Japanese fashion. In part, this is because Turner placed one of his own managers in Fujita's operation. According to Love (1995: 430), John Ashara, a Japanese–American who has worked with Fujita's company from the beginning, was responsible for introducing American management techniques:

> With Fujita's blessing, Ashara has built a young and creative operations team, which he has sheltered from the potentially stifling influence of Japanese management culture, where most power rests with more traditional senior executives. …He is continually on the look out for young and aggressive operations managers and he encourages their promotion ahead of more senior staffers – a direct challenge to Japanese traditions of promotion through seniority. He has even convinced the Japanese company of the wisdom of part-time floor managers. This practice is critical to efficiently managing the demand peaks and valleys of a fast-food operation but it is totally foreign to the Japanese.

Although Ashara is a highly influential figure in McDonald's Japan, he has no official title and maintains an extremely low profile. The combination of the American McDonald's operating system, management style and menu plus Japanese marketing has proved extremely successful. By mid-1986, McDonald's Japan had 550 restaurants and an annual turnover of $600 million; by 1995, this had risen to 1,482 restaurants and by 1998 to more than 2,400 restaurants. The Japanese market is now only second to the USA in terms of the highest turnover and is likely to remain so for some time. At the McDonald's twenty-fifth anniversary celebration in Tokyo, Fujita (now in his seventies) set a goal for McDonald's Japan to have 10,000 restaurants by 2006. It may be that the new deal recently agreed with the Nippon Oil Co. will play a part in this. They plan to establish 1000 drive-in restaurants at all their service stations (Martin, 1998).

Despite this success in overcoming cultural barriers, McDonald's has also had to face a considerable number of practical problems in taking its system abroad. In Europe, for example, Love (1995) suggests that there were problems with suppliers. European food processors did not have the basic skills for high-volume automated production let alone cryogenic meat freezing, which by the early 1970s was an essential aspect of the company's operations. McDonald's was faced with the prospect of either importing most of its food supplies or rebuilding the European food chain. When local suppliers could not be found or when local suppliers resisted changes or suggestions to improve their facilities, McDonald's turned to its established suppliers to build facilities in foreign countries, sometimes becoming a partner in these supply facilities. For example, the corporation spent $2 million in order to build Europe's largest and most sophisticated potato storage facility, and McDonald's England went into bun and syrup manufacture. Indeed, the corporation has gone to extraordinary lengths to ensure that its products are highly consistent wherever they may be.

The establishment of the first Russian restaurants involved the building of its own food chain. It trained local Russian farmers how to maximise their harvests, it indirectly managed cattle ranches and vegetable plots and imported its own beef semen and taught Russian beef farmers how to extend the cattle's feed cycle. It even imported and planted its preferred potato, the 'Russet Burbank', from the USA. It then constructed the world's largest food processing plant and dairy (around the size of five football pitches) to produce the beef patties, French fries and rolls. Four Russian managers were also sent to Canada for 8 months' training at the 'hamburger university', and for the first few years the operation was run by twelve McDonald's mangers from Germany, two from Hungary and three from the USA and Canada. In fact, the director of the Russian operation is an American who previously worked for Coca-Cola (Parker, 1992). In a similar way, Hong Kong was used as the staging post for the Chinese operation; McDonald's trained local farmers in China to improve production and to meet McDonald's standards (*The Economist*, 1989a, 1989b, 1990).

Structure and organisation in the European market

In 1997, between twelve and fifteen fast-food companies operated in more than one country in Europe, but by far the largest of these were the three American multinationals McDonald's, Burger King (Diageo) and Kentucky Fried Chicken (Tricon). Six or seven of the larger multinational companies affiliated to EMRA (the European fast-food employer's association) employ some 500,000 people. Therefore, a modest estimate of the total employment in the European fast-food industry as a whole must be well in excess of 1 million.

When McDonald's first came to Europe in 1971, it opened its first restaurants in The Netherlands and Germany. Restaurants were then opened in other European countries, as indicated in Table 2.1. In mid-1999, McDonald's employed approximately 200,000 people in about 3,700 restaurants in the seventeen countries of the European Economic Area (EEA). Until 1996, McDonald's had not made a huge impact on the Italian market, but in March of that year it bought out the eighty-strong Burghy chain of restaurants from Italy's Cafin group. This now makes McDonald's the main

Table 2.1 Year of entry, restaurants and proportions of franchises and employees in autumn 1999

Country	Year of entry	Total restaurants	Franchise restaurants (% of total)	Total employees	Franchise employees
Austria	1977	80	65 (81.3)	4,000	3,250
Belgium	1978	62	61 (98.4)	3,250	3,198
Denmark	1982	80	74 (92.5)	4,000	3,700
Finland	1984	85	54 (63.5)	4,250	2,700
France	1979	720	612 (85.0)	35,000	29,750
Germany	1971	1,000	650 (65.0)	51,000	33,150
Holland	1971	180	160 (88.9)	13,000	11,556
Iceland	1992	2	2 (100.0)	100	100
Ireland	1977	30	27 (90.0)	1,500	1,350
Italy	1985	220	187 (85.0)	10,000	8,500
Norway	1983	50	28 (56.0)	2,500	1,100
Spain	1982	161	130 (80.7)	8,000	6,460
Sweden	1973	151	101 (66.9)	7,500	5,017
UK	1974	1,000	275 (27.5)	56,000	15,400
Other EEA[a]		85	64 (75.4)	4,250	3,205
Total EEA		3,906	2,465 (63.1)	204,350	128,736

Notes
a Figures for some countries are not available and have been estimated.
Obtaining exact restaurant and employment figures is in any case difficult because of the continual level of expansion and high levels of labour turnover.
However, the above figures do provide a fairly accurate picture of the overall situation in late 1999.

competitor for the Italian fast-food market leader Autogrill. The USA has a smaller population than the EU, yet US citizens have between three and four times more McDonald's restaurants per person than their European counterparts. This suggests that the European market is likely to experience a lot more expansion in future. Although the world-wide proportion of franchise operations is 75%, in Europe it is closer to 65%. However, as we can see from Table 2.1, individual countries may have much higher percentages of franchise operations.

The UK is unusual in having only a relatively small proportion of restaurants as franchise operations. The first English restaurant was built in Woolwich in 1974 and was a product of a joint venture between Bob Rhea (a franchisee from Ohio) and McDonald's. In 1977, this had increased to thirty restaurants, and by 1982 this had reached 200 restaurants. In 1986, McDonald's bought out Rhea's 45% share for $38 million. Since that time, however, McDonald's UK has only slowly franchised parts of the operation. In 1993, this stood at only 11%, but by 1996 over 20% were franchise operations. McDonald's UK management state that they expect to have closer to 30% being franchises by early in 2001.

McDonald's official statements on the organisation structure suggest that each country has a head office which acts quite independently of the main head office in Oak Brook, Illinois, USA. However, repeatedly in this study, we found that the US head office is involved in major decisions, e.g. the setting up of the European Works Council (Chapter 8) or the replacement of senior human resource managers in Germany in the mid-1980s (Chapter 5). Indeed, it is clear that the US head office regularly monitors the activities of its overseas operations. It has an international division, and its US consultants sometimes take part in European meetings. Franchisees also have the opportunity to view the American way of doing things. Every 2 years, franchisees are invited to the world-wide convention in the USA to meet with senior management and to view the latest in McDonald's kitchen equipment or other technological developments authorised by the corporation. These meetings are well-attended social events which seem to be an opportunity to 'pump some more McDonald's ketchup into the veins' of their international franchise operators.

In addition, meetings frequently take place between various European heads to discuss matters of cross-national importance. In fact, the way that McDonald's organises its supply chains alone suggests that their raw materials and products often cross international borders; this may mean trucks loaded with buns or meat or cheese products supplying more than one country. There are regular meetings of European managers to organise logistics and to ensure the consistency and low cost of its supplies. In the early days of McDonald's European operations, senior managers were often sent to the USA for training. In fact, the training of managers in the USA or in other well-established 'hamburger universities', such as in Munich and London, is common practice and is seen as essential to guaranteeing that mangers will learn the

'McDonald's way' of doing things. For example, the Russian purchasing chief had previously worked at McDonald's in Yugoslavia (Uchitelle, 1992), and many managers in this study had been trained in other countries. As recently as the late 1990s, some Italian managers were sent to the UK for training.

The structure of restaurant operation and administration in each country tends to follow a similar pattern, but in some countries it appears to be more complicated than others. In some countries, some restaurants are operated as joint ventures or through holding companies. For example, in Germany, approximately 15% of McDonald's German restaurants are 'company-owned' (or McOpCo – McDonald's Operating Company) restaurants. A further 65% of its restaurants are managed as franchises, and the remaining 20% of McDonald's German restaurants are administered through holding companies. In Germany, these are called Anver restaurants (Anver Gewerbe- und Mietgesellschaft GmbH); technically, these are legally separate companies; however, in practice, they are 100% owned and controlled subsidiaries of the corporation. In Germany, they are split into six groups of outlets under the titles of Anver South, Southwest, Southeast, North, Northwest and West. However, these geographical distinctions bear only a slight resemblance to the actual location of the restaurants themselves. In France, the restaurants appear to be operated as company-owned restaurants, joint ventures or franchises. However, many of the joint ventures are 90% owned by the corporation, so to all intents and purposes they are company-owned restaurants.

In most of the larger countries such as Germany and the UK, operations are usually split into several regions and are administered through regional offices in the major cities. For example, in Germany in 1995, these were Hamburg, Berlin, Düsseldorf, Frankfurt and Munich. The capital city of each country is usually the location for the head office. Similarly, in the UK, the five regional offices are Belfast, Glasgow, Manchester, Birmingham and London. The heads of departments for each functional area are usually situated in the head offices (for example London and Munich), these functional areas being the executive, marketing, finance, personnel, purchasing, real estate, technical appliances and administration. Although there is a high level of central control, operations are normally administered directly from the regional offices.

Each restaurant is a profit centre. In both Germany and the UK, the corporation has access to turnover, profit, inventory and labour costs of every restaurant, whether it is a franchise, holding company, joint venture or a 100% company-owned restaurant. As we shall see, these financial reports are made monthly and budgets are set by head office each year that cover all aspects of the operation, including the amount of turnover the restaurant is expected to achieve by year end. Until recently, at McDonald's, sales data had to be manually 'touched' several times before they made their way to senior management. McDonald's is currently installing a new information system that uses PCs and web technologies to tally sales at all its restaurants in real time. As soon as someone orders two 'Happy Meals', a McDonald's marketing manager will know (*Financial Times*, 1999b). Any alterations to the system at restaurant level can only be made if authorised by head office. This ranges from the employment contract to uniforms and includes any aspect of basic operations. The central training centres are also located at the head offices, where training is established for the whole country. All salaried employees, second assistant or above, take their company examinations in either head offices or regional offices, whereas other employees are trained either in the restaurant or at regional offices.

McDonald's operates within a strict hierarchy that appears to differ very little across the globe, sometimes different names are given to the same posts but the findings suggest that the hierarchy at both senior management and operational levels is virtually identical. Examples are provided here for Germany and the UK. Each region has a 'regional' or 'market manager' (in Germany *Regionalleiter*) and each of the regions is split into a number of areas with area or 'operations managers' (*Gebietsleiterinnen*). These managers have responsibility for franchise and McOpCo. These areas are then further subdivided into smaller areas, with 'area supervisors' (*Bezirksleiterinnen*) supervising McOpCo and 'field consultants' (*Lizenzberater*) supervising franchise restaurants. These smaller areas usually consist of between two and eight restaurants. Below this level is the 'restaurant manager' (*Restaurantleiter*) and the franchise operator (*Lizenznehmer*).

Overall, the above analysis may suggest that the McDonald's system is very flexible in overcoming cultural, political and economic differences and obstacles in different societies. But can it maintain uniformity across countries in practice when it also has to deal with supposedly independent franchise operators, well-organised trade unions and different forms of legislative systems that are based on collectivist principles? The next chapter begins to unravel these issues by examining the relationship between McDonald's and its franchise operators.

3 The corporate paradox

McDonald's and its franchise system

If you come in and challenge the system you won't last very long, because the system is the system, is the system.

(McDonald's UK franchise operator)

The only way that we can positively know that these units are doing what they are supposed to…is to make it so that they can have no alternative whatsoever. You can't give them an inch.

(Ray Kroc in Love, 1995: 144).

Franchising may be more appropriate in some industries than in others and it is common in the service sector. The fast-food industry in particular is increasingly associated with the activity of multinationals and franchise operations (Felstead, 1993). Indeed, it is a form of international expansion that could be said to have been 'pioneered' by the McDonald's Corporation (Love, 1995). Chan and Justis (1990) suggest that maintaining uniformity while franchising across different societal cultures is particularly complex and difficult. The first question that comes to mind is why would multinationals use franchise operations as a method of international expansion? It is suggested here that there are four reasons for this. First, franchising provides multinationals with much needed capital for expansion. Second, it allows multinationals to share the costs and risks associated with international expansion. Third, it provides multinationals with the local knowledge of entrepreneurs. Fourth, franchise operations may be more efficient in driving down labour costs. A second question which arises is this: given that franchising internationally is complex and difficult and that franchisees are supposed to be independent operators, how can multinationals maintain the internal consistency and uniformity of their operations across societal frameworks?

The main focus of this chapter is to challenge the belief that McDonald's franchisees are truly independent operators and to argue that franchises are much closer *de facto* to 'subsidiaries' of the corporation. In legal terms, franchise operations are technically independent operators; they are usually considered to be self-employed and therefore not 'owned' or controlled by the multinational. However, this assumes that franchise operators enjoy a great deal of autonomy of decision-making over wide-ranging areas of the operation. Is this really the case? Who is really in control in the decision-making process? The McDonald's system is based on the 'format' franchise; this type of franchise is now more common than any other franchise system (Felstead, 1993). In this arrangement, the franchisor (McDonald's) not only sells his/her product to the franchisee but also lays down precisely the rules and procedures that have to be followed. This chapter examines these rules and procedures and the way in which McDonald's is able to ensure that such control mechanisms are maintained in practice. We begin with a brief review of the broader context in which franchising has developed.

The growth of the franchise

According to Felstead (1993), the origin of the word franchise dates back to the Middle Ages. In Norman England, barons were granted territories by the King in return for the payment of royalties and 'provided they met many other requests made by the Monarch' (Felstead, 1993: 39). The original meaning of the word comes from the French 'affranchair', meaning 'freedom from servitude or restraint'. However, as Felstead (1991) and the following sections will argue, the modern franchise is absolutely not about freedom from restraint or servitude. Why is franchising so popular? In addition to sharing risk, the key advantages for both parties appear to be that, first, a small locally based business can tap into, develop and maintain its contacts in the local community. Second, the personal involvement, commitment and investment of their own capital strengthens the franchisee's incentives to maintain a high reputation and develop customer loyalty. Third, personal attention to detail is also thought to be much greater under franchise ownership than under company ownership.

However, Landes (1986) argues that technological efficiency is not what matters in determining the organisation of production, but cost, efficiency and predictability and enforceability of output. Moreover, Reiter (1996) has argued that franchising is a good way to control managerial labour. Taken together with the capital investment that the franchisee must make, these arguments would suggest that its growth has more to do with the interests of the franchisor rather than the interests of both parties in some kind of equal partnership. Reiter also suggests that the big advantage for large corporations is that franchising allows companies to expand rapidly without large outlays of capital.

Felstead (1993) suggests that franchises can be categorised in two ways. The first, trademark franchising, is sometimes referred to as 'first-generation' franchising. This type of franchise usually means that the franchisee conducts business as an independent distributor, acquiring the identity of the franchisor through the product/trademark. The second type is that used by McDonald's, the format franchise. With this type of franchise, the franchisor sells the franchisee the product and/or service, but does so within a set of precisely laid down procedures or 'format'. The franchisee is in effect purchasing a carefully prepared 'blueprint', which minimises the risks involved in setting up a conventional small business. The key issue that differentiates the McDonald's franchise from others is that it is based not just on the supply of a tangible product but also on the supply of a way of doing business.

According to Felstead (1993), the format franchise has enjoyed unprecedented growth since the mid-1980s, not only in the UK and the USA but also in Europe. One reason for this may be that little experience is required. Second, this kind of franchise is well suited to those who have an interest in running their own business, but do not know what sort of business it should be. A survey of some 199 franchisees shows that existing franchisees had few ideas of their own on which to base a business (Felstead, 1993). These factors were also reflected in this study. The majority of franchisees who were new to the company stated that they had no clear idea what kind of business they should invest in, but they were impressed by McDonald's growth rate and the detailed training and commitment that a McDonald's franchise would require.

Official statements from the corporation and from other commentators have often suggested that McDonald's is a loose federation of retailers (*The Economist*, 1989a). However, much of the analysis from this study refutes the notion that the corporation is a 'loose federation'. This view does not take into account the relationship *between* firms and the reality of the format franchise relationship in particular.

The McDonald's franchise system

According to Love (1995), the McDonald brothers' restaurant system established in the 1940s gave rise to a large number of other fast-food hamburger stalls with different names and standards. Love suggests that many others tried to copy their system, including the future owner of Taco Bell, who was a regular customer at the McDonald brothers' stand. It was the McDonald brothers, not Ray Kroc, who first franchised their 'Speedee Service System' in 1952. With these first franchises, the brothers sold the right to use the name and the golden arches (if they wished), the blueprint to their building and a fifteen-page operating manual, all for a one-off payment of $1,000. There were no additional fees and no other specifications. The first franchise was sold to an independent gasoline retailer and then fifteen more followed, but most were failures. Franchisees would receive just 1 week's training and could then operate as they wished, and many did just that, typically failing to perceive the essentials which had made the brothers' system a success in the first place. By the mid-1950s, neither the brothers nor their competitors had developed any of their restaurants into an effective national hamburger chain. This failure undoubtedly reflected the low-involvement, simple, trademark franchise deal approach.

As we have already suggested in Chapter 2, the deal that Kroc made with the brothers to become their franchise agent was only on the basis that no changes could be made without their authorisation in writing. Love (1995) suggests that Kroc's main emphasis was on trying to maintain system-wide uniformity, but he soon concluded that the brothers' approach to franchising did not work and that a new approach would be needed. Kroc's new approach, Love (1995) suggests, was not to make a short-term killing from franchisees but to develop a long-term relationship with them. He established his first *Operations Manual* in 1958 and it ran to seventy-five pages. It spelt out exactly how the franchises should be run, and even in these early days Kroc's franchisees had to provide him with detailed reports on sales and costs. Love suggests that Kroc's plan was also different in that it was designed to encourage the success of his franchisees first because if they failed then he would fail. In addition, he was determined to avoid territorial franchises; at that time, it was the norm in the USA to sell a franchise perhaps covering a whole state or a major market for up to $50,000. The purchaser would then frequently pyramid his territory. It was an easy way to make a quick profit, but in that situation the franchisor had no control over the products that would be sold or the quality of the franchisees themselves. Kroc decided to sell only single-restaurant franchises, allowing him to retain tight controls over his franchisees. In addition, he retained the right to determine whether a franchisee should be granted a licence to operate a second or additional restaurants. Kroc's early system made its money from the 1.4% of restaurant sales that it collected as a service fee, making Kroc very dependent on the sales volume of the franchise restaurant.

Vidal (1997) points out that although this new system turned over a lot of money Kroc complained that his income was still being ploughed back into the business or paid in fees to the McDonald brothers (they received 0.5%). Real financial success only came when Kroc's company went into the real-estate business in 1956. Love (1995) suggests that this change is what turned the modern McDonald's business into a profit-making business and set it apart from all the other franchise companies. In the early days, franchisees either leased their own properties directly from a landlord or bought the land themselves. Many of the small operators that Kroc wanted to encourage could not afford this, so the first part of the solution was for McDonald's to adopt a 'sandwich position' on real-estate. McDonald's would lease the properties from the owner over a 20-year period and then sublease them to the franchisee. McDonald's would only agree to a flat monthly rent with the owner and would then make a 40% mark-up with the franchisee, and this was a minimum. The franchisee would either pay a flat rate equivalent to the 40% mark-up or if his restaurant was successful 5% of the restaurant's sales, whichever was the greater. To reduce any risk to McDonald's, they also insisted on a security deposit, which was originally set at $7,500, increased to $10,000 in 1963 and is now closer to £10,000 ($15,000). In the second stage, McDonald's then used this money to begin buying land and buildings outright. In 1970, the percentage was increased to 8.5% and it turned out to be a huge and stable source of income with another key advantage. The arrangement provided Kroc with the type of control over the franchisee that he could not get from a franchise agreement. In future, any violation of the franchise could automatically terminate the lease. According to Love (1995: 156–157), an excited Kroc reported to the McDonald brothers in early 1957:

> I have finally found the way that will put every single McDonald's we open under our complete control…if at any time…the operation does not conform in every way to the McDonald's standards of quality and service, this lease will be cancelled on thirty-day notice. Now we have a club over them, and by God, there will be no more pampering or fiddling with them. We will do the ordering instead of going around and begging them to co-operate.

Moreover, this arrangement also proved to be bullet-proof in the legal battles with franchisees that followed. Courts continually ruled that selecting and controlling locations was natural for the corporation and did not place the corporation's financial interest in conflict with that of its franchisees. McDonald's profitability now depended on its ability to increase the sales of its franchisees, building volume at existing sites rather than just building new restaurants. Today, McDonald's owns the property at 69% of its US units and at 35% of its international restaurants. McDonald's franchise agreement is a far more complex affair than that sold by the McDonald brothers. It includes the McDonald's 'fast-food bible', an operating manual that runs to some 600 pages covering cooking methods and procedures, standard food portions, daily cleaning requirements and quality control as well as specifying the organisation of production and the division of labour. However, restaurant managers and franchisees need not worry about acquiring the correct standard and quality of supplies, this is all dealt with by the company. McDonald's carefully control all their suppliers on all aspects of their products: specifications as to size, thickness, texture and quality of the food is carefully monitored (Love, 1995). The degree of monitoring required is substantial and highly developed. It consists of regular visits for experienced trusted franchisees usually once per month, some with no warning, but many more regular visits for new or less-trusted franchisees. McDonald's 'field consultants' generally conduct these visits. They are responsible for making sure of franchise restaurant quality. The restaurant is assessed on 500 items, using a standardised twenty-seven-page inspection form. A 2- to 3-day inspection is made once a year followed by an unannounced visit 30–90 days later before grades are assigned. Grades are based on an assessment of three key issues, quality, service and cleanliness (QSC), plus an overall grade on everything else, ranging from an 'A' to an 'F'. This is exactly the same in both Germany and the UK and appears to follow the same format in most other European countries in the study. These checks are also complemented by customer visits and the 'no warning' spot checks. In addition to the financial benefits of the franchise system, McDonald's has also benefited from the ideas and creativity of their franchisees. Some of their most successful products have come from franchisees, even Ronald McDonald himself (Franchise World, 1993; Love, 1995).

The financial costs and the application process

The amount of capital investment in acquiring a franchise is substantial. It consists of a security deposit of around £10,000, returnable when the 20-year licence expires, and a non-returnable franchise fee which includes money paid to third-party suppliers for equipment, fixtures and other fixed assets. On top of this, there is a monthly fee paid to the McDonald's Corporation of 12% of gross sales and an advertising fee of 4% of gross sales. By the late 1990s, a franchise in both the UK and Germany cost similar sums. This varied between £200,000 and £500,000, depending on the size of the restaurant, its location and age. Forty per cent of these costs must be provided from non-borrowed personal resources. Becoming a McDonald's franchisee is neither quick nor easy; many people show an interest in running a McDonald's franchise, but not so many will have either the financial backing or the required commitment to attain one. McDonald's is highly selective in choosing its franchisees, it does not often advertise to attract prospective franchisees (almost never in the USA and only in recent years in the UK). In a recent interview, the McDonald's UK Vice-President responsible for franchising stated (Franchise World, 1993: 35):

> The right person is more important than the money...we are looking for hands on involvement and personal commitment in what is a seven days a week business.

An ex-McDonald's manager, now turned UK franchisee, also confirmed this approach regards the selection of franchisees:

> People who are just looking at it to make a quick buck, are not the people who are going to be selected.

We can now examine these statements by looking at what is involved in obtaining a McDonald's franchise. There are two ways to obtain a franchise, either the traditional route as an outside investor or as a long-serving McDonald's manager.

Outsiders and insiders

Providing an individual has enough money and business experience, he or she is granted a 2-hour interview. If this stage is successful then the applicant must work for 45–50 hours at a McDonald's restaurant in a job experience programme. If they survive this then they are interviewed and evaluated again before beginning the 6- to 9-month basic operations course (BOC). Applicants are then re-evaluated by a licensing manager and McDonald's franchise consultants. The applicant will then be registered on the applicant's list, when he or she must then pay the deposit. Then the formal 6-month (full time) or 12-month (part time) formal training programme can begin. The applicant is trained for 20 hours per week in operations and management in an established McDonald's restaurant. The applicant must also attend four formal classroom sessions of 1 or 2 weeks' duration, the last one taking place at the 'hamburger university' (for example in London in the UK or in Munich in Germany). During the entire period, the applicant is not considered to be an employee of the company and receives nothing in terms of expenses or compensation for the time spent. He or she must achieve the standards laid down by the company. A prospective franchisee usually has to wait for 1 year after the deposit has been paid before his/her restaurant is opened. However, as the training usually takes at least 2 years (with the franchisee working for 2,000 unpaid hours), the new franchisee can usually expect to take over his new or established restaurant soon after his training is completed. On average only two-thirds of applicants will stay the course, the extensive time commitment and high attrition rate enables McDonald's to select highly motivated and capable franchisees.

If the franchisee fails to perform according to the rules and stipulations of the company, the £10,000 security deposit may be forfeited. However, this is quite rare. Love (1995) suggests that Ray Kroc decided early on that franchisees must be entrepreneurs willing to stake everything they owned for a chance to operate a McDonald's outlet. McDonald's does not allow franchisees to debase the trademark. As already mentioned, the licence can be cancelled at any time if standards are not met. These standards include the all-important quality, service and cleanliness (QSC), level of personal daily involvement, aggressiveness in local advertising and marketing, realisation of potential sales, depth and ability of management, level of reinvestment and the franchisee's co-operation and financial payment history with the corporation and suppliers. Finally, McDonald's generally prefers franchisees with no previous experience in catering. Some time ago, Shelton (1967) suggested that this was primarily to maintain the uniformity of the corporation's operations because, first, franchisees with no previous experience are likely to be much more dependent on the franchisor's know-how and, second, those with prior restaurant experience are likely to think that they know so much about the business that they might try to install practices other than those specified by the franchisor.

Long-term managers can also apply for a franchise, providing their employment record is of a high standard. The corporation also provides help in terms of loans to enable managers to acquire the necessary capital to take on a franchise. In the UK, the corporation operates a loan scheme for established managers called business-facilitated lease (BFL). This scheme consists of a 3-year lease and an extra percentage or rent is paid to the corporation. The advantage of this approach is that after 3 years managers can opt out of the deal without any significant loss. McDonald's normally insists that managers are at least at the level of area supervisor (normally responsible for several McOpCo restaurants in a given area) and have been employed by the corporation for over 10 years to be able to apply for this scheme. The numbers of 'insiders' tend to be in the minority, but providing their restaurants are profitable they provide a loyal franchise grouping for the corporation. 'Outsiders' are more likely to be the ones who will offer some resistance to the company's directives. In fact, it was a group of these franchisees that first established an institution to represent their own interests in the USA, the McDonald's Operators Association (MOA).

'Traitors within': the McDonald's Operators Association

The events surrounding the establishment of the MOA in the USA give us a useful insight into the relationship between McDonald's and its franchisees. The heavy growth and continued expansion of the McDonald's Corporation in the USA in the 1960s and early 1970s began to create problems for some of its franchisees. The corporation had also begun to increase the numbers of its company-owned restaurants under the McDonald's Operating Company (McOpCo). By 1975, there were some 1,100 franchise restaurants in the USA, but in the period 1968–75 the number of company-owned restaurants had increased from 9% to 31%. In 1965, the corporation adopted a regional organisation (which it still has today) with five major offices outside Chicago (head office). Franchisees were beginning to lose contact with those at head office and the personal relationship they had enjoyed with Kroc in earlier years. Some franchisees were coming to the end of their 20-year lease and were becoming concerned about renewal and some saw the increase in McOpCo restaurants as threatening, but the major concern for many was the 'impact' of loss of sales from expansion itself. Franchisees were not consulted when new restaurants were opened in their area, and often these new restaurants led to falling sales. According to Love (1995), the new regional management were inexperienced and autocratic, this together with falling sales and lack of consultation created a great deal of dissatisfaction among franchisees.

A group of fifty franchisees decided to take action and formed the MOA in 1975. When they received little interest from Kroc and other top management, they declared their intention to be an adversarial group and made several demands. Many of the demands hit at the heart of the whole system. These included: no new restaurants to be built that would have an impact upon existing franchise restaurants, major improvements to be paid for by McDonald's not the franchisees, automatic right to renew the franchise after 20 years and all new units in a market to be awarded to existing franchisees.

In effect, franchises were trying to attain lifetime security, guaranteed expansion and shelter from competition. These demands were completely contrary to McDonald's operating principles and were quite unacceptable to the corporation (Love, 1995). The corporation decided to try to improve consultation and communication with its franchisees by establishing the National Operators Advisory Board (NOAB). This board comprised two elected franchisee representatives from each region. It was to be an advisory committee, but it would cover all issues affecting the relationship with franchisees. A second step was to establish an ombudsman to investigate complaints as a 'neutral' third party. Apparently, this was an idea Ray Kroc had taken from third-century Scandinavian royalty (Love, 1995: 396):

> The Kings of Sweden, Norway and Denmark had begun to use advisers to plead the case of common people who had complaints about the treatment they received at the hands of the King's ministers.

This view of the McDonald's–franchisee relationship does suggest a dominant role for the corporation, perhaps with Kroc seeing himself as the 'King'. Kroc also became much more careful in opening new restaurants, spending time to discover what effect new restaurants would actually have on existing ones. The corporation also began making compensation payments to franchisees who had been most affected by the establishment of new restaurants in their area. In 1975, the corporation paid out $5 million in rent relief and also began providing loans for investment in new equipment or facilities for struggling franchisees. Of equal significance is the fact that Kroc increased the supervision over McDonald's regional managers to ensure that they retained the firm's original values.

These changes placated most franchisees and most of the more extreme demands were dropped. However, the corporation has had to go on paying compensation to franchisees ever since. This problem is unlikely to go away because the only way that the corporation can increase its sales in the American market is to go on building new restaurants (*The Economist*, 1996a). The MOA and individual franchisees continued to pursue some legal cases against the corporation, eventually winning them all; in fact, McDonald's was embroiled in a large number of lawsuits in the mid-1970s. As Love (1995: 403) states:

> When it came to protecting the operating basics, McDonald's has always refused to compromise with anyone.

In 1977, the MOA was effectively disbanded as an independent association and became part of the National Franchisee Association. Nevertheless, ombudsmen and associations such as the MOA still exist in most of the other countries where McDonald's operates. In the UK, the McDonald's Franchisee Association represented approximately 120 franchisees in 1994, and a similar association represents approximately 250 franchisees in Germany. The corporation has also encouraged the establishment of franchise associations in the old Eastern bloc countries. For example, a Hungarian franchise association was established in 1992 (Mendelsohn, 1992).

Additional committees for overseeing the McDonald's marketing budget are usually the norm in most countries. Because of its low number of franchise outlets, the UK was late when it introduced such a marketing co-operative in 1994. This committee comprises seven members, four franchisees and three corporation executives, and is based on similar committees in the USA, Canada and the rest of Europe. It gives elected franchisee representatives some say over how the marketing budget should be spent (*Franchise World*, 1994), but the amount of influence these associations and committees have is limited. Although they are consulted on most matters, the main area for consultation is marketing, and this tends to be advisory not co-decisional. Nevertheless, franchisees do suggest that having an independent voice of some kind is important and that if the number of franchisees increases they may gain more influence. A UK franchisee stated:

> You can try and get in with the right committees and the right people so that you can influence future decisions and that's the only way. Now that there are more franchisees coming in perhaps we'll have more say.

However, most interviewees suggested that such committees or associations could not achieve very much for franchisees. One recent example involved McDonald's UK's interpretation of the Transfer of Undertakings Act, which has implications for new franchisees taking over existing restaurants. In the past, franchisees had been able to choose their own *salaried* restaurant management from somewhere else and replace the existing restaurant managers. The original restaurant management would then have to be transferred elsewhere in the company. However, the Act has meant that these individuals can refuse transfer and demand a redundancy option; this has started to prove costly for the corporation over recent years. In 1994, the corporation made a unilateral decision to take away the franchisees' option to replace existing salaried management when they take over a restaurant. All franchisees were notified of the change by a statement from the Vice-President in a circulated memo. Another franchisee stated:

> It was just a statement by our vice-president so what do you do? We've discussed it at the franchise meeting, we've asked our representative to turn back and say we're not happy with this, but whether we'll get anywhere with it I doubt, because it does tend to be like a lot of things at McDonald's...end of story.

It appears that the same conflicts of interest that were evident in the 1970s are still evident today. However, the corporation has effectively kept franchise associations within controllable limits; any 'influence' for the franchisees is likely to be restricted to what the McDonald's system will allow.

Imposing uniformity

Kroc had already faced the problem of combining a centralised, standardised system with a decentralised franchise structure. In his autobiography, he states (Kroc, 1977: 86) that his aim was to:

> ...ensure repeat business based on the system's reputation rather than on the quality of a single restaurant or operator. This would require a continuing program of educating and assisting operators and a constant review of their performance. I knew in my bones that the key to uniformity would be in our ability to provide techniques of preparation that operators would accept because they were superior to methods they could dream up for themselves.

However, it is not only the superiority of the methods applied or the training given which maintain uniformity. It has already been stated that franchisees do not have autonomy in a wide range of areas, including hours of operation, pricing, product, supply of inputs and only limited say in promotion and pay levels. McDonald's also awards additional franchises one at a time, so franchisees have an added incentive to comply with regulations. Ray Kroc established a precedent of harsh punishments for any franchisee failing to meet standards. Additional franchises are refused if standards are not met and licences not renewed. Williamson (1985) argues that the asset specificity and the vertical integration involved in the compulsory supply network means that the franchisee is closely bonded to the franchisor. It is argued here that McDonald's success in maintaining uniformity is not only because of a highly effective method but also because of the highly specific cash investments in physical assets and human time and investments in training that are imposed by the corporation. When asked about the amount of freedom they had to make decisions, a typical reply was this from a UK franchisee:

> ...the one thing I've learnt in the last two years, is that the brand is everything, they won't let you do anything without it being checked tested and quality tested so many times...having a McDonald's franchise there is a frustration factor...changes that are made company-wise you have to go along with, they are foisted upon you, you have no say in what happens...we are an extension of the company.

This determination to retain uniformity has not changed since McDonald's early franchises under Kroc, as Kroc reported to the brothers in 1958 (Love, 1995: 61):

> Now damn it, we are not going to stand for any monkey business [from franchisees]…once they sign [the franchise] they are going to conform and we are going to hold to it that they do conform.

Franchisees often run more than one restaurant, established franchisees may run between two and five restaurants and in the USA they may run even more (some have over twenty). None of the franchise operators interviewed in the study had more than two restaurants, and it was not unusual for franchisees to operate with only one restaurant each. However, all the franchisees interviewed did hope to and had definite plans for additional restaurants if their existing businesses succeeded. In fact, most had already applied for a second or third franchise and were awaiting a suitable site and final authorisation. In cases where the franchisee begins to run more than one restaurant, franchisees tend to adopt a similar managerial hierarchy as the corporation. Quite often, the restaurant manager in the first franchise would be promoted to the equivalent of an 'area supervisor', monitoring the performance of all the franchisee's restaurants. However, the final authority on performance of the franchisee's restaurants still rests with the corporation and their 'field consultants'.

In addition to the residual profit motive, it is arguably the tremendous risk of losing the right to the franchise (or additional franchises) that *imposes uniformity* and quality throughout the system. The corporation uses the incentive of acquiring an additional franchise to ensure that franchisees conform and are aggressive competitors. Michael Quinlan, the ex-CEO of the McDonald's Corporation, insists that for franchisees to qualify for expansion they must meet even tougher standards of performance. This is especially so in the USA, where any growth must come from the competition not from expansion. He encourages strong franchisees who are trapped into small markets to buy out weak franchisees who are 'underexploiting' larger markets. Williamson (1985) suggests that the usual problem limiting the growth of large organisations is the need to add hierarchical layers, making information more costly to transmit. However, McDonald's is able to disperse information and impose its will on the system through the franchisee.

The distinction between the franchisee and the company restaurant manager

It might be assumed that the amount of autonomy enjoyed by the franchisee and the company restaurant manager would be considerably different over a wide range of issues. Indeed, although there is some technical variation in individual agreements required to take into account differences in national law (Buschbeck-Bülow, 1989), the outcome is the same. Control and monitoring of franchisees is so tight that they have very limited autonomy over the running of their restaurants. McDonald's monitors performance of its franchises through their 'field consultants', whereas company-owned restaurants are monitored by an 'area supervisor'. In all the countries in this study, the same kind of monitoring structure is evident, e.g. in Germany and Austria these positions are called *Lizenzberater* and *Bezirksleiter* respectively.

In general, there is less frequent monitoring of both franchise and McOpCo restaurants if they consistently produce high sales volumes. Those that underperform will receive much more detailed and frequent scrutiny. This may therefore have some knock-on effect on the autonomy enjoyed by individual franchisees and company restaurant managers, and this may also be dependent on the personal relationship between the area supervisor and manager and between the field consultant and franchisee. Nevertheless, the areas in which the franchisee has more control is very limited. Table 3.1 sets out the key differences and similarities, with areas of discretion split into three categories: no control, some control and total control. When asked what the key difference was between being a franchisee and a restaurant manager, one UK franchisee (who had previously been a long-serving company manager) stated:

Table 3.1 Differences and similarities in franchise operator and company-owned restaurant manager autonomy

Level of control	Restaurant managers	Franchisees

No control	Suppliers
	Basic operating system
	Product mix
	Pricing
	New expenditure
	Capital purchase
	Appointment of
	  salaried management
		Suppliers
		Basic operating system
		Product mix
		Pricing
		New expenditure
		Capital purchase
		Appointment of salaried
		  management

Some control	Promotions, marketing,
	  small contracts
	Planning and staffing levels
	  for part-time and hourly
	  paid employees
	Crew training
	
	Pay and conditions
		Promotions, marketing
		
		Planning and staffing levels
		  for part-time and hourly
		  paid employees
		Crew training
		Recommendation for
		  promotion of salaried
		  management, but not
		  training or appointment
		Pay and conditions
		
		Small contracts

Total control	Part-time and hourly paid
	  employees (floor/swing
	  manager and below)
	Recruitment
	Promotions
	Small pay increases based on
	  performance
		Part-time and hourly paid
		  employees (floor/swing
		  manager and below)
		Recruitment
		Promotions
		Pay based on performance

In terms of how the operation runs, y'know very little. McDonald's are very strict in their operating standards, very strict in the way that they deal with franchisees.

Similarly, a German franchisee stated:

If you want to change anything, there are various committees organised for every possible facet of McDonald's that you can imagine, whether it's new products, marketing, equipment, personnel policies etc. …they would want it in writing and then they let you know.

Capital expenditure, marketing and small contracts

The restaurant manager must implement any capital purchase or new expenditure deemed necessary by his area supervisor. In theory at least, the franchisee can refuse to implement capital purchase and new expenditure and should be able to appoint and promote his own salaried managers and set wage levels. However, the reality is somewhat different. Refusals to meet requests for new expenditure are rare. If they do occur, then the field consultant, rather than command, will explain the 'importance' of the expenditure and try to persuade the franchisee. A German ex-manager, now franchisee, states:

Yes, whereas here, for example McDonald's wanted me to invest in another piece of equipment a very different approach is taken. If it has happened that new equipment is needed, if its for the sake of food safety, then McDonald's will push the issue more so.

However, if this persuasion doesn't work then the area manager or even regional manager can be called in. If the corporation wants something done, they do have the ultimate sanction of revoking the franchise, and it is difficult for the franchisee to make excuses because, first, the corporation knows exactly whether or not a franchisee can afford a new purchase or not. A UK franchisee stated:

Obviously McDonald's have access…one of the agreements in the franchise document is that McDonald's have a copy of my profit and loss statements, completed monthly, so they are very well aware of the financial position of each franchisee.

Second, if there is financial difficulty, loans can and will be provided. This is something that the corporation first introduced in the mid-1970s and still does today; franchisee again:

If the company realises that an investment is needed that someone can't financially meet, they will offer assistance, not necessarily pay for it, but offer a loan to pay it back over a longer term, or whatever, they are fairly accommodating.

In practice, therefore, it is very difficult for franchisees to refuse new expenditure on capital if the corporation insists on it. Franchisees do have some freedom with promotions and marketing, e.g. they can spend more on promotions, but they cannot spend less because they pay a fixed percentage of sales. In addition, franchisees do have more control in the area of small contracts for such issues as window cleaning, refuse collection and garden services.

Franchisees: working the employees harder?

By the 1960s, the incumbent McDonald's chairman, Fred Turner, began to change things, converting franchises into company-owned restaurants based on the idea that the corporation would then earn full profits. However, Turner reversed this process when he realised that the long-term profitability and competitiveness of the company depended on the franchises. Turner then limited the number of company-owned restaurants to 33%; today, it stands at about 20% in the USA and at about 25% on average world-wide. As Turner states (Love, 1995: 292):

> Lacking the incentive and drive of entrepreneurial owner–operators, company restaurants rarely equalled the profit margins of franchised units. Company owned restaurants tend to do far worse at low volume sites where managerial efficiency is essential for success.

Shelton (1967: 1257) also argues that franchises perform better than McOpCo restaurants. In a study of twenty-two fast-food restaurants, Shelton suggests that franchise ownership turned loss-making company-owned outlets into profit-making franchisee-owned ones:

> ...franchisee-owners just watch the little things closer; they utilise the cooks and waitresses better; they reduce waste.

It is because the fast-food industry is labour intensive that a great deal of emphasis is placed on maximising labour output. With the franchisee, McDonald's has a large supply of highly committed, 'non-shirking' competent managers. They are likely to be more motivated than employed managers and to work themselves and their workforce harder. The corporation may argue that franchisees are better at motivating their employees, but this is not the only explanation. The findings from this study suggest that in practice this may mean working with smaller numbers of employees and not always adhering to the minimum pay and conditions set by collective agreements.

In fact, the levels of staffing and the pay and conditions of employees is one key area where franchisees do have more control than the managers of company-owned restaurants.

Appointment, promotion and training

Both managers and franchisees have total control over the selection, appointment, promotion and training of the part-time and hourly paid employees. The main differences appear to be in the way in which this is carried out. Correct procedures for this are all stipulated by the corporation; the management in company-owned restaurants are supposed to adhere closely to the corporation's rules and regulations, including the use of an 'observation check list' (OCL; see Figure 3.1).

PREPARATION AND TOASTING		Possible	Actual
1	Buns are selected using FIFO	3	
2	Empty as well as full bin trays are stacked where they are not a hazard and sorted according to colour code	2	
3	Trays of buns are stacked so that buns are not crushed	3	
4	Appropriate bun board used and toaster set at 420°F (± 5°F)	3	
5	Bun trays are flat, clean and dry	3	
6	Macs/Regulars: Buns person directs grill person to achieve perfect timing and co-ordination. Buns are never pre-staged in toasters	3	
7a.	Regular bun crowns or Big Mac club and heel sections: placed in toaster immediately on call from production person	3	
b.	Quarter bun crowns: placed in toaster immediately; after 30 seconds duty timer sounds		
8a.	Regulars and Quarters: when buzzer sounds, toaster handle is lifted immediately and heels are placed in toaster before crowns are removed	3	
b.	Big Macs: when buzzer sounds, toaster handle is lifted immediately and crowns are placed in toaster before clubs are lifted out using a spatula, and placed on tray with heels. Tray is placed on dressing table		
9	Bun surface is caramelised to a uniform golden brown	3	
10	Bun is not crushed by excessive compression or damage in any other way	3	
11	Bun person keeps up with product demand	3	
12	Good communication and teamwork exists (i.e. 3 Cs: Communication, Co-operation and Co-ordination)		

GENERAL

1	Uniform is neat and clean (wearing apron). Name badge is worn	3	
2	Hands are washed before commencing work on this station	3	
3	Clean white/blue border cloths are used and kept in the appropriate pan	2	
4	Only countable waste is placed in the red bin	1	

OVERALL GRADE

(A)	× 0.75 =	(C)	
(B)	× 0.25 =	(D)	
OVERALL	= C + D		

Pass = 90%

TOTAL (pass = 40)	44	
SCORE (A)	100%	

COMMENTS

_____

_____

Figure 3.1 An example of an observation check list (OCL) used for the toasting and preparation of buns

Franchisees are supposed to use OCLs to adopt best practice, but it is not an issue on which the corporation is likely to discipline them. Some adopt their use simply because they feel that they are something positive for the employees. Most of the franchisees in the study have used them at one time or another, but often erratically and some hardly at all. Employees are given a grading on an OCL that is supposed to reflect their performance, and these grades are then used as the criteria for decisions about the employee's overall performance, which in some countries then determines whether or not they receive a small increase in pay. In fact, even in company-owned restaurants, OCLs were rarely completed at the correct times or even at all in some cases.

Some managers and/or franchisees were simply more 'diligent' in their use than others. Restaurant managers cannot appoint or recruit full-time salaried staff (i.e. assistant managers or above). Within McOpCo restaurants, any promotion to a salaried position can only come from regional or more senior management. In theory, franchisees can select and promote their salaried management. However, salaried management have to be trained by the corporation, so promotion can only be authorised after individuals have passed the corporation's exams, which are held at regional or head offices. Since the European legislation on the Transfer of Undertakings, if franchisees take over an existing restaurant then they are obliged to take on the existing salaried employees of the restaurant.

In a number of European countries where a works council is in place, franchisees and the corporation may theoretically have to inform and consult the works council and, in some cases, gain the council's consent with regard to appointment or promotion of staff. However, as we shall see in Chapter 6, in practice it has been very difficult to establish effective works councils in most European countries. Franchisees who take over new restaurants are to some extent free to select the assistant managers and restaurant managers that they want for their restaurant. However, in practice, the franchisees often choose individuals recommended by the company and they are often managers with whom franchisees have already worked while they carried out their training. In addition, franchisees usually go to the company for any additional salaried managers they may require.

Staffing levels, pay and conditions

The restaurant manager and franchisee can determine the number of part-time and hourly paid employees, who make up 90% or more of the workforce, in a similar way. However, it is the more senior management outside the restaurant who set guidelines for labour costs. Both managers and franchisees must not exceed those guidelines. Franchisees usually have some leeway in being able to exceed these labour cost percentages. However, this is one of the few areas where franchisees have some freedom of action to be able to increase their profitability. They are therefore unlikely to exceed the guidelines set by the corporation; they are more likely to be trying to keep them under control, particularly because poorly performing franchisees are likely to come under pressure from the corporation with regard to their licence.

In the UK and Ireland, there are no collective agreements in place. In the remaining eleven European countries covered in this study, McDonald's employees are covered by national, sectoral or, in some cases, company-level agreements on basic pay and conditions. Franchisees are not likely to pay their staff a great deal less than in the McOpCo restaurants, but, as the analysis in the following chapters indicates, franchisees do tend to be much tighter in controlling wage levels and in pushing the boundaries of labour costs to their limit. Rather than reducing basic pay rates significantly, franchise operators tend to keep employees in lower wage groupings than those to which they are entitled, miscalculate sick and holiday pay and overlook health and safety regulation. In any case, in some countries, such as the USA, the McDonald's starting wage is often the same as the legal minimum wage. As we shall see in Chapters 6 and 8, franchises are also often at the centre of problems with national systems of worker representation, such as works councils.

The franchise operator: employer or employee?

This analysis suggests that the franchise is a much more subtle way of exercising power than one might have otherwise assumed. The franchisor (in this case McDonald's) can enlist the support of franchisees for the intensification of work rather than directly speeding up the pace of work themselves and then take a part of the increased revenues generated. As one franchisor put it (Burck, 1970: 120):

> ...franchisees can expect to work like hell put in long hours, follow every rule – and make a lot of money.

But the franchisor also acquires the consent of the franchisee. Edwards (1990) has stressed the importance of consent as well as coercion in achieving control over labour because total elimination of worker's discretion is impossible. As Burawoy (1979: 27) puts it, '...coercion must be supplemented by the organisation of consent'. The franchisor does acquire the consent of his franchisee to work hard and to drive hard those he employs. However, the franchisee does not have an employment contract but a commercial contract; the franchisee works for a profit not a wage. However, the appearance of the franchisee investing large sums in the purchase of the physical means of production and the hiring of their own workforce does not mean that franchisees are unambiguously capitalists. In one court case in Germany, the Labour Court of Appeal in Düsseldorf ruled that one group of 'franchisees' was actually employed by the company Jacques Wein-Depot. According to Albrecht Schulz Sigle *et al.* (1988), in tightly controlled franchise agreements, similar to those found at McDonald's, the franchisee only differs from an employee in that he can set his own work hours and holidays and does his own book-keeping. It is becoming clear from the analysis so far that the franchisor does not bargain with the franchisee as an equal. Franchisees are relatively powerless right from the beginning of the relationship. In contrast to the free market view of franchise contracting, the relationship between the franchisor and the franchisee is arguably one that is closer to the employee and employer relationship. As Wright (1976: 37) puts it:

> The owners of fast-food franchises could be seen as occupying a contradictory location between the petty bourgeoisie or small employers and managers. While they maintain some of the characteristics of self-employed independent producers, they also become much more like functionaries for large capitalist corporations.

The inability of the franchisee to be able freely to sell the franchise and McDonald's extensive control over most aspects of the operation suggests that franchisees are much closer to 'subsidiaries' of the corporation rather than truly independent operators. As one franchisee put it:

> You can try out your own ideas as long as they come within the scope of what McDonald's will allow you to try.

Taken together with the ease with which McDonald's can terminate the franchisee's contract, the above analysis suggests that, as Rubin (1978: 225) puts it:

> ...the definition of the franchise as a separate firm, rather than as part of the franchisor, is a legal and not an economic distinction.

The format franchise system operated by McDonald's is not about devolved decision-making. Franchisees do not have autonomy over a wide range of issues, and even in areas where McDonald's franchisees do have some control or influence their freedom of action can be threatened at any time. In many aspects of the operation, the franchisee is just as restricted as the restaurant manager.

In McDonald's official biography, Love (1995) repeatedly suggests that the key to success for McDonald's in international markets was the same as it was in the USA: 'local control by local owner operators'. For example, in struggles with trade unions in Ireland, the company emphasised the fact that its franchisees were Irish and that the original McDonald brothers were descendants of Irish immigrants in the hope that it would dilute the connection with the American head office in the eyes of the public. They came up with the slogan (Love, 1995: 443) 'Our name may be American but we're all Irish'. However, as we have shown, franchisees may be 'local' but they are nevertheless 'McDonald's people'. The careful selection, and the extensive training and socialisation of both franchisees and managers, eliminates those with opposing values and inappropriate attitudes. Love perhaps inadvertently makes this clear when he also states that, despite their diverse backgrounds, common threads run through the backgrounds of most McDonald's managing directors and franchisees overseas and that this provides an insight into the chain's unique success on foreign soil. Love (1995: 429–30) states:

> ...while most of the international partners are foreign by birth, virtually all of them are not traditionalists in their homeland. Indeed, most have an affinity for American business practices and American entrepreneurs, and most have spent considerable time in the United States. 'Coming to the States was a vitamin injection' recalls Swedish partner (franchisee) Lederhausen. 'Americans seemed more alert more aggressive and were more willing to try new things'. And Australian Chairman Ritchie took his job with McDonald's because he wanted to be involved in an American business. 'I always admired the US approach to things... American companies seemed more efficient and aggressive than Australian companies'.

Franchisees may be 'local' in the sense that they understand local issues, local culture and the kind of obstacles likely to confront the McDonald's system. But rather than meaning 'adaptation', being local is more likely to mean having the ability to impose the McDonald's system on local arrangements more effectively. The interfirm relationship, especially the relationship between the franchisee and the franchisor, is a key intervening variable which can just as easily represent a strengthening as much as a weakening of corporate control. To suggest that the legal separation of the franchise signals a loss of control for the large organisation overlooks the reality of this kind of franchise relationship. The franchise is, therefore, no obstacle to controlling uniformity and, if anything, aids uniformity because of the strictly controlled and highly motivated franchisee.

Franchisees only enjoy freedoms when it benefits the corporation; then, McDonald's is willing to turn a 'blind eye' to the franchisee's activities in return for higher sales volumes and better profitability. This often means pushing down labour costs. In most European countries in this study, it was often (but not exclusively) the franchisees who infringed employee and trade union rights and health and safety legislation, and in most cases it was the franchisee who did not adhere properly to collective agreements. However, where the actions of franchisees endanger the brand and the long-term profitability of the corporation, they are usually brought into line. As we shall see, for example, in Chapter 6, when French managers at a McDonald's franchise were imprisoned for infringement of trade union and employee rights in 1994, the corporation soon moved to repair the damage to its public image. However, this action did not alter the nature of the relationship with its franchisees, nor did it improve the lot of the majority of its workers who are employed in franchise operations. Where higher profit margins can be maintained without damaging the corporate image, McDonald's will not interfere with franchisees because it directly benefits from these more 'efficient' operations.

Indeed, the issue of maintaining low labour costs and high profitability is at the centre of the next chapter, which provides an analysis of the nature of work, the employment relationship, corporate culture and typical workforce characteristics at McDonald's. This analysis should help us to understand how the socialisation of management takes place in practice and how both company mangers and franchisees are able to gain the control and consent of the workforce in the day-to-day operation of the restaurants.

4 McDonald's at work

I've often said that I believe in God, family, and McDonald's and in the office that order is reversed.

(Ray Kroc, quoted in Vidal, 1997: 37)

It's (McDonald's) been successful because every individual knows what's expected of him, whether he's a supplier to us or someone who works for us: it has to be right, it has to be the best, it has to be exactly when required – and if it isn't, as far as he's concerned that's it, he's gone.

(Director of McDonald's Russia, quoted in Parker, 1992: 343).

The organization cannot trust the individual; the individual must trust the organization

(Ray Kroc, quoted in Love, 1995: 144)

This chapter examines the restaurant hierarchy, the nature of the work, the employment relationship and the characteristics of the people who work at McDonald's. How does the corporation 'manage' the control and consent of its employees and managers? How does McDonald's deal with considerable differences in the availability of different kinds of workers in different labour markets? Can the concept of corporate culture help to maintain the uniformity of its employee relations practices across a variety of societal frameworks? We begin with a brief analysis of the restaurant hierarchy and the work itself.

McOrganisation

The hierarchy in McDonald's restaurants in all the countries in this study appears to be remarkably similar; where differences do exist, they appear to have a minimal impact on the corporation's basic American operating system. Figure 4.1 sets out the basic restaurant hierarchy below. The majority of employees are called the 'crew', and in fact this term appears to have been universally accepted; we have yet to find a country where this term is not in use. The term 'crew' was apparently used by the brothers right from the beginning of their 'Speedee Service System' in 1948, when they trained their

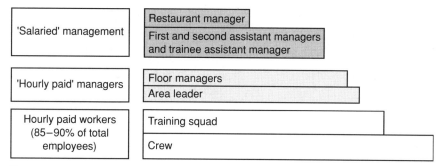

Figure 4.1 Job titles and hierarchy in the restaurants

twelve-man 'crew' to work like a 'crack drill team' (Love, 1995: 16). The idea
that the employees should be trained like the military was also promoted by
one of Ray Kroc's early franchisees, Sandy Agate, who opened his first
restaurant in Waukegan near the Great Lakes. Agate carefully selected the
crew, preferring mostly Navy chefs from the nearby Naval Training Centre.
Love (1995: 82) states: 'During peak periods, Agate barked out production
orders as a skipper might order sailors to their battle stations'.

In every country in this study, crew jobs are fragmented into different
stations, e.g. working on the till, cleaning tables and emptying bins, garnishing
burgers and monitoring fries, bread machines or the grill. Again, this goes
back to the McDonald brothers' early system. Love (1995: 18) states that as
the brothers refined their techniques members of the crew became specialists:

> There were three grill men who did nothing but grill hamburgers; two
> shake men, who did nothing but make milk shakes; two fry men who
> specialized in making French fries...three countermen who did nothing
> but fill orders....

Although some flexibility across different jobs is called for, kitchen workers
usually remain in the kitchen and till workers on the till. The 'training squad',
as they are called in the UK, or 'crew trainers', as they are called in Germany,
France and most other European countries, train other crew. They are
supposed to know all the stations and to monitor the work of normal crew
and, as mentioned earlier, they are supposed to do this with the use of an
operation checklist (OCL).

When training squad members are aged 18 years or over and are able to
work enough hours, they can be promoted to area leader (*Vorarbeiter* in
Germany and Austria; *Responsable de Zone* in France; *Ayundante de área* in Spain).
Further promotions would take them to floor manager and then shift-running
floor manager (*Schichtführer* in Germany; *Assistente de turno* in Spain). In The
Netherlands and France, these more senior floor managers are usually known
as 'swing managers', just as in the USA. These floor managers are still,
nominally at least, hourly paid workers and some are qualified to run a shift

by themselves, i.e. to distribute cash register drawers full of money and to deal with customer complaints. They look more like salaried managers because they usually wear a blue or white shirt or blouse with tie or bow and black trousers, whereas the crew and training squad usually wear some kind of T-shirt. The salaried managers are the restaurant manager and first, second and trainee assistant managers; they are employed on a permanent contract and are usually only appointed by regional management. Regional management normally determines promotion to salaried management positions in franchise operations, but franchisees can, and do, 'poach' existing salaried managers employed in company-owned restaurants. Promotion is dependent on employees passing the McDonald's training courses which managers in Italy, Germany and the UK suggest, it seems without exception, are based on the same format as in the USA. The German personnel director stated:

> The system is the same as in the USA, Basic Operations Course (BOC), Intermediate Operations Course (IOC) and the Advanced Operations Course (AOC) and its the same here.

Salaried managers enjoy greater employment security, benefits and monthly salaries. However, the issue of 'hourly paid' versus 'monthly paid' workers is not always that helpful. In some countries where collective agreements apply, as in Italy for example, all employees are paid on a monthly basis even if they only work a few hours per week.

McWork

As we have already suggested in Chapters 2 and 3, virtually all aspects of the business are highly standardised and rigorously monitored. Assembly line techniques are used to produce and serve identical products; standardisation and higher productivity are ensured through new technology and the systematic planning of each job, broken down into the smallest of steps. The corporation's industrial engineers measure and plan the equipment layout and scheduling in terms of seconds of working time using computerised time study methods. The worker's skills are eliminated and the work is labour intensive with the machinery making the cooking decisions. Lights and buzzers tell workers when to turn burgers or take fries out of the fat. Computerised cash registers do most of the thinking for till and window workers, separating the hand and the brain in classic scientific management style (Braverman, 1974).

The modern ketchup dispensers are little changed from the McDonald brothers' days: they squirt a measured amount of ketchup or mustard on each burger. Workers learn a routinised job in 1 day. For example, to prepare and bag French fries, workers follow nineteen carefully calculated steps; the French fry scoop enables workers to fill a bag and set it down in one continuous motion and helps them to gauge the proper serving size. All the jobs can be learnt with no previous experience or with the minimum of training. Operations are monitored and controlled using the *Operations and Training Manual* or the 'bible' as some McDonald's managers call it. It is some 600 pages in length and extremely comprehensive, it includes full colour photographs which, among other things, illustrate the correct placement for ketchup and mustard in the preferred five-point 'flower' pattern and it determines the correct size of pickles to be placed on each type of hamburger. Rules and procedures cover everything, eliminating decision-making for workers and, as one respondent put it, makes the job 'virtually idiot-proof'. One German floor manager stated 'Anyone can learn this job. There's no challenge for workers, only speed and exactitude'. When the assembly line output of burgers slackens because the restaurant is quiet, it does not mean that the workers are allowed to take a break. Ray Kroc was obsessed with cleanliness, he insisted that his staff should be constantly cleaning areas that no one else would even think about, with the cleaning cloth becoming an essential tool for every crew member. As Kroc frequently reminded his staff (Love, 1995: 143), 'If you've got time to lean, you've got time to clean'. So, although the work can be easily learnt, it would be a mistake to think that it was easy. A UK assistant manager emphasised the intense and hard nature of the work:

> Many people are not prepared to do the work that it entails, you've got to be a very strong-minded person to be able to handle it. A lot of people who think, 'oh this will be so easy', they totally underestimate it…it's often students who can't hack it, they don't want to work that hard for the money.

Moreover, the work is not just for the ordinary crew who do the bulk of the work but is also for the managers. One UK crew member stated:

> It is very stressful especially for the managers. I don't think I could work here full-time. The stress of trying to keep the happy face of McDonald's, that's what you've got to keep, or try to, even if you're having a bad day with the restaurant manager on your back, you've still got to be nice to customers, it can be difficult.

The majority of workers in most countries in this study work part time, so some may only do one full (8 hour) shift per week. However, if the restaurant is busy or short-staffed, workers are frequently asked to stay and work longer hours. In some cases, employees may end up working 10 hours or more; in fact, it can be much longer. Some full-time Finnish workers reported that they often worked a 14-hour day, and in one 2-week period they had worked 110 hours. Some workers may be quite happy to take the extra hours; in other cases managers may tell workers that if they refuse they may not get work on other occasions. In all European countries, hourly paid employees are supposed to get rest breaks; in some countries where collective agreements apply, these breaks may be longer or more frequent than laid down in the law. However, despite more stringent European regulation, workers from several countries reported that when the restaurant is busy breaks are cut short, workers have to get permission to leave the floor and managers are often reluctant to let employees go when their contracted hours are finished. In these situations, workers would sometimes aid management by 'controlling themselves', staying on longer so as not to 'let their colleagues down'.

Although there are rules and tight procedures for everything and managers usually working alongside closely monitor the work, workers do sometimes find short cuts. The research revealed that in several countries workers sometimes cheat on the system. They find short cuts when the restaurant is busy and when working within the system cannot cope with demand. In the UK, some employees were referred to as 'cowboys'; these workers would find short cuts in exactly the same way as assembly line workers in other industries in order to create some porosity in an otherwise hectic schedule. One UK floor manager stated:

> Yeah, some of the lads, the 'cowboys' have figured out how to save time on cleaning, missing out some of the steps but getting the same results. Or sometimes they make more burgers than are required by the shift leader on the wrap and call station, so that they get a short break.

In addition, some workers have reported on more deviant forms of behaviour, which might be akin to physical sabotage (Taylor and Walton, 1971). One example was what some young male employees called 'sweating competitions'. The hot kitchen conditions were used to see who could sweat the most over the products, apparently as a way of relieving the frustration or boredom or as a way of seeking revenge on unpopular managers or the customer. Nor is this the only example; one worker reported that he purposely did not wash his hands after a visit to the toilet, whereas others would apply their nasal fluid onto the products as a way of getting back at customers and managers.

Sometimes, mustard and ketchup dispensers clog up and then too little or no sauce is placed on the burger, pickles are missed, sometimes food falls on the floor and, if the manager isn't watching, it sometimes ends up with the customer. Buns, burgers and fries are taken out before the buzzer has buzzed, sometimes fries are kept longer than the regulation 7 minutes. Indeed, similar findings have also been reported by Leidner (1993) in her study of McDonald's restaurants in the USA. In some cases, it appears that managers adopt an 'indulgency pattern' (Gouldner, 1964); when restaurants are short-staffed, managers may turn a blind eye to some of these behaviours, providing that customer demand is met.

Managing control and consent at McDonald's

How does the McDonald's Corporation contrive to attain the consent and control of the workforce in practice? Schuler and Jackson (1987) suggest that different types of organisations adopt different approaches to the control of their workforce, depending on how they compete. They argue that there are three main bases for competitive advantage – innovation, quality and cost – whereas strategies revolving around quality and innovation are usually associated with a committed workforce. For organisations where costs are the most important part of the question, *control* is likely to be a more important factor than commitment. Although some level of consent is always necessary, control is high on the agenda at McDonald's. Control at McDonald's is not merely achieved by direct supervision, machines, the physical layout of the restaurant and the detailed prescription of rules and procedures but also through recruitment.

Applying for a job at McDonald's is usually the same process in most countries. The applicant fills in an application form and, if successful, will be invited for an interview. Until the 1970s, the corporation routinely put applicants through a half-hour lie detector test in some US restaurants, largely to determine whether or not they had any sympathy for trade unions. This practice was only ended after threats of legal action and changes in American labour law (Vidal, 1997). Above all, it appears that having the 'right attitude' is the most important attribute to obtain employment at McDonald's. Indeed, Fred Turner (an ex-CEO of the corporation) also suggests that the 'right attitude' is crucial. According to Love (1995), Turner was extremely impressed with the way that Japanese employees worked. However, he complained about the difficulty of achieving control over his American employees (1995: 426):

> ...with our Yankee mentality...(US) grill men don't give a damn about the system...But in Japan, you tell a grill man once how to lay the patties, and he puts them there every time. I'd been looking for that one-hundred percent compliance for thirty years.

Even unskilled workers have some power to disrupt the efficiency of the operation by withdrawing co-operation from the production process, disrupting the process or by simply leaving the organisation. Employees may submit to the authority of the employer, but are always likely to retain a strong interest in the use of their labour. Studies of work group behaviour show how workers often combine and co-operate with each other not only to bargain over wages and working conditions but also to control or influence the pace of work (Turnbull, 1988). Employees and management are, therefore, to some extent *interdependent*; management cannot rely solely on coercion or even compliance to secure high performance, management also needs to secure active employee consent and co-operation.

When workers' efforts are extracted through an elaborate systems of rules, including rules about grounds for promotion and for punishment, employers arguably establish more control over workers' personalities and values than when their efforts are extracted through direct exhortation or force or through the design of equipment (Edwards, 1979).

The customer can also play a significant role in this kind of process. The McDonald brothers were able to bring the customer into the equation early on with the introduction of their see-through building or 'goldfish bowl'. This was not lost on later building designs, which reveal not only the workers at the cash tills but also the workers in the kitchen to public view, leaving them few hiding places. Benson (1986) argues that where management is dependent on workers' expertise in dealing with customers, workers' culture may be a powerful impediment to managerial control. However, where extreme routinisation lessens workers' leverage or where management successfully inculcates its own values, workers' culture may be stunted or co-opted. So, the nature of the relationship between customers and workers will have an effect on the ability of workers to resist managerial demands effectively. The involvement of the customer in the work process replaces the usual two-way struggle between management and labour with a triangular pattern of shifting allegiances and interests among workers, managers and customers. Benson (1986) suggests that each of these three groups pursues its own ends in opposition to pressures from the other two, but under the right conditions would ally with one another against the third.

In some cases, workers can exercise control over customers not only when organisational rules dictate customer behaviour but also when workers' interests depart from those of management by the denial of useful information or the withholding of personal charm and effort (Benson, 1986). They can also be vengeful: deliberately spilling drinks on customers (Hochschild, 1983) or more violent action using 'techniques' such as the 'Disneyland seatbelt slap' (Van Maanen and Kunda, 1989). The McDonald's system offers very few opportunities for workers to control customers and similarly few ways in which customers can be punished, although there are examples of customers receiving food which has been spoilt or tampered with, e.g. burgers dropped on the floor and then placed in the serving bins.

What is more significant is the extent to which customers can control workers in this industry. They can act as informal supervisors, reprimanding workers for behaving rudely, dawdling or avoiding work. For example, Edwards (1979) suggests that customers can control work in a number of ways. They can direct workers by specifying their preferences; if the connection between work activities and service outcomes is well understood and immediately observable, customers can evaluate the workers and they can reward or punish them either with thanks or insults or with tips or complaints to superiors. The customer is also used to control the managers. Consumer surveys and other means of off-site management are increasingly being used by corporations as much to control *middle management* as to control workers. Indeed, this has become an increasing concern for American trade unions as managers use customer reports to discipline staff and link such criteria to salary (Fuller and Smith, 1991).

The service interaction at McDonald's may be limited, but the efforts of employers to standardise personality traits are often more direct than Edward's (1979) analysis indicates and the attitudinal and expressive requirements are much more specific. The diminution of workers' 'breathing space' is, therefore, even more drastic in some organisational programmes which attempt to train standardised workers. These attempts amount to a different form of worker control altogether, distinct from direct, technical and bureaucratic means of control; when employers such as McDonald's directly subject workers' attitudes, demeanour, self-concept and ways of thinking to standardisation, this control arguably goes beyond bureaucracy and into the realms of subjectivity.

Managing subjectivity

Hochschild (1983) argues that questions of subjectivity are not separable from the analysis of actual work practices in interactive service work because employers actively manage workers' *identities*. Workers and customers vie with management in a three-way contest for control and satisfaction. Hochschild (1983) emphasises the distress felt by workers subjected to organisational exploitation of their feelings and personalities; however, Leidner (1993) argues that not all workers resist the extension of standardisation to their inner-selves. Rather, many attempt to construct interpretations of their roles that do not damage their conceptions of themselves. As we shall see in the following sections, this 'cognitive dissonance' (Festinger, 1962; Hughes, 1984) may explain why some workers remain with the corporation for longer periods of time. Leidner (1993) also argues that in some situations service routines provide *workers and customers* with benefits which help account for their frequent acquiescence in managerial designs. However, Leidner (1993) does not suggest that the routinisation of service work and the standardisation of personality are benign, nor do workers, customers and employers necessarily benefit from these processes in a happy congruence of interests. These manipulations are often invasive, demeaning and frustrating for the workers and sometimes for the customers who experience them.

The importance of emotional labour in interactive service work, even of the limited kind found at McDonald's, should not be underestimated. Employers who standardise the service interaction exert a cultural influence that extends beyond the workplace. Hochschild (1983) and James (1989) argue that when workers are estranged from their own smiles the company is laying claim not just to physical motions but also to their *emotions*. Their organisational control strategies reach deeply into the lives of workers, encouraging them to take an instrumental stance towards their own personalities and towards other people. McDonald's employees working on a till, for example, although only involved in limited service interactions, are expected to control themselves *internally* by being pleasant, cheerful, smiling and courteous to customers, even when customers are rude and offensive. This applies to all McDonald's workers and their relations with fellow workers and supervisors, with whom they are expected to show obvious pride in their work and employment. How does McDonald's manage subjectivity and attain 'emotional labour' from its workforce? The findings suggest that a great deal of emphasis for satisfaction or dissatisfaction is placed on the relationship between individual managers and individual employees. An NGG (Gewerkschaft Nahrung Genuss Gaststätten) representative gave his opinion as to why German employees who stayed long term at McDonald's appeared to be reasonably satisfied and loyal:

> McDonald's give people a value, who in the normal German labour market have no or only little value, they say, 'we value you and are happy to work with you', of course these people recognise this and they are therefore much more tightly bound to the organisation and more loyal. A second point is that compared to other employers in the hospitality industry, McDonald's management are extraordinarily well trained and instructed in Human Resource Management. They place an extremely high value on leadership, McDonald's takes extreme care over the management of its workforce, it is patriarchal, ...despite being a system it has an extremely polished and personal relationship with its employees.

Reiter (1996) suggests that management in fast-food enterprises pursue a management approach that focuses on isolated individuals and concentrates on their needs and wants, which suggests that job satisfaction can be attained through adequate leadership and the efforts of management. With this view, job satisfaction is not attained through good pay and working conditions but through the less tangible area of psychological concepts. A good manager is one who will solve the problem of employee discontent through adequate communication. This is strongly reflected in the advice given to McDonald's managers in both countries. In the UK basic training manual, it states, for example:

> Employees who understand what is going on and who feel part of restaurant life, develop a sense of loyalty and pride. As a result they work harmoniously with management.

When asked how they motivated employees, both UK and German managers at restaurant and senior management level stressed the importance of good communication. Managers are encouraged to apply and concentrate on Herzberg's (1966) 'motivators': 'achievement', 'responsibility', 'growth' and 'recognition'. This may take the form of 'employee of the month' awards, day trips and cash bonuses or of encouraging workers to strive for promotion and take on responsibility. One UK training squad commented:

Really we're all brainwashed by their little procedures and incentives, they offer little carrots like the 'stars' and little pay rises or going for promotion to training squad.

On the one hand, the striving for promotion locks managers' and employees' loyalty into the system; on the other, it may offer real opportunities for advancement which may be hard to come by for those with poor academic backgrounds. Managers are encouraged to discount the importance of Herzberg's (1966) 'hygiene' factors, such as pay and conditions of work. Managers have no control over these issues because they are dictated by the system. Training reinforces the view that pay and conditions do not really matter; what really does matter is their 'positive' management style and leadership. Job satisfaction is thus defined as a phenomenon determined through the area of psychological concepts, not through good pay and conditions. A good manager will therefore 'solve' the problem of resistance or discontent through good communication. Managers in the UK refer to the three Cs (in Germany, the three Ks), co-ordination, co-operation and communication, as the basis of the solutions to all problems

McDonald's Germany training materials suggest that workers become resistant to management prerogative for the following reasons: a lack of communication; inadequate praise, recognition and staffing levels; incorrect management style; and mistakes in calculating pay, sick pay and holiday entitlements. Managers are frequently reminded that they must provide the necessary 'vision' for employees. Part of the list of competencies required for providing leadership are given in a (1994) UK management training package:

[Manager] clearly defines and communicates vision of greatness for restaurant...links restaurant vision to regional and corporate vision...ties vision to day-to-day actions and demonstrates personal belief in the vision through behaviour...demonstrates commitment to live out the vision.

Identification with the restaurant and other crew members is fostered through the creation of a new form of collective. If 'us and them' is still recognised, it is reinterpreted to mean 'us' as the management and crew and 'them' as the customer. Workers are encouraged to think of themselves as part of a team and managers are encouraged to equate restaurant management with coaching a team. The result of this form of 'teamwork' seems to be that individuals are often loath to be seen by their peers as making extra work for other people by not doing their share. Even the more resentful employees, who had what management saw as 'negative' attitudes, would still work hard to keep the respect of their peers. A typical feature of management style was the repeated use of certain kinds of language, with paternalistic expressions such as the 'McDonald's family'. Management and employees in both countries used the term to describe their work environment. Many responses reflected the strongly paternalistic nature of the employment relationship which management worked to foster. This was especially evident among foreign workers in Germany, one crew member in his late thirties stated:

> I am very happy here, my supervisor will understand if I have any problems, if there is something wrong I can go to the Schichtführer [floor manager] or the boss [franchisee].

When asked what he would do if something was wrong and the complaints he put to his boss found no response, he replied: 'I don't like to argue with my supervisors'. It would be wrong to assume that the manager's task of keeping workers happy is an easy one: to provide workers with feelings of achievement and recognition while they are themselves tightly controlled by their seniors. Their freedom of action is curtailed by stringent scheduling rules and by the needs of the restaurant that must come before those of the individuals. The carefully planned approach to managing the workforce, which requires managers to show consideration and give praise and recognition, often breaks down under the strain of meeting difficult targets. One UK floor manager commented that management tended to fluctuate from good to bad with the moods of the managers. Although managers were trained and able to give the appropriate 'leadership', it was often not put into practice:

> Getting praise makes it all worth while, but there's not enough of it, the managers don't always notice when I do things. Whenever I go to Regional HQ for training it's always superb, and I think what a wonderful company then you come back to the restaurant and...its like when we get a mystery customer inspection, if we get a bad one we hear about it for weeks afterwards, if we get a good one, it's rare that anyone gets a pat on the back.

As already suggested, achieving promotion within the restaurant inevitably means longer and longer hours and more responsibility. This includes the restaurant manager who will often have to work longer hours than anyone else. It was not uncommon for restaurant managers in this study to regularly work from 6.00 a.m. to 6.00 p.m. However, rather than this resulting in good management, it tended to result in unreasonable expectations and poor morale (UK floor manager):

> The main problem is crew morale, there is always somebody upset, people really take it out on others here and it can be very nasty. Managers just have the wrong attitude to other people, they can be very autocratic. [Salaried] Managers work such long hours and they expect everyone else to do the same, it breeds a culture... even when we're not busy there is an atmosphere in the restaurant which you can cut with a knife.

Although all restaurants are closely monitored and the head offices are very keen to train managers in developing the right leadership style, the ultimate emphasis is not on how the employees are managed but first and foremost on the profitability of the restaurant and its QSC (quality, service and cleanliness). One UK floor manager commented:

> They have inspections but they focus more on cleanliness, appearance and profitability. In a full-field inspection you'll have people here all night, it will be spotless, hygiene is always a very high standard, but problems of crew morale are only considered if profitability or QSC are affected.

Typically, employees will blame their immediate superiors rather than the company for their bad treatment. Satisfaction, resistance and consent are in a state of flux, but the all-powerful 'system' and the one-sided nature of the communication processes (see Chapter 6) usually mean that grievances and complaints are often waved aside or sometimes forgotten in the rush to satisfy the customer. Given the way in which the employment relationship is managed at McDonald's and given that there is an asymmetry of power in the employment relationship, it would appear that the only way in which McDonald's employees could be represented effectively would be through the mobilisation of collective interests. In theory at least, most European systems of industrial relations would appear to offer a number of ways in which the collective interest might be mobilised, e.g. well-organised trade unions, compulsory minima provided by sectoral or national level collective bargaining and worker-friendly labour legislation providing rights to consultation, information and, in some cases, co-determination. Such rights and systems are created and supported by societal culture and the values of individuals who have developed particular assumptions about the nature of the employment relationship in their societies. For example, German works councils and unions find a considerable amount of acceptance among the German business community (Eberwein and Tholen, 1990) and broader German society at large (Lane, 1989, 1994). Is it possible for these typical German norms and values regarding such institutions – derived from outside the workplace – to be immobilised or suspended so that multinationals can maintain an adequate level of uniformity across societies? The answer may lie with the issue of corporate culture.

McCulture

> We cannot trust some people who are non-conformists…we will make conformists of them in a hurry.
>
> (Ray Kroc, 1977)

It is not within the scope of this chapter to provide an analysis of culture and corporate culture *per se*,[1] this is more than adequately dealt with elsewhere (for example Smircich, 1983; Schein, 1984; Meek, 1988; Willmott, 1993; Anthony, 1994). Although the McDonald's Corporation may indeed 'have' a 'strong' organisational culture, there remain the questions of to what extent senior managers can influence it and of whether or not individuals within the organisation will internalise its basic assumptions. Willmott (1993) argues that the degree to which individuals may be prepared to see themselves as members of a corporate culture and internalise its norms and values may depend on their assessment of its moral character. Willmott (1993) also suggests that employee commitment is at best partial and that management attempts to expand control by trapping employees into a vicious circle of cynicism and dependence. Furthermore, much of the protagonists' writing on corporate culture and for that matter comparisons of international culture (for example Hofstede, 1980) are based on paradigm assumptions of unity, which ignore subcultures and individual perceptions within different levels and compartments especially in large organisations.

However, as Sathe (1983) and Anthony (1994) both point out, managers may not be interested in whether or not norms and values are internalised, providing they get the required *observable* behaviours. German restaurant management frequently referred to the inappropriateness of works councils and unions in the McDonald's system (Royle, 1998, 1999a). We suggest that 'getting on' at McDonald's does mean some demonstration of adherence to McDonald's values. At crew level, bureaucratic and mechanistic controls are more likely to be to the fore. For managers, however, corporate culture may be more significant in bringing about an unconscious and deeper transformation of behaviour. This would then make *external* controls unnecessary by persuading managers to control themselves *internally*. One UK assistant manager (a graduate), who had worked for the company for nearly 2 years and who had by now accepted the regular 60- to 70-hour weeks she worked, stated:

> ...There's not even an attempt to schedule for 40 hours. So I mean if you were scheduled for 40 hours you would stay on and do extra hours anyway because that's the kind of culture that it is. But the fact that you are not even consulted on the matter and you're scheduled for 50 hours and you stay for another 10 on top of that a week. ...I mean when I first started the job, oh my god my body felt just utterly exhausted. But you really do get used to it. You don't have time to think about being tired to be honest. I know that sounds like an exaggeration. ...But the one thing that the company has taught me is self-discipline.

This kind of statement suggests that the subjectivity of individuals is successfully manipulated, to the extent that the turkey not only sacrifices itself for the Christmas dinner but also helps to lay the table. In this sense, a 'strong' corporate culture is achieved by advocating a *systematic* approach to creating and strengthening organisational values in a way that *excludes* and *eliminates* all other values (Willmott, 1993). As Fred Turner, ex-CEO of the corporation, stated: 'Top executives are psychologically committed' (TICL, 1987: 15). This not only demands loyalty from employees but it also excludes, silences or punishes those who question its creed. In other words, the 'strength' of a corporate culture means its lack of contamination by rival 'ends' or values to which the discretion of employees might otherwise be 'misdirected', such as involvement with trade unions (see Chapter 5; Royle, 1998, 1999a). Those that come in from outside the organisation into a position of responsibility may find that the process of transformation is painful. When asked how her feelings about the company had changed in the last 18 months, a UK assistant manager stated:

> Well I hated it, loathed it and despised it when I first started, I used to go home crying everyday for the first two weeks, I hated it. …The reason why I stayed with the company then was because I was so bloody-minded. I couldn't bear to think that a company like McDonald's could break me. Y'know what I mean? I just couldn't bear it. I thought I have got to see this through because if I can't stick this out then I'll never be able to do anything for the rest of my life.

When basic assumptions are already shared about the nature of the world and more specifically the correct way to do business, adapting to the culture may be less traumatic. What is striking is the extent to which the same kinds of management practices dominated over different societal norms. There were several examples of restaurant management being disciplined for 'losing their way'. One such example was the case of a Danish assistant manager who having worked a 70-hour week took a day off in the following week. This right was clearly established in the Danish collective agreement; nevertheless, when this was brought to the attention of senior management the assistant manager concerned was strongly admonished. She later reported to the Danish union representative that her manager had shouted:

> What's going on here? Are we starting that now? Is that what we are doing? Taking time off?!

There is an unspoken rule that management work long hours over contract but that those hours are not noted down anywhere. This is further exacerbated by intense competition fostered between managers to do their administrative work in fewer and fewer hours. The hours allocated for such work are never adequate but managers do not want to be seen to be falling behind other managers, so they simply do the work (unpaid) in their own time. Only when these basic assumptions are not shared is resistance likely to arise.

The method of recruiting through the ranks may also help to support the 'strength' of the corporate culture, promoting through the ranks means that individuals are arguably already socialised into the way of doing things.

McDonald's claims that it strongly encourages a promotion from within approach. In the USA, Wildavsky (1989) suggests that more than 50% of the corporation's restaurant managers and almost 40% of its corporate officers started as hourly paid workers. German management estimated that 30% of salaried management had started as crew; in the UK, this was estimated at 35%. From the interview and questionnaire sample, the percentages of employees who had started as hourly paid crew and had been promoted to a *salaried position* (i.e. second assistant or above) generally supported these estimates.

Explaining labour turnover

Despite the similarities of the operations in terms of jobs, hierarchies and the apparent consistency of the way in which employees are managed in most countries, there are some noticeable differences in the numbers employed in restaurants in different countries. For example, the average number of employees in an average city centre restaurant in the UK was sixty-five, whereas in Germany it was only fifty-two. According to Lane (1989) and Prais (1981), German business organisations manage with a lower overall staffing level than do UK organisations. Despite these differences, the proportion of hourly paid crew, training squad and floor managers to salaried assistant managers is usually similar. There were also differences in labour turnover in several different countries. How can we account for these differences? The fast-food industry is well known for its high level of labour turnover. Figures provided by McDonald's German and UK management show that in 1989 (the year the first German collective agreement was established) annual labour turnover figures were high for hourly paid employees in both countries. However, by 1993, turnover in the UK had virtually doubled, but in Germany turnover had nearly halved. Table 4.1 gives labour turnover figures for both the UK and Germany.

According to senior German management, McDonald's Germany enjoys one of the lowest employee labour turnover rates in McDonald's world-wide. Although exact figures were not available for all the other countries in this study, similar variations were evident. The impact of collective agreements and other aspects of labour legislation may be part of the explanation for these variations (see Chapters 6 and 7). However, in some cases, labour turnover also varied considerably within countries. In Italy, for example, labour turnover was much lower in the south of Italy than in the north. Another part of the explanation for this is likely to be variations in the level of unemployment. For example, a German first assistant manager stated:

> We've had particularly low turnover in the last two to three years [since 1991], mostly since the first collective agreement, it brought better conditions, but of course there's more unemployment so there's no shortage of workers.

Table 4.1 Labour turnover percentages in Germany and the UK

Year	1989	1990	1991	1992	1993	5-year average
Salaried management						
Germany	20.0	23.0	17.9	17.5	12.6	18.2
UK	16.3	19.0	28.3	28.6	28.3	24.1
Hourly paid employees						
Germany	103.0	108.0	99.0	79.0	52.0	88.2
UK	105.9	122.0	105.0	162.7	191.0	137.3

Low labour turnover is often associated with high unemployment (Rothwell, 1995); Germany has experienced increasing levels of unemployment since reunification (Sauga *et al.*, 1996). Although unemployment undoubtedly is a factor in the variation in workforce numbers employed in restaurants, another part of the explanation could be the proportion of part-time and full-time workers employed.

Part-time work

Part-time and temporary working is central to the way in which fast-food companies operate. In the USA and the UK, something like 80% of all McDonald's workers are part time, but at McDonald's in Germany and Austria it is closer to 65%. The whole emphasis of the McDonald's and other fast-food systems is the flexibility of the workforce. McDonald's defines part-time workers as who regularly working less than 35 hours per week and full-timers as those who are scheduled to work more than 35 hours per week. However, the distinction between part time and full time is not always clear cut. Individuals may work different hours at different times of the year; part-time or full-time status may therefore shift, depending upon individual circumstances. The hours worked by crew vary greatly; typically, school pupils or those at college or university will often work full time in the vacations and then part time during term time for just a few hours per week. However, anyone wanting more hours has to compete and prove that they are 'worthy' through consistently good job performance. Cutting back an employee's hours is a standard way for managers to show their displeasure for poor job performance or having a 'negative' attitude. Leidner (1993) also made similar observations in her analysis of McDonald's in the USA.

Since the early 1990s, there has been increasing interest in the issue of part-time work at European level. The European Commission, for example, has encouraged more extensive use of flexible working time as one means of reducing unemployment in the European Union (*Labour Research*, 1994a). Demands for increasing flexibility from employers is also arguably driving the increase in part-time, temporary and seasonal working across a wide range of industries, but particularly so in the service sector. A major criticism of part-time work has emphasised the disadvantageous conditions associated with this form of employment. In the UK, for example, criticism has focused on the way in which the thresholds of hours affect the application of basic employment and social security entitlements. Discrimination based on length of service is still common in the UK (Grahl and Teague, 1992; *Labour Research*, 1994b), although the situation is gradually improving with, first, the House of Lords ruling in March 1994 and, second, the Employment Relations Act to be implemented before April 2000. This legislation will be introduced in order to comply with the EU directive on part-time workers. This should guarantee that part-time workers are treated 'no less favourably' than full-time workers (*Labour Research*, 1999b). Levels of part-time and temporary work vary considerably in different countries. Table 4.2 provides figures for the growth in part-time work in six European countries as a percentage of the total labour force.

In Ireland, Italy, Spain, Portugal and Greece, part-time work is the exception, but one-fifth of all work is temporary. In contrast, almost one-quarter of the employed workforce in the UK, Denmark and The Netherlands are part-timers, but temporary jobs are comparatively rare. Germany, France and Belgium have more moderate levels of part-time work but have all experienced an increase in recent years (Maier, 1991; Eurostat, 1993), particularly in Germany (O'Reilly and Bothfeld, 1998). According to Gregory and O'Reilly (1996), three major factors can be identified which account for differences in the use of part-time work in different countries. First, the nature of employment regulation; second, the concerns of the particular business in question; and third, the characteristics of available labour supply. However, it will be argued in the following sections that, despite the restrictions of employment legislation and quality of labour supply, large companies such as McDonald's, which pursue a highly centralised and controlled system with deskilled work, will be able to operate their systems with the minimum of adaptation. It is probably fair to say that few firms compete in similar global markets and there may be only a limited number of firms who can operate in this way.

The German labour market is more highly regulated than in the UK and it allows for an additional category of part-time workers called *Geringverdiener* or low earners. About one-third of the McDonald's part-time workforce are classified as *Geringverdiener*, and they are not allowed to earn more than DM620 (approximately £225 per month) over 1 year and they have restricted weekly hours (14–20 hours). Until 1 April 1999, companies did not have to make social security payments on behalf of these employees, thereby considerably cutting their labour costs. In addition, many students who fall into this category can earn and work more hours than the standard restriction in the summer months to help to fund their studies without having to worry about tax and insurance payments. However, after that date, and in a move that has raised a good deal of criticism and angered many German employers, the Schröder government has changed the law so that employers will now have to pay these social security costs (*Handelsblatt*, 1998; Sodan, 1998). However, this decision does seem to have affected McDonald's to its fullest extent. Union officials at the NGG state that McDonald's reacted immediately to this new situation by writing to all the 15,000 or so employees affected, telling them that their employment contracts have been changed. These changes allow McDonald's to deduct 50% of the social costs from employees' wages. The NGG estimates that this would mean a DM50–70 (£18–25) reduction in a worker's monthly wages (and a huge saving for McDonald's). Union officials suggest that only in restaurants where union-supported works councils are established have they been able to stop employment contracts being changed. In those restaurants where workers continue to receive their

Table 4.2 Growth percentages in part-time work in Europe

Year	The Netherlands	Denmark	UK	Germany	France	Belgium
1983	28.1	26.7	22.4	15.3	10.3	11.3
1985	29.3	26.5	24.2	15.2	11.9	12.5
1987	34.6	26.3	24.7	15.1	12.9	14.3
1989	36.6	25.2	26.3	16.0	13.4	14.9
1991	37.0	24.6	24.5	18.1	13.4	16.3

Source: Eurostat (1993: 77).

full wage, workers have been notified that McDonald's still intends to change the calculation of their wages. Although differences in labour market regulation may account for some differences in the part-time workforces at McDonald's, it still does not explain why there appear to be larger proportions of full-time workers in Germany. To answer this question, we need to examine the characteristics of the workforces in each country.

Workforce characteristics

The data only provided for a detailed study of the workforce characteristics in Germany and the UK, not in all the European countries under examination. Nevertheless, together with some figures and some anecdotal evidence, a fairly clear understanding of the role of workforce characteristics can be attained. The first and most obvious finding from the German and UK data is that the UK workforce is much younger. According to management, some 65% of the British workforce are under 20 years, with some 30% under 18 years. This is similar to McDonald's in the USA, where 70% are 20 years or younger (BNA, 1985). In Germany only 24% are under 20. Part of the explanation for the lower German turnover figures could be because they have an older workforce. Rothwell (1995) suggests that older workforces tend to have a lower labour turnover than younger ones. Why is the German McDonald's workforce older? Part of the explanation for this is that the majority of German workers under the age of 20 years are still in full-time education or undertaking an apprenticeship. McDonald's management stated that in 1994 there was only a tiny number of employees under 18 years and these were only in franchise operations. The reasons for this appear to be that German youth legislation (*Jugendarbeitsschutz*) makes employment of workers who are under 18 years old unattractive. First, their hours and conditions of work are tightly restricted and regulated; as a senior German manager put it, '…under 18s are too inflexible, they're no use to us'. Second, McDonald's Germany believes that employing large numbers of under 18 year olds would be bad for the company image. This is in marked contrast to the UK and the USA, where young workers are actively encouraged (BNA, 1985). One UK franchise operator stated: 'Most of my staff are kind of 17, 18, 19. It's not hugely different from the school environment'. Employing under 18 year olds undoubtedly reduces McDonald's UK labour costs because they are able to apply lower wage rates to younger workers. This has not altered since the introduction of the minimum wage in 1999 because it does not provide a minimum wage for under 18 year olds and only a lower rate for under 21 year olds. However, the absence of under 18-year-old workers in Germany is not the only explanation. Something like 25% of the German workforce are students; so why is the average age of the German workforce so much higher? Part of the answer is due to differences in the German and British education systems. German students tend to be older than British students because many do not begin their university education until they are in their early twenties, and the completion of the German A level equivalent (*Abitur*) does not necessarily stop at 18 or 19 years of age. Most German nationals have to undertake either military service or its civilian equivalent and a fair number of students also undertake an 'apprenticeship' (*Lehre*) before they take their degree, which can add on another 2–3 years. There is nevertheless another part of the explanation and that is the issue of foreign workers.

Foreign workers

The German McDonald's workforce is made up of a large proportion of economic or political migrants, especially from the old Eastern bloc (*Aussiedler*), and other foreign workers (*Gastarbeiter*). Most of these foreign workers tend to be older. Unions have criticised American multinationals in the past for excessive use of migrant or guest workers. This strategy is said to create a more compliant workforce and to help to keep down labour costs (De Vos, 1981). *Gastarbeiter* or guest workers are nothing new in Germany, where there has been a long tradition of foreign workers. Ardagh (1987) suggests that by the late 1980s there were some 4 million foreign workers in Germany: about one-third from Turkey, with Italians, Yugoslavs, Greeks and Iberians as the next most numerous. In recent years, the numbers of *Aussiedler* from the Eastern bloc have increased considerably. In the 5 years to 1993, something like 2.5 million *Aussiedler* settled legally in Germany (Emmott, 1993). Many are of German origin, but very few speak German adequately. Some have a lack of education, but more commonly they have problems with the recognition of their qualifications. They often find it difficult to get work elsewhere in Germany. The following were typical comments from foreign workers at McDonald's Germany:

> I was a school teacher in Poland…but there's no chance to get a teaching job in Germany, there are problems with the recognition of my qualification, there are language problems and there's too much competition. Everyone knows that only foreigners work at McDonald's.
>
> (Female German floor manager)

> I have a university degree in accounting from the Philippines but there are problems with the recognition of my degree. I don't think I could get a job anywhere else.
>
> (Crew member)

> I was a sales manager in a department restaurant in Poland but I can't get that kind of work here.
>
> (Floor manager)

There are many foreigners here…language is always a problem in other kinds of jobs.

(Crew trainer)

Although there are a significant number of employees from EU countries, especially in more senior positions, the majority are from countries with 'weaker' economies than that of Germany, such as Finland, Greece and Italy. At every level, the numbers of foreign workers outweigh the numbers of German nationals. This appeared to be particularly marked in restaurants in large cities. In one company-owned restaurant, 90% of the workforce were of Turkish descent, and works councillors interviewed in the study referred to a number of such restaurants in one city as the 'Turkish mafia'. However, the NGG suggests that because Turkish workers were becoming more integrated into German society than other foreign workers they were gradually becoming less common at McDonald's, their jobs were now being taken by *Aussiedler* from the old Eastern bloc. One German restaurant manager stated that it was often difficult to employ German nationals at all and especially in big cities; but this was not seen as a problem in itself:

A lot of Germans would rather be unemployed than work at McDonald's, and anyway the motivation of foreign workers is usually a lot higher.

If a 'higher level of motivation' exists among foreign workers, it may in part be explained by Eastern bloc workers associating McDonald's with the 'success of the West'. An NGG representative made this comment about such workers:

McDonald's is the West and everything is good in the West. People who have spent 40 years under those conditions [Communism] are a lot less critical and see everything with 'coloured balloons'. …What is also important is that in contrast to the West German environment where they are marginalised in society, this job is 'home'…this job gives them a chance to find recognition.

This may be more obvious where multinationals operate in countries with severe economic difficulties and extreme levels of unemployment. In Russia, for example, McDonald's received 27,000 applications for the 600 jobs initially on offer at its first Moscow restaurant (Frantz, 1993; Vikhanski and Puffer, 1993). Nevertheless, it is perhaps not all that surprising that such foreign workers are happy to work at McDonald's. In 1995, it was estimated that about half a million foreign workers were working illegally in Germany, of whom 300,000 were reckoned to be from the Eastern bloc. They work for wages well under the legal minimum wage, sometimes for less than £1 an hour (Pollack, 1995). McDonald's offers close to £5 per hour in Germany, which probably seems quite attractive. One crew member from the former Yugoslavia commented:

> There's a lot more competition for jobs than when I first came to Germany
> five years ago, Germans have a very different opinion about McDonald's
> than we do, they don't really like to work here, they can earn much more
> money working in a factory.

Additionally, the number of unqualified and low-skilled jobs in Germany
has been falling for some time. According to *Der Spiegel* (1996), by 2010 the
number of jobs in the German economy that require little or no qualification
will be halved. Meanwhile, the numbers of individuals leaving school without
the most basic qualification (*Hauptschulabschluß*) is increasing; some 30,000
individuals left school with no qualifications in 1994. In addition, almost 75%
of all those who are unemployed in Germany have only a basic education and
there is an excess of demand for skilled workers. Second, there is a
disproportionately high rate of unemployment among women (SVR, 1994).
These factors would suggest a large and 'ready made' workforce for a company
such as McDonald's.

Indeed, a recent article in *Stern* (1999) magazine suggests that many
foreign workers specifically brought over from countries such as Bulgaria
and Rumania under the auspices of the German Federal Employment Service
(see Chapter 7) signed contracts with McDonald's before they had left their
homelands. When they did arrive in Germany, they found that the
accommodation they received was organised by the corporation. The article
states that the accommodation was 'seedy' and that, in one instance,
McDonald's was renting a 40-square-metre flat for DM1,000 per month but
was subletting it to up to four or five workers at DM500 each (*Stern*, 1999:
122). It also suggests that accommodating the workers themselves in this
manner was also a very effective way of controlling them. When workers
needed to extend their visas, the restaurant manager went with them himself
and is reported to have said: '...We must agree that we will always be at the
disposal [of the restaurant]'. Since that time, alleges the article, the restaurant
manager regularly phones the flat to make the Eastern Europeans go to work
when the restaurant gets busy (*Stern*, 1999: 122).

One additional feature of the German workforce relates to German
nationals predominantly filling floor manager and assistant manager
positions. Although small in number, respondents referred to those that
had been 'washed up' in the German labour market, using the term
Angeschwemmte. These individuals were often working at floor manager or
assistant manager level rather than as crew. For example, those who had
dropped out of their degree courses often entered as trainee managers and
those failing A levels (*Abitur*) or apprenticeships might be working as floor
managers. The German labour market is extremely competitive in terms of
skills and qualifications and management posts are always subject to high
levels of competition. It appears that this type of employment may offer
individuals a second chance to gain a management position.

'Coasters' and ethnic minorities

The UK workforce is much younger and does not have any significant number of foreign workers, but it does appear to have a large proportion of ethnic minorities. This proportion varied considerably from one restaurant to another, with more than 50% in some restaurants and less than 10% in others. According to the General Municipal and Boilermakers' Union (GMB), ethnic minorities are twice as likely to be employed as White workers are in the UK hospitality industry in general (Quiney, 1994). This is also reflected in North America; according to McDonald's own web site, it is the largest employer of African–Americans in the USA.

There appears to be some variation in the workforce characteristics of the other European countries examined in this study. In Austria, trade union officials suggest that McDonald's has a very similar workforce to that found in Germany. Something like 60–70% of McDonald's Austrian workforce are non-EU citizens. In most of the other countries, McDonald's workforces were closer to those found in the UK, with large proportions of younger workers, students, ethnic minorities and second-income earners. In countries such as Finland, youth unemployment is very high and many students also work full time or part time at McDonald's to pay their way through college.

Flexible hours and part-time work may be attractive for students, school pupils and second-income earners such as married women, but the data revealed that there are a number of employees who work full time at McDonald's and who do not move on to other jobs that quickly. Why do these workers stay when the pay is often lower than can be earned on the local supermarket checkout? Even managers admitted that working full time at McDonald's was not seen as a particularly good job, and one UK franchisee stated: 'As far as full-timers are concerned I sometimes think it's looked on almost like a last resort job'.

Gabriel's (1988) study of fast-food employees suggests that, on the one hand, workers may feel as if they are somewhat exploited but, on the other hand, they are often resigned to having to do this kind of low-skilled work because of few other job opportunities in the labour market. In addition, workers find satisfaction in activities outside the workplace. Some 20% of full-time hourly paid employees in the questionnaire sample had four or more GCSE qualifications, some also had A levels and had been working at McDonald's full time for 1 year or more as crew. In this situation, perhaps unsure about what they want to do with their lives, workers appear to be 'coasting'. One UK assistant manager stated:

> ...Most of the full-timers that I've come across, there's probably only 1 in 20 that's a bit slow or the kind of person who wouldn't achieve academically. And the rest of them are really bright street-wise people who are just coasting because they can't be arsed to do anything else or they didn't find themselves at school. I look at them and I think what are you doing here? Why are you doing this?

One UK part-time training squad also commented:

> There are only limited career possibilities as a full-timer, you might get to floor manager if you can stick it out for long enough but it's difficult beyond that. That's why you've got a lot of coasters, they need a job for a couple of years and this is a good way to earn your £130 or whatever you need to live on and you get a good reference if you work hard. That's why you get coasters because that's probably how the company works, they must realise that that's what a lot of people do.

When 'coasters' gave their reasons for working at McDonald's, their responses suggested an element of cognitive dissonance (Festinger, 1962). In other words, some individuals may have attempted to construct inter-pretations of their own work roles that do not damage conceptions of themselves (see also Hughes, 1984). Some of the full-timers are those who may not have done well in education and are looking for a career with the company. In the UK questionnaire sample, 18% of assistant managers had no GCSEs and 42% had a vocational qualification. Only 33% had one A level or more, only 16% had Higher National Diplomas (HNDs) and only 8% had a degree. All of the restaurant managers in the questionnaire sample had at least four or more GCSEs, although one restaurant manager in the interview sample had only two GCSEs. The majority of the floor mangers and crew with qualifications were students. These are workers who, although dependent on the company for their livelihood, see no point in all the extra work and responsibility that promotion to management would bring. As one long-serving UK training squad member commented,

> My title is senior dining host, but I'm really more like training squad. I'm not really interested in promotion, why have a lot more stress and worry becoming a floor manager? I get the same sort of money as floor managers get because I've worked here seven years, I'd be responsible for the safe and things like that, I don't have all those worries.

Disabled workers

In the USA, where the fast-food market is far more saturated, employers are having problems finding suitable employees and have turned to other sectors of the labour market such as retired people and considerable numbers of mentally and physically handicapped workers (BNA, 1985). McDonald's introduced its McJobs programme for disabled employees with visual, hearing, learning, mental and physical handicaps in 1981, although it had begun employing disabled workers in the 1960s (Wildavsky, 1989). By 1991, McDonald's USA had employed some 9,000 disabled employees. McDonald's also receives federal state funding for its programme; in 1991, it received on average $800 for each disabled employee it trained. As Laabs (1991) points out, this is the first job for most of these individuals and they are often very dedicated and loyal to the company that gives them such an opportunity. In Germany, the law stipulates that all companies must employ a small percentage of disabled employees or pay a levy if they choose not to do so. No disabled employees were working in the German restaurants in this study, and, when challenged on this, one franchise manager stated that none had applied but that in any case it was simpler for him to pay the levy than to have to accommodate disabled employees. In the UK samples, there were a small number of individuals with learning difficulties. However, both UK franchisees and managers made positive comments about employing those with learning difficulties:

> I don't think they need to be terribly academically competent in all honesty to do a crew member's job. But I've taken on people with learning difficulties and found that they've been excellent at applying themselves to the operation. People like the guy who works on the dining area here and he's quite slow, he had learning difficulties at school, but y'know he's brilliant, he works hard, he works like a workhorse.

However, despite these claimed benefits for employers, the numbers of disabled employed in Germany and the UK were either small or non-existent. It could be argued that although there are continuing high levels of unemployment and no shortages or difficulties in acquiring 'loyal' McDonald's employees, there is little incentive for the corporation to employ disabled workers in these countries.

Previous work experience

Leidner (1993), in her study of McDonald's crew in the USA, suggests that 60% of workers said that McDonald's was their first job. However, although some workers in this study had no previous work experience, the proportion is much lower than in Leidner's study. In fact, the questionnaire sample suggests that the majority of crew in both countries do have previous work experience, some 75% in the UK and 63% in Germany. The US labour market has an even larger percentage of youth workers employed in the fast-food industry than the UK. What is perhaps of greater significance is the type of previous work experience that the respondents have had. In the UK, 74% of previous work was unskilled, whereas in Germany it was a mixture of semiskilled, skilled manual and even some professional, with only 28% having previously had unskilled work.

These findings support the earlier argument that the German workforce is a much more varied and older workforce with a significant number of *Aussiedler* who have skills from previous jobs. However, these are skills and experience that are not recognised in the highly competitive German labour market. In the UK, the workforce is much younger, with individuals often still at school, college or university. These young workers have not had enough time to develop skills in previous jobs, which tend to be mostly low-skilled and seasonal jobs and casual work. Some employees have worked in much worse places with even lower pay. One 19-year-old UK crew employee had previously worked for £1.50 per hour in a badly run family restaurant, but at the time of the interview she was earning £3.10 per hour at McDonald's.

Recruited acquiescence?

At a time when many Western economies are desperate to create new jobs, this relatively new and rapidly expanding industry does exactly that. Germany and the UK offer two very different labour markets for multinationals. However, this industry is strongly rooted in Taylorist/Fordist principles and provides jobs that are predominantly part time, low skilled and low paid, so the issue of adequate skills resources is not an issue. What is of significance is how differing societal frameworks constrain multinationals in determining whom they can employ and how they are employed in practice.

On one level, there are some differences between the German and UK McDonald's workforces. The UK workforce is mostly made up of students, school pupils and second-income earners who want flexible hours; 71% of the workforce are aged 20 years or under. The flexible hours, fast pace of the work and the emphasis on 'fun' is undoubtedly attractive to younger workers wanting to work with people of their own age, especially when they have so little experience of any other work. However, there is also a number of people who work full time and for longer periods of time with McDonald's. First, there are those who have qualifications and could find something more demanding elsewhere, but appear to be 'coasting'. Second, there are those who have not done well academically and stay on because of the lack of alternatives, some of these workers may be seeking a career with the corporation.

The German workforce appears to be slightly different, having an older workforce dominated by foreign guest workers and economic migrants. McDonald's provides a 'family' atmosphere for foreign workers and a badly needed job that does not require qualifications or language abilities. There is currently a much lower labour turnover level among the McDonald's German workforce. This appears to be the result of the improvements in working conditions introduced by the collective agreements since 1989, but is also a reflection of the higher levels of unemployment and very limited job opportunities for foreign workers in Germany.

For those who have been 'washed up' in the labour market because of inadequate qualifications, McDonald's may provide one of the few chances to attain a career and a 'management' position. These opportunities are likely to remain as long as the corporation continues to expand. On the one hand, McDonald's offers an employment opportunity that would not otherwise exist for a section of society that is on the periphery of the labour market. On the other hand, the similarities between the two workforces suggest that McDonald's is able to take advantage of weak segments of the labour market regardless of differences in market regulation.

The detailed analysis of the German and UK workforces, and that of the other European countries, suggests that McDonald's workers in most European countries are unlikely to resist management control. First, because of their weak labour market position and possible career aspirations, those who really need these jobs are unlikely to put their jobs on the line by complaining about company policy. Second, young workers who have very little or no previous work experience have little else with which to compare their working conditions. In any case, the majority do not intend to stay with the corporation. Like second-income earners, who often have family responsibilities, young workers still in education are less likely to be financially dependent on the company as they often live with others who support them. As one UK student (training squad) stated,

> I think full-time workers are exploited here. I don't know how they stick it so long, if it was my career I would kick up a fuss, but it's not worth the hassle because I'm not staying with the company after my degree, I'm only a part-timer.

It is argued that in any employment relationship there is always a dynamic balance among control, consent and resistance. McDonald's appears to manage this relationship across societal borders in a remarkably similar way through exceptionally rigid and detailed rules and procedures, a paternalistic management style and an 'acquiescent' workforce. Indeed, Reiter (1996: 145), in her study of Burger King in Canada, argues that '...it is not consent that is produced but acquiescence'. Edwards (1986) has also used the term 'acquiescent'; here, the author uses the term 'recruited acquiescence'. There are also parallels here with what Maguire (1986) calls 'recruitment as a means of control'. The importance of recruiting suitable individuals into an organisation should not be underestimated. As Beaumont (1993: 57) argues,

> The design of the selection system...supports the overall organisation strategy, the monitoring of the internal flow of personnel...matches emerging business strategies.

Whether recruited acquiescence is a predetermined, planned strategy is unclear, and in any case the whole concept of 'strategy' is problematic (Mintzberg, 1994). Nevertheless, as we shall see in the following chapters, despite differences in societal frameworks, it seems that the corporation is able to take advantage of workers who share common traits. More often than not, they appear to be able to 'weed out' those who may question managerial prerogative, have notions of worker solidarity and/or have an interest in trade union representation. This is increasingly likely to be of concern to trade unions. The study by Disney *et al.* (1998) suggests that employees who begin life in a non-union firm are more likely to remain non-union in later jobs, and there seems no doubt that the growth in non-union workplaces such as McDonald's is an important contributory factor in this regard. Resisting managerial prerogative often runs hand in hand with trade union organisation. However, as we shall see in the next chapter, gaining union recognition or access to McDonald's workers, even in the countries of mainland Europe which generally have well-organised unions, has not been a straightforward matter for the unions of Europe.

5 'There's no place like home'

The impact of trade unions and collective bargaining frameworks

McDonald's is basically a non-union company and intends to stay that way.
(Michael Quinlan, CEO of the McDonald's Corporation until 1998)

This chapter examines the extent to which trade unions have been able to unionise McDonald's restaurants in several European countries and the extent to which differing national arrangements for collective bargaining have had an impact upon the corporation's 'home country' employment practices. We provide a brief analysis of the broader context of union organisation and collective bargaining in Europe and then move on to examine the impact that the trade unions and collective bargaining frameworks have had on McDonald's European operations. But we first begin by examining McDonald's experiences with unions 'at home' in North America and then in some other countries around the world.

McDonald's and the unions in North America

Union membership in the USA is reckoned to be the lowest in the Western world (Wheeler and McClendon, 1998). A review of industrial relations in the USA by Kochan and Weinstein (1994) revealed that historical hostility displayed by American employers towards unions has been actively reinforced by new trends in work reorganisation. Union density continues to decline in the USA together with a considerable investment in coercion against trade unionists, especially in the private sector. According to Kochan *et al.* (1984: 18), union avoidance in the USA is deep rooted:

> Many companies now make union avoidance or union containment a very high priority. The pluralistic assumptions of industrial relations researchers that independent worker organisations have a legitimate role seemingly are not shared by the majority of American employers.

Towers (1999a) suggests that most American employers resist union organisation because they regard unions as unacceptable restrictions on the right to manage, and genuine partnerships involving power sharing with unions are rare. The McDonald's corporation has a well-documented anti-union stance (Dowling *et al.*, 1994; Love, 1995; Vidal, 1997). In 1991, Michael Quinlan (the Chief Executive of the McDonald's Corporation until 1998), stated (BNA, 1991: 66):

> McDonald's is basically a non-union company and intends to stay that way. ...I do not feel unionisation has interfered with employees' loyalty to McDonald's, or to the company's philosophy of service and employee motivation...unions do not bring much to the equation.

In fact, McDonald's has a long history of anti-unionism that is well illustrated by the role played by John Cooke, McDonald's US labour relations chief in the 1960s and 1970s. According to Love (1995), Cooke was technically employed to 'educate' US employees about unions; however, in practice, his job was to keep the unions out. He organised 'flying squads' of experienced McDonald's restaurant managers who were dispatched to a restaurant the same day that word came in of an attempt to organise unionisation. He trained managers on how to deal with employees and union representatives. As Cooke himself made clear (Love, 1995: 397), '...unions are inimical to what we stand for and how we operate'. Vidal (1997) states that McDonald's also ran into trouble in the American courts in the mid-1970s for using lie detectors to weed out trade union sympathisers in San Francisco. Indeed, he suggests that the practice only stopped because new laws made this practice illegal in the USA. Vidal (1997: 231) also quotes a memorandum from Cooke to top McDonald's executives that stated:

> I think [the union] was effective in terms of reaching the public with the information that we do use polygraph tests in a Gestapo-type manner.

In fact, attempts by unions to organise workers in the US fast-food industry have met with little success. Despite remaining non-union, McDonald's restaurants in the USA have experienced worker resistance and union organisation attempts. In the early 1970s, one US restaurant was unionised for 4 years in Mason City, Iowa, but there have been no real successes in the USA since that time. For example, in April 1998, in Macedonia, Ohio, some twenty McDonald's workers managed to stage the first ever strike of a US McDonald's. Teamster union members (trade union grouping: local 416) had joined the workers on their picket line during the strike. The 5-day strike ended when McDonald's officials agreed to adjust pay scales, offer 1-week paid holidays for full-time workers and hold crew meetings and employee appreciation events. Two employees who led the dispute were hoping to unionise the restaurant when they returned to work; indeed about half of the forty workers (mostly college students) had signed union cards with the Teamsters. However, the two strike organisers were fired 2 days after they reported to work with 'Go union' written on their faces in glitter paint and argued with restaurant managers who tried to photograph them. In fact, the franchise owner operating their restaurant reduced the basic starting wage from $5.50 to $5.25 per hour and it is alleged that management were discriminating against those workers involved in the strike. The two workers hoped that remaining workers would pursue the unionisation attempt, but by June 1988 four pro-union workers had left allegedly under pressure from management. The National Labour Relations Board became involved in the dispute when the two workers filed unfair dismissal claims; however, before the case was due to be heard on 16 February 1999, the McDonald's franchisee made an out of court settlement for an undisclosed amount on 29 January 1999. The remaining workers did not pursue a further unionisation attempt (*Buffalo News*, 1998; Robb, 1998, 1999). Similar actions have also taken place from time to time in Canada. Vidal (1995: 234) reports on the management's response to one such occasion in 1993 when a 16-year-old Canadian worker signed up a majority of workers to a union in one restaurant in Ontario:

> ...managers organised a bizarre and nationally controversial 'anti-union' campaign, which included creating a climate of fear against pro-union staff, getting some of the workers to lie outside in the snow forming the word 'NO' (to unions), putting on special anti-union video and slide shows and temporarily allowing improved conditions in the run-up to a secret ballot in the restaurant for union recognition.

The attempted unionisation failed. More recently, in July 1998, when two 17-year-old workers tried to organise their McDonald's restaurant in Squamish, British Columbia, they were met with intense resistance from McDonald's management. Within 4 days after contacting the Canadian Auto Workers Union (CAW), the two workers had managed to sign up more than the 55% of their co-workers required to gain union 'certification' under the local labour legislation. The day after the workers began their campaign, the restaurant hired twenty-eight new workers and challenged the certification, stating that these new workers should also be allowed to vote. In addition, a local lawyer challenged the certification on the grounds that he represented some workers who had now changed their minds about wanting a union. He also claimed that under the Province's Infants Act they couldn't join a union without their parents' permission. However, these challenges were to no avail, and on 19 August 1998 the Squamish restaurant was unionised. Currently, the workers are bargaining with management, but a CAW official states that she expects it to be a long and tough process, with McDonald's taking the opportunity to delay negotiations whenever it can.

International Union of Food, Agricultural, Hotel, Restaurant, Catering Tobacco and Allied Workers' Associations (IUF) officials also report other cases. They state that in February 1998, 2 weeks after being laid off, sixty-two workers at a McDonald's restaurant in Saint-Hubert, Quebec, had been certified as Teamsters union local 973 by the provincial labour commissioner. After a year of legal stalemate, on the day that the commissioner delivered his decision, the franchisee concerned faxed the commissioner to announce that he was not opposed to union accreditation. IUF officials state that the closure of the franchise restaurant was not based on a financial decision but was clearly intended to avoid unionisation. Canadian labour legislation is probably more favourable than that found in the USA, but in fact the majority of attempts to organise McDonald's workers there have also failed. From the snippets of research that have been carried out on McDonald's in other countries around the world, it is also clear that McDonald's would prefer to operate without trade unions.

It's cold outside: McDonald's and unions around the world

In 1999, McDonald's had over forty outlets in Russia, some thirty-one of which are in the Moscow area, and employs some 6,000 workers. McDonald's Canada owns 80% of the operations in the Moscow region through a closed joint-stock company, the remaining shares are held by the food service administration of the Moscow City Government. Unlike other fast-food multinationals, the corporation draws on an extensive system of local suppliers and processes most of the materials at the Moskva McDonald's plant. McDonald's Canada senior chairman, George Cohon, was originally a US citizen who adopted Canadian nationality during McDonald's early troubled years in Canada in the late 1960s and early 1970s, apparently to help persuade Canadians that McDonald's in Canada was a Canadian business (Love, 1995). In his autobiography, *To Russia with Fries*, Cohon (1999) states that it is his firm conviction that a union at McDonald's would answer no need and would only complicate things. Interestingly, the foreword to Cohon's book is written by Mikhail Gorbachov, who credits McDonald's with furthering 'the development of civilised modern markets' and with helping the Russian people to build a 'democratic society'. However, this does not appear to extend as far as fully respecting international labour standards.

   If there was a honeymoon period in the first few years of the McDonald's operations in Russia, it seems to have come to an abrupt end in August 1998 when the economic crisis forced McDonald's to lay off factory staff and reduce wages (Blundy, 1999). A deputy representative claimed that many of the people who signed voluntary redundancy forms did not get a pay-off. In 1999, IUF officials state that a group of workers at the Moskva McDonald's processing plant, which supplies the corporation's Moscow restaurants, decided to form a trade union. Unions allege that the plant management responded immediately with a campaign of intimidation and harassment. Union supporters were threatened with loss of salary and benefits, workers who refused to sign letters denouncing the union were transferred to more difficult positions and the elected representative's work telephone line was cut. A deputy union representative at the factory stated (Blundy, 1999: 14),

We have been told that if we form a union they will take away our benefits…they have organised our lunch breaks so that we can't get the message across to our colleagues.

In an official statement, McDonald's denied the allegations. IUF officials state that together with the local Commerce and Catering Workers Union they protested to the city government and the corporation. The government of Moscow initiated tripartite negotiations, which resulted in formal recognition of the union. However, McDonald's has as yet resisted negotiations for a collective agreement. Despite continued pressure on union members, the union has begun to establish relations with workers at McOpCo restaurants. Ironically, the workers suggest that things were better when most managers were American (Blundy, 1999: 14): '… Nowadays they are mostly Russian and the regime is very strict and unfriendly'.

According to IUF officials, a similar picture also emerges from McDonald's activities in a number of countries. In Australia and New Zealand, for example, much of the early union opposition has been crushed, and restaurants have remained largely non-union. Indeed, until recently, government policy promoting 'flexible' labour markets in those countries has tended to support the McDonald's approach to labour relations. The IUF also reports that in the 1980s there was a considerable degree of conflict in Mexico, with pickets standing outside McDonald's restaurants. Much of this early conflict was over the minimum wages and conditions of work; more recently, the IUF report that the trade union representing McDonald's workers in Mexico has been taken over by a company-friendly organisation. The IUF also reports similar conflicts around McDonald's activities in Lithuania and other Eastern European countries. However, as we suggested in Chapter 1, the countries of Western Europe have industrial relations systems that arguably provide more protection for employment rights and trade unions than in the rest of the world. With this in mind, how has McDonald's approached its labour relations policies in its European operations?

Trade unions and collective bargaining in Europe

Despite the relatively strong position of most European unions compared with those in the USA, it is clear that the 1990s have not been good to European trade unions. Problems of rising and high unemployment, job restructuring and increased international competition have all led to a decrease in union bargaining power and lower levels of union membership. In particular, Germany, which experienced the stress of reunification, has experienced a sharp fall in trade union membership, which has fallen from 12 million in 1991 to 8.6 million by the end of 1997 (Bowley, 1998). As a whole, European trade unions lost nearly 11% of their membership between 1990 and 1995 (Visser, 1998a), with European membership declining twice as fast as in the USA during the 1990s.

Continued high levels of unemployment have plagued many European states; by 1997, unemployment in the EU reached 11%. However, this is not the only concern; unions are also faced with the continual restructuring of work and labour markets. Visser (1998a) estimated that by the mid-1990s in Western Europe 45% of union membership was in the public sector, 40% in mining manufacturing and construction and only 14% in private services. The private services sector is growing rapidly in most Western economies, and yet unions have been unable to make any real progress in increasing union membership in this sector. In particular, European trade unions are most under-represented in the 'most flexible' segments of the labour market, where temporary contracts and part-time work abound. This may be partly explained by the declining and low levels of union membership among younger workers (Visser, 1998a). In addition, increasing numbers of women are entering the labour market, particularly in the private services sector. Although the unionisation rate among women is increasing in most Western European countries, it is not having a large impact in unionisation in the private services sector. European unions are still, by and large, failing to focus enough resources on this new and growing sector. Part of the problem may be a 'conservative bias' among the richest trade unions, which are frequently found in declining sectors. Visser (1998a) suggests that the fact that unions tend to describe part-time and temporary work, so frequently found in many jobs today, as 'atypical' is itself ideologically loaded. In other words, many unions are still focused on the predominantly male standard employment contract as the norm. Nor have peak associations been able to change this perspective significantly or influence recruitment drives, and even where they have prevailed they have usually failed (Pankert, 1993).

Exacerbating these trends is the continuing level of interunion rivalry. Although political and ideological divisions tend to be internalised in one dominant federation in Britain, Ireland, Germany, Austria and Greece, where conflict is not suppressed it tends to be channelled through specific factions. Such conflict tends to be more open in Spain and France; indeed, ideological differences are stark in France, with French unions experiencing increasing fragmentation in recent years. In Italy, independent unionism is endemic and has sometimes been interlaced with political movements and interunion rivalry. In the 1980s, relations between the three main union confederations were poor, but in the 1990s things improved and they now work much more closely together. Unlike most other countries, the main issue dividing Scandinavian unions is across the 'collar line'. Three federations usually represent blue-collar workers, with other employees or higher educated managerial and professional staff being represented separately. The answer would appear to be to merge across the 'collar line'; some talks have begun but formidable obstacles still remain.

Merger activity is, in any case, on the increase even in countries such as Germany and The Netherlands, where sectoral and/or industrial unionism is well established. The numbers of industrial unions in Germany has already reduced from sixteen to nine in recent years. But it is unlikely to end there; an official at the German main peak association, the DGB (Deutscher Gewerkschaftsbund) [the German equivalent of the Trades Union Congress (TUC)] suggests that by 2001 further merger activity will reduce the number of industrial unions in Germany to four or five. This is mostly the result of the planned merger of five unions to create a new service union called 'Ver.di' that will have around 3.2 million members (*Labour Research*, 1999a). Similar trends are also evident in several other European countries; in particular, Sweden, Switzerland, Ireland, the UK and The Netherlands all either have undertaken merger activity recently or have it on the agenda.

There are also increasing questions about the ability of European unions to deal adequately with the challenge of multinationals. Despite the merger activity within nation-states, there is no real indication of mergers across national borders. In view of the continuing if not increasing diversity of differing European national industrial relations systems, this is perhaps not very surprising. The tendency of the European Trade Union Confederation (ETUC) to keep out of national union issues and focus on lobbying at supranational level precisely reflects this diversity of interests (Goetschy, 1998a). The fourteen or so transnational European sector organisations have made some attempts to monitor and inform the progress of national unions in their struggle against multinationals, and they may become the focus of cross-border union mergers if this day should arise at some time in the future. Despite the possibilities for international labour networking provided by recent legislation such as the 1994 European Works Council Directive, there seems little doubt that unions are still, as Ramsay (1991) lamented, lagging well behind employers in their ability to co-ordinate their activities across national borders. Visser (1998a) appears to be optimistic that the European Works Council Directive of 1994 is likely to provide for closer, more direct links between European unions and for improved labour networking. This may well be the case for unions in well-organised sectors, but, as we shall see in Chapter 8, where unions are unable to have any effective influence on such bodies then the future does not look so bright. Nevertheless, according to *Labour Research* (1999a), there are some grounds for optimism. In 1995, unionisation in Western Europe stood at 31% and was still over twice that in the USA (at only 14%), and there are now some European countries where union membership has increased.

Although union membership may provide some indication as to the 'health' of the union movement, it is really the influence that it has through the regulation of collective bargaining or other worker representation arrangements which arguably determines a union's power in the workplace. For example, the withdrawal from employers' associations and attempts to derecognise mainland European unions does not necessarily free an employer from the provisions of collective agreements.

European collective bargaining and the organisation and role of trade unions have developed in different ways, so, for example, there are major differences in who is legally able to negotiate collective agreements and the level at which bargaining takes place. The differences between the industrial relations systems in mainland Europe and the UK became more marked during the 1980s and early 1990s. The UK has seen major changes in its system of industrial relations since that time, and these changes have allegedly seen a shift away from traditional patterns of collective bargaining towards a new emphasis on the role of the individual. There has been a decline in union membership, an increase in labour market deregulation and a decentralisation of collective bargaining (Edwards *et al.*, 1998).

These differences are also reflected in the structure of national union confederations. Essentially, European states can be divided into three different models. First, states with a single confederation that includes all or most unions, e.g. the UK, Ireland, Austria and, to some extent, Germany. Second, there are states such as Denmark, Finland, Sweden and Norway with several confederations that are divided on an occupational basis, usually between manual and non-manual workers or between public and private sectors. Finally, there are countries with several competing confederations usually divided on political grounds, such as France, Spain, Belgium, The Netherlands and Italy. In some countries, the larger union confederations are referred to as the 'most representative unions' and by law are entitled to sign collective agreements or to put forward candidates for works council or union delegate elections. This distinction exists in Spain, Italy, France and Belgium.

Unlike in the UK, in most mainland European countries industry-level bargaining between unions and employers' associations, at least in terms of the numbers of employees covered, is still the most important level. There may be a single agreement or a number of regional agreements covering all employees deemed to be employed in particular industries, e.g. banking, hotels and restaurants, engineering. However, there are further variations, e.g. collective bargaining is highly structured and the Belgium state has become increasingly involved in collective bargaining; in 1993, it intervened to impose a freeze in real wages until the end of 1996. Similarly, in Finland, arrangements have been made which can cover the whole economy and which may fix pay increases over several years. Since 1987, similar arrangements have also been established in Ireland, with a series of 3-year pacts dealing with pay and broader economic and social issues at national level, the most recent of which being 'Partnership 2000'. However, unlike Belgium, these pacts have no legal force, and employers' organisations and unions are expected to discipline their own members.

Even in countries such as Germany and Sweden, where industry-level bargaining still dominates, employers are increasingly demanding more flexibility of arrangements at company or plant level. For example, in Germany, there have been an increasing number of *Öffnungsklauseln*, deviation clauses within sectoral agreements which allow employers to bypass agreements by winning concessions from workers at plant level (*EIRR*, 1997a, 1999a). Some commentators have interpreted these and other changes as a potentially serious undermining of the existing German industrial relations system (Flecker and Schulten, 1999). However, as yet, these changes appear to be only minor changes in the way unions operate and collective bargaining is conducted (Wever, 1997; Bowley, 1998, Jacobi *et al.*, 1998).

Like Ireland, collective agreements in the UK have not been binding in law. Indeed, until 1982, the regulation of UK union activities had been minimal with rules governing bargaining being established by custom and tradition and only loosely defined, arguably leaving UK workers without legally guaranteed rights (Terry, 1994). The coverage of UK collective bargaining has continued to fall throughout the 1980s and early 1990s. By the mid-1990s, only a minority of the UK workforce was covered by collective agreements; nevertheless, collective bargaining is still the predominant form of pay setting for some groups of employees (Brown *et al.*, 1995; Ackers *et al.*, 1996). However, when the new 1999 Employment Relations Act comes into full force, it will raise the possibility of legally binding collective agreements for the first time since the failed Industrial Relations Act of 1971. However, unionists fear that the way in which the new Act has been drawn up suggests that legally binding agreements could be a two-edged sword for trade unions and workers.

In most mainland European countries, by contrast, collective agreements are usually legally binding and can often be extended to cover all employers in an industry. In Germany, for example, collective agreements have the force of law, are binding on all those who have signed them and can be extended to cover all employers if the state[1] deems it necessary (*EIRR*, 1997a, 1999a). The effect of which is that German collective agreements tend to act as a minimum wage and they still cover between 80% and 90% of the German workforce. In Belgium and the Scandinavian countries, collective agreements generally cover the entire economy, whereas in most other countries agreements can usually be extended to cover all employers by one means or another. To add to the complexity of this issue, in some countries, such as Spain and The Netherlands, company-level negotiations exist alongside industry-level negotiations. Although formal agreements may technically cover most employees in countries such as France, actual pay levels tend to be determined much more by the decisions of employers rather than negotiated settlements. Furthermore, as we shall see in the following sections, the depth and the scope of collective agreements can vary considerably, so that in some countries they are of only limited effect.

McDonald's and the European unions

It appears that when the corporation first came to Europe in the 1970s McDonald's tried to carry out the same non-union employee relations policy that it had in the USA. Nevertheless, over time, it has had to make some adaptations to national systems in the countries of mainland Europe. However, in the more 'westerly' Anglo-Saxon-orientated countries of the UK and Ireland, there has been no need to make any real adaptation to their

Table 5.1 Union density in McDonald's European operations

Country	McDonald's stores	McDonald's workers	Main unions/union confederations representing the fast-food industry	Union density country (1999)	Union density private sector (1999)	McDonald's union density (1999)
North						
Denmark	80	4,000	RBF	79.1	68.0	6.0
Finland	85	4,250	HRHL	78.4	65.0	7.0
Norway	50	2,500	HRF	57.7	45.0	3.5
Sweden	151	7,500	HRF	87.6	78.0	15.0
West						
Ireland	25	1250	SIPTU	46.2	37.0	0.0
UK	1,000	56,000	GMB, T&G, USDAW	32.1	21.0	0.0
Centre						
Austria	80	4,000	HGPD	40.3	b	20.0
Belgium	62	3,250	AHS-FGTB, CCAS-CSC	51.9	b	1.5
Germany[a]	1,000	51,000	NGG	28.0	25.0	4.0
The Netherlands[a]	180	13,000	Horecabond-FNV	29.0	19.0	4.0
South						
France[a]	720	35,000	CFDT, CGT, FO, CGC	9.0	6.0	1.5
Italy[a]	220	10,000	FISASCAT, UILT, FILCAMS	38.0	32.0	20.0
Spain[a]	161	8,000	FECOHT, FETESE	23.0	b	1.0

Sources: *Labour Research* (1999b) and Visser (1998b).

Notes
a Obtaining exact figures is almost impossible because of the often high rate of labour turnover. In all cases, the McDonald's figures are based on the various unions' own estimates; however, some were not available. The figures for union density by country and sector do not include union members who are unemployed, self-employed or retired.
b Figures not available.

'American' employee relations practices. However, in the countries of mainland Europe, McDonald's has faced quite a different challenge. The levels of union membership provide some indication of the ability of unions to organise McDonald's workers. Table 5.1 sets out the numbers of employees and restaurants and compares the union density rates per country, per hotel and restaurant sector with the union density rates at McDonald's. Even where unions have been relatively successful, in some countries union density figures are much lower than the national average. This is not entirely surprising because union density figures are usually lower in the hotel and restaurant sector than in other industries. In fact, the figures provided by the unions in this study suggest that union density figures are lower still in the fast-food sector than in the hotel sector, although part of the problem is that complete and accurate figures are not always available for comparison. For example, the figure for union density in the UK hotel and restaurant sector in 1995 is only 8%; in Finland, it is around 65%, with density in the fast-food sector estimated at around 8% (LFS, 1996). Nevertheless, in most European countries, the union density figures at McDonald's appear to be lower than in the hotel and restaurant sector and often even in the fast-food sector itself. One might have expected that the Scandinavian countries, especially Sweden, Denmark, Finland and Norway with the highest union density rates in Europe, would also have the highest union membership rates at McDonald's. But this is not the case. It is actually Italy and Austria that have the highest union density within McDonald's European operations. The following sections will look at the distinct experiences with unionisation in each country and try to unravel the reasons for the low levels of membership and the variations in trade union density across countries.

'Do it your own way': the UK and Ireland

The kind of approach to employee relations that McDonald's would normally operate in the USA, i.e. a strictly non-union policy, has not been problematic in the UK. The first McDonald's restaurant was opened in the UK in 1974, but it was not until the early 1980s that the corporation really had a significant number of employees. By that time, the British trade unions were finding life difficult under the new neo-liberal government of Mrs Thatcher. Until then, the UK industrial relations system had had a long history of voluntarism and, in comparison with most European countries, was weakly regulated (Edwards *et al.*, 1998). In a context of huge increases in unemployment and a government actively undermining the position of unions, it is hardly surprising that McDonald's had few problems in operating its usual non-union system. In fact, as Table 5.1 indicates, union membership in the UK was at zero or close to it. The three main trade unions with some interest in representing workers in the UK fast-food industry are the Union of Shop Distributive and Allied Workers (USDAW), the Transport and General Workers' Union (TGWU) and the General Municipal and Boilermakers' Union (GMB). The

GMB is probably largest of the three unions in the fast-food industry (TICL, 1987). Despite the fact that these unions have been trying to target part-time workers and students in recent years, none of these unions has had any real success in organising McDonald's workers in the UK. Sid Nicholson, ex-personnel chief in the UK, stated in an interview with the industrial editor of the *Daily Mirror* in 1986 (Vidal, 1997: 233) that 'We will never negotiate wages and conditions with a union and we discourage our staff from joining'. The 1999 Employment Relations Act is also unlikely to achieve union recognition for McDonald's UK workers. While it halts the tide of anti-union legislation introduced by successive Conservative governments from 1980 to 1993, it has serious weaknesses as far as the unions are concerned, with the new procedures still arguably being heavily in favour of companies (LRD, 1999; Towers, 1999b). For example, there are likely to be problems with gaining adequate union members and problems over the definition of the 'bargaining unit' at McDonald's. Furthermore, the new Act is said to move closer to the model of recognition in the USA, which is in itself seen as partly responsible for the decreasing level of unionisation there (Adams, 1999). It seems likely that the new statutory recognition procedure envisaged in the Act is unlikely to trigger recognition in an aggressively non-union industry of this kind.

A similar story also emerges in Ireland. McDonald's opened its first restaurant in Dublin in early 1977; over the next 2 years, the Irish ITGWU union managed to recruit a few McDonald's workers (between six and eight) and issued a claim for improvement in wages and conditions. The company did not respond. Union officials state that as soon as somebody joined or showed some interest in joining the union they were put under pressure by management and often dismissed. In March 1979, the union balloted its then six members for strike action. The company was given 1 week's notice of the strike action. Three more workers joined the union and the strike took place. The Bakery Workers' Union stopped bread supplies in a sympathy action and mass pickets were organised outside the two restaurants. By now , the union had recruited thirty members, but McDonald's managed to get a High Court injunction to limit the number of pickets to three per restaurant. The strike went on for 6 months, until finally the Labour Court issued a recommendation in favour of union recognition. Some of the pickets who had returned to work were dismissed not long afterwards and union members were not allowed to wear union badges or to put up union notices in the restaurants. ITGWU officials state that their members were being continually reprimanded and that this effectively amounted to harassment. They also report that by the end of 1981 the company had systematically 'got rid' of nearly all their members. Later attempts to organise restaurants simply ended in dismissal. A number of cases were taken to the courts in the mid-1980s; the union won most cases and compensation was paid, but the attempt to organise the restaurants failed. Once union members were removed from McDonald's, the union effectively lost its right to recognition. Union officials now state that McDonald's will meet them in joint labour management catering committees, but not on their own. Since that time, McDonald's in Ireland has remained totally non-union. SIPTU (Services, Industrial, Professional and Technical Union) officials state that McDonald's is not seen as the worst employer in the fast-food sector, but that the new compromise on union recognition procedures (Partnership 2000) in Ireland (*EIRR*, 1999b) is unlikely to make any difference to their non-union stance and in practice will have no effect on union membership.

Unions in the centre: Germany, Austria, Belgium and The Netherlands

In 1991, the McDonald's chairman, Quinlan, suggested that McDonald's must adapt to local conditions where labour relations are concerned and that the corporation had 'learnt its lesson' (BNA, 1991: 66): 'McDonald's has had some horrible union fights around the world, ...do it their way not your own'. An analysis of the corporation's operations in Europe certainly helps to provide one explanation for Quinlan's statement, with a similar pattern of 'adaptation' emerging in most European countries. The McDonald's operations in Germany are a good example. Its first German restaurant was opened in 1971; as more restaurants were opened, McDonald's found itself increasingly in conflict with the German trade unions. By the early 1980s, McDonald's was facing a major public relations crisis over its employment policies. The German union NGG (Gewerkschaft Nahrung Genuss Gaststätten) was increasingly criticising the company in the press over its pay and conditions of employment: one article described conditions in the restaurants as being like the 'Wild West' (*Der Spiegel*, 1981). Things probably came to a head with the publication of the book *Ganz Unten* by Walraff (1985). Walraff (1985) reported a McDonald's memorandum that detailed recommended recruitment procedure for restaurant managers. This explicitly instructed that recruitment procedure was to ascertain whether or not the applicant had any membership or interest in a trade union. If this was found to be the case, the interviewing manager should (Walraff, 1985: 80):

> ...bring the interview to a close after a few additional questions and tell the applicant he will receive a reply in a few days...of course the applicant should in no circumstances be employed.

The company later distanced itself from this statement, stating that its source had been one overzealous manager and that the statement in no way represented company policy. The Walraff (1985) incident appears to have been the 'final straw' as far as avoiding collective agreements was concerned. As one German franchisee, an ex-senior manager with the corporation in the mid-1980s, stated:

> McDonald's has to pay attention to public opinion. In the middle of the

1980s we were strongly attacked by the unions concerning working conditions and it was given a lot of support in the media, but we cleared that up eventually. We were compelled to do something about our image, to get a better position in public opinion.

After the continuing build-up of bad publicity, the corporation apparently decided on a shift in policy. Union officials and McDonald's managers suggest that the McDonald's 'Germany' did not make the final decision alone but with the American parent. Around 1986, three American managers were sent to Germany to make a decision about whether or not the company should negotiate with the NGG and accept a collective agreement. According to these respondents, the corporation's major concern was to balance the effect of the involvement of trade unions on labour costs with effect on public image and therefore sales. As most bargaining in Germany takes place at industry level, this would normally mean joining an employers' association. DEHOGA (the German hotel and guesthouse employers' federation) was already well established and represented a wide range of employers in the hospitality industry. However, according to a DEHOGA representative, works councillors and NGG officials, McDonald's had not enjoyed a good relationship with DEHOGA. The fact that McDonald's was frequently being 'dragged through the mud' by the unions over its labour relations had not endeared the company to other DEHOGA employers. An NGG official states that in the mid-1980s the chairman of DEHOGA, a hotel owner, had openly denounced the company, deriding them as 'chip fryers and meatball roasters'.

Ultimately, McDonald's decided to establish a new fast-food employer's federation, the Bundesverband der Systemgastronomie (BdS). After some 15 years of conflict, the company finally entered negotiations which eventually resulted in the first collective agreement with the unions some 3 years later. Discussions began with other 'fast-food' employers and with the NGG for a collective agreement. Union officials and work councillors allege that on many occasions the chairman of the BdS, Thomas Heyll, has been very much involved in developing the McDonald's anti-works council strategy. According to *Stern* (1999), in the 1970s Heyll actually worked 'on the other side' for the German Commerce, Banking and Insurance Union (HBV). In 1979, he joined the German salaried employees' union federation (DAG), where, together with the large German newspaper publishing group Springer, he led a campaign against supposed communists in the HBV (*Stern*, 1999: 128). He took over chairmanship of the BdS when it was established in the late 1980s.

The membership of the BdS has changed somewhat since its inception. However, in early 1999, the BdS included McDonald's, Burger King, Tricon, DINEA, Häagen-Dazs and Train Catering (a subsidiary of Mitropa – previously the German railways' catering company, DSG). The allegedly poor relationship with DEHOGA may have had a small impact on the decision to establish the BdS, but other explanations seem more likely. Traxler (1991) suggests that employers' associations tend to have more conflicting interests than those of trade unions and will often 'specialise' by forming separate associations. It seems quite likely that McDonald's interests could simply be better represented away from hotel employers, who offer a somewhat different form of service than that provided by fast-food restaurants. It may also be that McDonald's wanted to position itself as a clear leader in its own sector, not merely in terms of sales but to be seen also as setting 'high standards'. For example, before 1989, McDonald's had usually paid a small amount above the minimum wage collectively agreed with DEHOGA. Individual employers' associations also have other advantages: the BdS may have been established to provide a lobbying vehicle. De Vos (1981) suggests that such associations are important for developing channels of communication with government agencies. The establishment of the employers' association and collective agreements might suggest that anti-unionism would now be a thing of the past. Indeed, the German personnel director admitted that McDonald's early labour relations image was poor, but suggested that the relationship with the unions had now improved:

> We had a bad image, but today we're accepted by the unions and that's very important, trade unions are our partners, it's absolutely no good if we try to work against each other. But of course we have to watch that we stay in existence here in Germany. Because the wage levels are already crazily high, the trade unions have allowed the wage rates to explode.

This is not the way that the unions see it. NGG officials are adamant that the collective agreements, although welcome, were merely a pragmatic decision to improve the organisation's image and did not represent any change in the underlying non-union stance of the corporation. One NGG official stated:

> On the outside the company appears to be friendly to unions, but when it comes down to it they're as hard as nails, exactly as before. No influence is to be allowed in, on the inside the union is kept out. It's two sides of the same coin. They do it so that they can say they are not against unions, to stop public criticism. Within the company they make propaganda against the union and the works councils. They use the old tactics just as they have before to avoid either the works councils or union membership in the restaurants.

Indeed, as we will see in Chapters 6 and 8, the activities of McDonald's with regard to both national level works councils and the European Works Council suggest that the 'leopard has not changed its spots'. It appears that McDonald's has also provided plenty of work for the German labour courts. According to *Der Spiegel* (1997), some 335 employees in five Dortmund restaurants have brought more than 200 legal proceedings against McDonald's. That there is continuing trouble is not very surprising if the report in an article in the German magazine *Stern* (1999) is anything to go by. The article (*Stern*, 1999) suggests that workers are forced to work through their breaks and that when a manager has 'clocked' the worker 'out' he has to go on working. *Stern* (1999: 122) also suggests that clocking-out times had been tampered with afterwards in order to reduce payments to workers. The article quotes a disenchanted German assistant restaurant manager who was demoted from restaurant manager for allowing his staff to elect a works council: '…I've done that myself in some cases, it also happens regularly in other restaurants'. Indeed, it appears that in four cases presented to the labour court in Dortmund a restaurant manager was accused of falsifying employment contracts to prevent workers from taking time off to which they were entitled.

In another surprise move in April 1999, McDonald's Germany allied itself with the trade union Ganymed, which according to IUF officials falls under the umbrella of a union with a 'Nazi' history, the German Association of Commercial and Industrial Employees (Deutscher Handels- und Industrie-aangestelltenverband; DHV). The DHV is affiliated to the CGB (the Christian Federation of Trade Unions), which in total has fewer than 300,000 members (Jacobi *et al.*, 1998). It appears that, with the help of the DHV, McDonald's has been able to place employer-backed candidates on the workers' side of the bipartite body that administers the accident insurance fund for workers in the food and HRC sectors, which was created in the post-war period. Since that time, the NGG has proposed a list of candidates, representing the employees, to sit on that body every year. In 1999, the NGG agreed to the participation of other candidates proposed by the DHV, only to learn, as the election was in process, that the signatures legally required for participation in the election had been gathered at the instigation of McDonald's Germany. Of the 1,700 signatures collected for the list, most were McDonald's employees; the NGG alleges that the company had sent directives to local managers instructing them to gather signatures. NGG officials state that in effect McDonald's has now created a seat on the employees' side, thereby destroying the legal principle of administrative parity between employers and employees. As if this was not enough, the Ganymed union has also featured in negotiations between the NGG and the employers' association (the BdS) in this year's collective bargaining round. McDonald's is offering a 1.5% pay rise for each of the next 3 years (4.5% over 3 years – well below the level of inflation). NGG officials involved in the talks state that McDonald's representatives have threatened that if the NGG does not accept the offer it will no longer negotiate with them, but will conclude a deal with Ganymed. The NGG has organised members to demonstrate outside McDonald's German restaurants to complain about the low level of existing wages (see Chapter 7). The Ganymed union is extremely small, having around 1,500 members and being administered by five staff in an office in Bonn. According to an article in *Stern* (1999: 128), a spokesman for the CGB stated that '… Membership figures will certainly rise if we do business there'. The

Ganymed union leader, Horst Albers, must be well aware that a deal with the BdS and McDonald's would have a major impact on the fortunes of his union, and he has apparently been making the appropriate statements (*Stern*, 1999: 128): '... Partnership instead of class struggle'. The conflict looks set to continue.

In Belgium, union officials from both the restaurant and hotel unions affiliated to the FGTB (General Belgian Trade Union Confederation) and the CSC (General Christian Trade Union) state that it has been impossible to have any kind of meaningful dialogue with the corporation. Although collective agreements are automatically imposed on the corporation, unions have been unable to negotiate a company-level agreement. Union membership is a big problem and there is very little effective union representation in the restaurants. They have been unable to establish works councils and only have a small number of union delegates in the restaurants. Unions report problems of collective agreement infringements and unfair dismissals. Overall, the unions report that McDonald's is essentially anti-union in its approach, but that it will respond quickly if its image is threatened. In this situation, it is very difficult to establish effective union representation in the restaurants and to ensure that the sectoral agreement is properly applied.

McDonald's came to Austria in 1977, and by 1998 had approximately eighty restaurants and 4,000 employees. Some 80% of these restaurants (about sixty-five restaurants) are franchise operations. McDonald's was automatically covered by a sectoral collective agreement from the first day that it began business in Austria, but until the mid-1990s the corporation refused to deal with the trade unions. Despite this, it appears that here too McDonald's experienced considerable conflict with the trade unions. In Austria, trade union officials at the HGPD (Hotel, Gastgewerbe, Persönlicher Dienst) described the first 17 years of the 'relationship' with McDonald's as 'war': 'They were like a red rag to a bull for us...we were regularly beating each other over the head in the newspapers'. However, after continued pressure in the media and apparently losing the public relations battle, in 1994, some 17 years after opening their first restaurant in Austria, McDonald's finally changed its approach. The McDonald's senior Austrian human resource manager was replaced and both sides began talks. Since that time, McDonald's appears to be taking a more pragmatic approach towards the unions and the relationship with the unions has apparently improved considerably, with union officials able to state that '...the war is now over'. Part of the deal now allows the HGPD to recruit union members actively in the restaurants, which union officials suggest has rapidly increased the numbers of its members at McDonald's. On one level, its relationship with the unions has definitely improved; however, officials state that there is a huge difference between McDonald's McOpCo restaurants and the vast majority run by franchisees. There are still problems with getting franchisees to apply the collective agreements correctly and, as we will see in Chapter 6, the unions have been unable to establish any co-determination rights through works councils or a supervisory board in either McOpCo or franchise restaurants. This is significant because without a works council in the restaurant they are unable to ensure that workers' rights are guaranteed.

According to union officials at the Dutch Federation of Trade Unions (FNV)-affiliated Horecabond (the Dutch trade union for hotel and restaurant workers), the relationship between McDonald's and the union was also very poor from when it entered the Dutch market in 1971 until the mid-1980s, although union officials also suggest that this may in part be a result of the activities of some left-wing youth groups associated with the Voedingsbond FNV. Nevertheless, something like 13 years went by before McDonald's 'toned down' its outspokenly anti-union policies in The Netherlands. Increasingly coming into conflict with the unions during that time, it faced more and more bad publicity. After losing a number of court cases involving infringements of the national collective agreement, McDonald's made public pronouncements that it would thereafter agree to recognise the trade unions and take part in and adhere to collective agreements. Since that time, both its public image and its relations with unions in The Netherlands have improved a good deal. The corporation has also benefited from positive publicity in working with the union in encouraging more people to take up part-time work. Benders and Mol (1998) suggest that the improvement in this relationship could be explained by a more consensual orientation prevalent in Dutch society (d'Iribarne, 1989). However, they also point out that a major part of FNV's policy has been to redistribute work by encouraging part-time employment, fighting unemployment and increasing access to work for ethnic workers and women, precisely the kind of employment offered by McDonald's. Interestingly, it was in 1982 that the Accord of Wassenaar was signed. More than union resignation to economic hard times (real wages had already been frozen by statutory restraint in 1980 and1981), Visser (1998b) suggests that this agreement marked a victory for the moderate faction within the FNV, the dominant union confederation. The sharp and apparently unstoppable rise in unemployment pushed the FNV into adopting a jobs first policy, abandoning its goal of redistributing income and power in favour of workers (Visser, 1998a).

Union officials state that, in 1997, of the 13,000 or so McDonald's employees only eighty were union members. After a 6-month campaign ending in early 1998, the union successfully increased its membership to what is now around 500 members. However, because of the high level of labour turnover, improving on or even maintaining this small figure will not be straightforward. Visser (1998b) also suggests that unionisation is particularly low in The Netherlands among women and young workers in the service sector. Despite the co-operation with McDonald's management, a survey conducted by the union in late 1997 and early 1998 suggests that a considerable number of problems still remain. In particular, there was a general complaint that relations between managers and workers were not good, that there was inadequate notice of working hours, incorrect sick pay calculations and a considerable problem with McDonald's classifying workers into a lower pay grouping of 'apprentice fast-food worker'. This 'grade' does not exist in terms of the collective agreement. Union officials state that these problems frequently occurred in franchise restaurants, where 90% of McDonald's Dutch workers are employed. McDonald's claimed that the survey was unrepresentative because it did not include salaried employees and did not match the results of their own survey. Nevertheless, McDonald's stated that it would take the claims seriously and the details were also reported in the Dutch press (*Algemeen Dagblad*, 1998; *Delftse Courant*, 1998). In an attempt to deal with these kinds of problems, the corporation agreed to meet with the union at least twice per year or more to try to iron out any difficulties. Although co-operation on these issues is helpful, the corporation appears to be less keen to deal with the issue of works councils. As we will see in Chapter 6, the union has been unable to establish any significant numbers of union representatives or works councils in the restaurants. This may be even more significant in the Dutch case; Dutch unions have typically organised at industry level in a way in which union activity at plant level (or in this case restaurant level) is neglected, leading to a power balance in favour of employers (Visser, 1998b).

Unions in the south: France, Spain and Italy

Only 3 years after Quinlan's statement about 'doing it their way', French McDonald's management appeared to be doing just the opposite. As in The Netherlands and Austria, McDonald's was automatically covered by a sectoral agreement in France. However, for over 15 years, McDonald's adopted an 'empty chair' policy in the French fast-food employers' association (SNARR – Syndicat National d'Alimentation et de la Restauration Rapide) and refused to recognise the trade unions. Once again, things appeared to have to come to crisis point before McDonald's would change its approach. By 1994, McDonald's had an increasingly significant public profile and 250 restaurants in France. It was around this time that the most surprising and well-publicised case of conflict hit the headlines, being reported in both the French and the UK newspapers (*Libération*, 1994; Sage, 1994). It appears that twelve McDonald's managers were arrested at their place of work and put under judicial investigation. They were accused of union discrimination, breaching union rights, breaching the right to display union documents, failing to hold monthly meetings for employee representatives and irregularities in the organisation of union delegate and works council elections (see Chapter 6). As one official from the union CFDT (Confédération française démocratique du travail – French Democratic Federation of Labour) stated (Sage, 1994: 16): 'The company has a resistance to unions that is incredible'. After continuing bad public publicity associated with these events, McDonald's finally not only joined the employers' association but also became its president. The corporation now stated that it wanted to follow the 'logic of consultation and partnership' rather than pursuing a 'logic of confrontation' (*EIRR*, 1997c: 20). Between April and June 1996, McDonald's and the CFDT concluded a company-level pay deal for the, at the time, thirty-seven French McOpCo restaurants. In addition, McDonald's also signed a 2-year recognition agreement with the CFDT in October 1996 that covered all trade unions represented in the company. Although the company-level agreement improves slightly on the pay and conditions determined under the sectoral agreement already in place (see Chapter 7), the company agreement only covers the 10% of McOpCo restaurants and not its joint venture and franchise operations. McDonald's stated that it hoped that the deal would provide a model for the franchises to emulate. However, since that time, union officials state there has been little evidence of any 'emulation' by franchisees. Although they see the appointment of a more union-friendly human resources manager as an important step, it does not represent any major change in the 'values' of most McDonald's management. In an interview in 1999 a CFDT official described the corporation's 'change' on employment relations policy as little more than a public relations exercise.

McDonald's first arrived in Spain in 1982; it has refused to recognise the trade unions ever since and very few workers are members of any union. FECOHT is affiliated to the CCOO (Comisiones Obreras) confederation, which is one of the two main trade unions representing the food and drink industry. Its officials estimate that just 1% of McDonald's workers in Spain are union members. They also state that neither they nor any other trade union has had any success in establishing any kind of meaningful relationship or dialogue with McDonald's or its franchisees. In fact, they allege that McDonald's has actively tried to prevent the presence of trade unions in its restaurants. Although a sectoral level agreement automatically applies to McDonald's in Spain, it has not had a great impact on the normal mode of operation of McDonald's. It does not cover pay and only covers some aspects of working conditions; also, as it applies to all the employers in the hotel, restaurant and leisure industry, some of its provisions are not very relevant to the particular problems of fast-food. In fact, most sectoral level agreements in Spain have not covered pay since the mid-1980s, but Spain does have a legal minimum wage normally up-rated each January (IDS, 1996). Large and medium-sized companies normally have their own company-level agreements covering pay and conditions. Most of McDonald's company-owned restaurants (about thirty) are located in or around Madrid, but these are only a minority of restaurants, the remaining 130 restaurants outside Madrid are run by franchisees. No union has been able to negotiate any collective agreement with the corporation. However, at least two company-level agreements do exist which have been concluded by allegedly 'company-friendly' works councils (see Chapter 6). One of these agreements is for the company-owned restaurants in Madrid and the other covers a number of franchise restaurants operated by one franchisee. FECOHT officials state that the pay levels and conditions concluded in those agreements are very poor, but that wage levels and conditions in other franchise restaurants are even lower. FECOHT officials suggest that McDonald's has achieved this situation by being able to capture Spanish works councils for a managerially sponsored agenda (see Chapter 6).

The situation in Italy is somewhat different. The Italian unions have, with Austria, the highest union density rate in McDonald's restaurants in Europe. Part of the explanation for this is that many of McDonald's restaurants were previously owned by national food chains and were already unionised. A second explanation is that labour turnover is not so high because unemployment levels have remained high, especially in the south of Italy. Third, representative unions have the right to enter premises and they have managed to establish a fair number of union delegates and some works councils. McDonald's is automatically caught by a sectoral collective agreement, but union attempts to negotiate a company-level collective agreement have so far failed. Union officials and McDonald's workers complain that 20% of workers are not paid in accordance with the correct pay grouping and allege that union delegates face regular harassment and poorer working conditions than non-union workers. Typically, there are many more problems in the franchise restaurants than in the company-owned restaurants, and in particular workers complain of unsatisfactory health and safety procedures and working conditions. Even as recently as May 1999, McDonald's Italian workers went on strike, shutting restaurants on consecutive Saturdays in a number of Italian towns and cities, including Milan and Bologna. Once again, union membership is much higher where works councils or union delegates are in place.

Unions in the north: Denmark, Finland, Iceland, Norway and Sweden

The history of the relationship between McDonald's and the Scandinavian unions is somewhat mixed. In Denmark, Finland, Iceland and Norway, McDonald's had initially refused to recognise unions. The only exception to this is Sweden, where McDonald's appeared to adopt a more union-friendly approach from the beginning. In fact, in Denmark, the dispute between the unions and McDonald's was rather acrimonious and long running. There are approximately 4,000 employees at McDonald's Denmark who are employed in about eighty restaurants, seventy-four of which (over 90%) are franchise operations. From the beginning, when McDonald's opened its first restaurant in early 1982, McDonald's would not come to an agreement with the unions. By summer 1983, seven McDonald's restaurants had opened, all as franchise operations with four different franchise owners. McDonald's was the only multinational in the Danish fast-food sector that had not signed a collective agreement or joined the employers' association. After several months of demonstrations against the corporation by a trade union youth organisation, the main hotel and restaurant union took the initiative in the summer of

1983. One lawyer represented all four franchisees and it became clear that McDonald's would not allow individual franchisees to sign an agreement, only an agreement covering all seven restaurants would be accepted. By September 1983, negotiations had broken down; in particular, McDonald's would not accept any regulation of working time regulations. The unions began a boycott campaign and organised daily demonstrations outside the restaurants. According to Danish (RBF) union officials, a McDonald's spokesman confidently stated in 'Dalek-like' tones that union resistance would be useless:

> McDonald's has as much money as there is water in the sea, we will not give in to an agreement, industrial action is useless.

The corporation was initially successful in acquiring a court ruling prohibiting the use of any poster or leaflet which included their trademark symbol on it, in this case the McDonald's 'M'. In spring 1985, McDonald's once again refused to take part in negotiations with the unions. This time, the unions responded with a broad trade union boycott campaign that would stop deliveries of some items to McDonald's restaurants. The conflict really came to a head in 1988. There was frequent and extensive coverage in the newspapers and there were daily demonstrations outside the restaurants. The Danish graphics workers refused to deal with their advertising material, brewery workers refused to deliver beer and construction workers refused to build any new McDonald's. The unions were particularly pleased with a poster designed for them by a Danish graphics worker which portrayed a dog urinating on the McDonald's 'M' symbol; this illustration was used to make T-shirts, leaflets, placards and badges. The Nordic unions met in January 1989 to discuss the problem, and at the end of January the Finnish unions warned McDonald's Finland that a Danish agreement would have to be put in place by 15 February 1989. This was not forthcoming, so in February 1989 the Finnish unions organised sympathy action. The extending of the dispute to Finland was given considerable publicity. It was reported on TV, on radio and in the newspapers. The largest Finnish trade union confederation (SAK) asked that all affiliated organisations take part in the boycott. Large-scale information campaigns were organised in Finnish schools, and student and youth organisations distributed leaflets asking people to boycott McDonald's. There were also plans to broaden sympathy action in the other Nordic countries. McDonald's finally caved in May 1989; it joined the Danish employers' association for the hotel and restaurant sector and accepted a collective agreement. By this time, McDonald's had twelve restaurants in Denmark. This agreement appears to have achieved considerable improvements over McDonald's normal basic terms.

Since that time, Danish union officials state that the relationship has not really changed and that McDonald's frequently breaks the collective agreement, particularly in the area of working hours and overtime payments and on several occasions it has tried to undo the basic agreement concluded in 1989. One such instance occurred only 2 years after the first agreement had been signed. In 1991, during annual negotiations with the unions over pay and conditions, McDonald's startled union officials at the RBF by offering them 100% union membership at McDonald's Denmark. In return, McDonald's wanted the unions to renegotiate the basic company agreement concluded in 1989, reducing the extra payments for evening work, Sundays and public holidays. An RBF official alleges that a senior McDonald's manager stated:

> ...We will make all the employees join your union if we can pay less for these flexibility allowances.

The union refused the offer because, as an official pointed out, '...it would have been too cheap a way to get members'. Management attempts to undo the first agreement are perhaps not very surprising; as we shall see in Chapter 7, the allowances negotiated in the Danish agreement for unsociable hours appear to be much more generous than those negotiated in many other countries. It has also been very difficult to establish union delegates in the restaurants; at present, they only have one in eighty restaurants, union membership is still very low and co-operation committees simply do not exist (see Chapter 6; Royle, 2001).

Arriving in Finland in 1984, McDonald's was automatically bound by the existing sectoral collective agreement and it decided to join the Finnish employers' association. Officials at the Finnish hotel and restaurant workers union (HRHL) are not entirely satisfied with the current agreement because it is based on the hotel and restaurant sector and does not, therefore, adequately deal with some of the issues in the fast-food sector. Furthermore, there are frequent problems with the proper application of the collective agreement. In fact, HRHL officials report that McDonald's has so far been unwilling to negotiate directly with them, so there is little in the way of any 'relationship'. As in many other countries, it appears that the role of union representatives (or works councils) in the restaurants is the key to recruiting union members. However, HRHL officials report that it has been difficult to establish representatives and that union membership is still low. In fact, as we will see in Chapters 6 and 8, it appears that McDonald's has tried to hinder the election of union representatives. However, the unions have had some success recently with a recruitment campaign and with a new union information leaflet specifically aimed at young workers. There are no workers' committees or councils and no union representation on a supervisory board, but there is a health and safety committee.

In a similar approach to that adopted in Denmark, when the first McDonald's restaurant was opened in Iceland in 1993 the owner announced that it would not join the employers' association or conclude any collective agreements with the trade unions. McDonald's eventually gave way on some general principles, but union officials still report workers being dismissed for having contact with the trade unions and regular infringements of the sectoral collective agreement.

McDonald's came to Norway in 1983 and once again ran into trouble with the unions. Although a sectoral agreement automatically applies to McDonald's in Norway, the basic framework is based on an old agreement dating back to the 1930s and 1940s and relates to the wider hospitality industry. The Norwegian union (HRAF) has therefore tried to establish a company-level collective agreement for every franchise operation and for those employed in the McDonald's company-owned restaurants. The idea behind this approach was to make sure that workers would know their rights and take 'ownership' of the collective agreement. However, the unions have not been very successful; franchisees in particular have been unwilling to negotiate company-level agreements. A major problem for the Norwegian unions is that they must have union members in a restaurant before they can get recognition for collective bargaining. The high level of labour turnover and mostly very young workforce and what union officials describe as an anti-union policy make this difficult. For example, in 1992, a previous union campaign for an agreement covering three franchise restaurants in Oslo collapsed when the unionised workers left McDonald's for other jobs. In 1993, when twelve cleaners joined the union, the union demanded a collective agreement. HRAF officials state that McDonald's responded by dismissing all twelve workers. After negotiations, the workers were reinstated, but after a few months they came under pressure to leave the company. Only after strike action was threatened and there was considerable coverage of the conflict in the media did McDonald's finally give in to an agreement for workers employed in its McOpCo restaurants in Oslo in October 1993. At present, there is just one company-level agreement at restaurant level, covering all of McDonald's company-owned restaurants. Union officials state that the attempt to get franchisees to the table has not succeeded and, furthermore, that there are frequent problems with franchisees not following the agreements over basic issues in employment contracts, such as scheduled work hours, correct pay rates, overtime and holiday pay errors. There have also been problems with young workers being employed illegally. Recruiting union members among so many young workers is a continuing problem; there is always the danger that if union members leave the restaurant then the union may lose its recognition rights. Norway has a similar industrial relations system to Sweden, so there is no scope for separately elected works councils; however, union officials estimate that there are around twenty-five union representatives in about fifteen of the fifty restaurants in Norway. The union is most concerned about those restaurants that do not have any union representatives because it is in these restaurants where most of the infringements of the agreements are taking place.

Sweden was the first Scandinavian country to experience McDonald's, which opened its first restaurant there in 1973. The reaction to the company was extremely hostile, with Lederhausen, the Swedish businessman who opened the first franchises, receiving regular hate mail and his restaurants being smoke bombed by left-wing groups complaining of what they termed 'creeping American imperialism' (Vidal, 1997: 41). Despite admiring the American way of doing things (Love, 1995), Lederhausen perhaps decided that to take on the Swedish unions, who have the highest union membership rates in Europe, would be a recipe for disaster. In any case, the restaurants would automatically be caught by a sectoral collective agreement concluded for the whole hotel and restaurant sector. As a result, the relationship with the Swedish unions is probably the best in Europe: provided with a separate office, a union delegate works full time on union matters in the McDonald's head office in Stockholm. However, problems still remain, union membership levels are extremely low compared with Swedish norms. Union officials at the HRF union state that relations between them and the McDonald's senior management are good; indeed, the policy of McDonald's central management in Sweden is that restaurant management must stay on good terms with the union. However, union representatives report that life in the restaurants is something else and that the managers in the restaurants often try to undermine their position with the workforce, with some managers being more hostile to union representatives than others. One union representative (a floor manager) working outside Stockholm commented: 'I think that they can't be bothered to fight with the union since the union is so strong in Sweden'. Another union representative in a company-owned restaurant stated that there are sometimes problems with getting managers to pay people within the correct pay grouping in accordance with the collective agreement. However, the main problem appears to be finding enough people to be union representatives at all. Where representatives do exist, infringements are less likely, and awareness of employment rights among workers is much higher. But among the majority of workers, and especially among foreign workers located in the big cities such as Stockholm and Gothenburg, the knowledge and awareness of employment rights and collective agreements is low. Where union representatives are established, union membership can increase dramatically; workers report that in one restaurant outside Stockholm, for example, union membership increased from around 5% to 75% once a union representative had been established.

Explaining low union membership

The often geographically disperse, small unit, temporary, part-time and low skills base of the jobs in the wider hospitality industry have typically fostered high levels of labour turnover. These factors, together with the employment of ethnic minorities, young and female employees, make union organisation very difficult. From a UK and US perspective, union organisation in the wider hospitality industry has always been low (Lowery and Scott, 1996). It often reflects the 'Bleak House' of industrial relations (Sisson, 1993) and highly 'individualised' employee relations, resulting in high dismissal rates, accidents and absenteeism, high labour turnover, large numbers of grievance procedures and low pay (Lucas, 1996). However, unions themselves may also be somewhat to blame. Perhaps because of these difficulties, unions have not always been willing to focus adequate resources on recruitment in this industry. The fast-food 'portion' of this sector is at the vanguard of this form of 'atypical' work. In fact, this kind of work is no longer atypical, but increasingly represents 'typical' work for a growing sector of the labour market. The previous sections also suggest that despite the high levels of union membership and state regulation often found in most European countries the problem is that union membership in McDonald's is still very low. The following sections attempt to explain why this is by examining some of the responses from McDonald's workers and managers in Germany and the UK.

Management attitudes towards unions

The earlier analysis suggests that negative management attitudes towards unionisation are part of the explanation. In Chapter 4, it was suggested that the basic assumptions (Schein, 1984) of the McDonald's corporate culture remain strongly grounded in anti-unionism. But to what extent are these assumptions transmitted and internalised by senior level and restaurant management in different countries? As we have already suggested, whether values are actually internalised may not be very significant in practice. However, interviews with German and UK management do suggest that certain values are indeed transmitted across societal borders to management at senior and restaurant level. The following comments from UK and German senior managers were typical:

> Unionisation has risen its ugly head over the years, but you know, we feel that we don't need unions. I think we've seen that the unions' power within business has been eroded quite considerably over the last 15 years, we've managed to get rid of them.
>
> (Senior UK manager)

> We don't see the need for unions. McDonald's has shown that it's not necessary in this industry. We already have a good system of communications. Unions are less important than they used to be.
>
> (Senior German manager)

Perhaps less outspokenly, anti-union restaurant management also uttered similar comments. The following comments from German and UK restaurant salaried and 'hourly paid' management were typical:

> Unions are asking too much as far as wages are concerned, the claims they are making on our economy are unsupportable, they should think

more of the unemployed and more in the interests of the employer, they won't work in our system.

(German restaurant manager)

Of course unions play an important role in society, but they are unnecessary in the McDonald's system, we don't need them here.

(German shift-running floor manager)

Unions can cause problems if they get out of control, I don't think they need to get any stronger. Unions should be there as an advisory function, I would like to think that there would be no need for them in the future. But I can't see it, because not everyone is as honest as the managers in this restaurant, so I think there will always be a need for them. We don't need them in this restaurant because we do things right, manage them right.

(UK first assistant manager)

I think unions have an important role to play, but in the restaurant where it's only one on one there's no need for them. I've never thought of joining a union, never been in a union, my initial feeling is, it's not worth bothering.

(UK shift-running floor manager)

German salaried management tended to be better informed about which union would represent the industry and about the role of unions in general. In the UK, salaried managers typically had no personal experience of unions and appeared to be poorly informed about their current strength relative to employers and their wider role in society. UK managers typically saw UK trade unions as powerful and dangerous and there appeared to be very little concrete knowledge of the changes in union legislation introduced in the 1980s and 1990s. The following comments by young UK salaried managers in 1994 and 1995 were typical:

I think they've got too much power at the moment, nobody wins strikes, they are getting their members over a barrel. I must admit, my knowledge is very limited, I didn't know about the changes in legislation on unions.

It's as if they have the power to say right we're on strike, it's as if they have control over employers.

I think they are more political than they used to be. I think they lobby for a lot more than their predecessors did. I think they are a lot stronger than they were. They've got all these lawyers looking for loopholes now, that they never used to and outside help. They've got a lot of money and a lot of backing, so they can do a lot of damage, that's the main reason why I'm against them, well not against them, but I think they can do a lot of unnecessary damage.

Some managers in both countries did make a few positive comments, but these tended to be accompanied by the caveat that either unions were unnecessary at McDonald's or that any role they could perform with McDonald's would have to be tightly restricted. One German floor manager commented:

> Unions can be useful in dealing with conflict situations in large organisations, but we don't need them at McDonald's.

One comment made by a UK restaurant manager unwittingly reflected previous events in Germany: he suggested that unions could perhaps play a useful role in improving the McDonald's public image by representing workers over pay. However, he also made it clear that this might lead to unsupportable rises in labour costs that would be unacceptable:

> The company is not interested in unions, it is its own boss. The company has got its own ideals and doesn't want an outside organisation stepping in. The only issue I think unions could get involved in is pay, because it might improve its image with the public and its employees, the only trouble with that is it might get out of hand.

The majority of German managers were much more negative about unions and stated that with 'good' management they could imagine a future in which unions would become extinct. Both German and UK managers suggested that it would be quite possible to do without unions provided employees were managed properly. One German floor manager commented:

> With good management it is possible that there will not be unions in the future.

Less surprisingly, this notion was also strongly reflected in comments from UK respondents. One UK restaurant manager commented:

> Well we must take on the role of the trade union and protect the employees. It comes back to the motivation thing, if we protect them and look after their interests they are going to be motivated, there's no need for trade unions at McDonald's because we are two organisations in one. I can't see a problem with having no unions in society if each business had a philosophy of looking after their employees like McDonald's, but then, that's Utopia isn't it?

These responses suggest that regardless of societal differences the McDonald's corporate culture is quite effective in moulding the required responses of management. Willmott (1993) argues that strong corporate cultures 'exclude and eliminate' other values, such as, in this case, the acceptance of unions. The emphasis placed on the importance of 'good' management suggests a moral tone. Willmott (1993) suggests that the extent to which individuals may be willing to internalise these norms may depend on their assessment of a company's moral character. The McDonald's 'culture' appears to be one that encourages managers to see unions as an unwarranted interference which will 'destroy' the corporation and the 'good' management practice they carry out.

Franchises: the benefits of small operations

As we have already argued in Chapter 3, the high proportion of franchise operations (some 65% of its restaurants in Europe and as high as 90% in some countries) is not an obstacle to maintaining control and the consistency of its operations across societal borders. Franchisees are motivated by profits not by a wage. They pay much more attention to fine details of the operation and may be much better at eradicating waste and keeping labour costs low. In this sense, franchisees provide the corporation with highly motivated 'managers' of small business operations, yet paradoxically retaining tight control over them. Franchisees foster the kind of paternalistic relations that allow them to keep a close eye on the activities of their employees. One UK franchisee stated:

> I like people to tell me every little incident in detail that goes on because if there is a problem I can react to it.

Abbott (1993) makes the point that large organisations find it more difficult to stop unionisation because of the distance between senior managers and employees, whereas small operations make it more difficult for unions to recruit members. Commenting on the third Workplace Industrial Relations Survey (WIRS) (1990), for example, Blyton and Turnbull (1994) suggest that *ceteris paribus* non-union firms in the UK are more likely to be small, single-plant establishments and located in the private (especially service) sector. Indeed, this has also been evident in a number of other studies (Rainnie, 1989; Holliday, 1995). Abbott (1993) suggests that the majority of small business owners in the UK often comment that they do see the need for unions in society in general, but see no need for unions in *their* businesses. Typically, he suggests, this was because they believed that they were good employers. Abbott (1993) also suggests that small businesses would interpret any interest in union involvement by their employees as a failure of management. This was also strongly reflected in responses from franchisees in this study. German and UK franchisees made the following comments:

> If they wanted a union here I would take it personally, I'd feel a little bit insulted and think, well, why do they want one?
>
> (German franchisee)

I don't think they are necessary. If crew wanted to join a union I would feel disappointed, because it would mean that I had failed in my efforts to look after them. I'd feel I'd not been doing my job properly. I think because of the damage other employers have done to some employees unions will stay popular, I don't think they will die off overnight in those old industries. Fast-food is a new breed.

(UK franchisee)

In addition, franchisees are well aware that inviting unions into restaurants would not sit well with the values of the corporation. They are unlikely to do anything that might attract the corporation's criticism and risk losing their licence or the chance to add additional restaurants in the future. McDonald's have the best of both worlds: willing 'partners' in sharing the costs and risks of development and highly obedient and motivated operators spreading the corporate message and leaving little room for union involvement.

Workforce characteristics and workers' attitudes

As we have also suggested in Chapter 4, the reason for the low union organisation rates in the McDonald's European operations is not entirely to do with an anti-union corporate culture and close monitoring of employees. The characteristics of the workforce itself are also an important factor. In most European countries, the majority of McDonald's workers are very young, many are still at school and many are students. Young workers tend to have very little previous job experience; if they have worked before, it is often in similar kinds of low-skilled work. Many of the young employees only work for 'pocket money', do not intend to stay long with McDonald's and therefore tend to have highly instrumental attitudes. In addition, they tend to have very little knowledge of trade unions and often do not see their relevance. In addition to frequently hostile management attitudes towards unions, this makes union recruitment of young workers extremely difficult. The following comments from young German and UK McDonald's workers are typical of responses from young McDonald's workers in other European countries:

Unions are not important for me personally at the moment, here at McDonald's, but maybe later when I get a better job.

The company see it as big happy family sort of company. I think some people would join a union if there was a choice but I wouldn't bother.

The problem of young workers and union recruitment at McDonald's seems to be a particular problem for the Scandinavian countries. In the UK, in particular, the majority of young workers were simply not well informed about the current status of unions, union roles or priorities or what services unions may be able to provide for them. Not one of the UK interview respondents within the restaurants at any level could say which union would be responsible for the fast-food industry or knew which union they should approach if they had wanted to. The following comments from UK workers was typical:

> I just don't know enough about them, I tend to associate unions with strikes but I don't know a lot about it.

> I don't know, I've never really thought about unions, it's not something I think about. I don't know really, don't know what they do. I've never been told or given anything about unions.

In the Scandinavian countries, the unions enjoy much better access to McDonald's workers, but still find it very difficult to recruit young workers. Danish and Finnish union officials suggest that McDonald's restaurant management would often try to persuade young employees that the reasonably good pay and conditions they enjoyed had nothing to do with the trade unions, 'who were only trouble makers', but were the result of a benign and generous employer. When asked why she had taken the unusual step to become union representatives in her restaurant, one Finnish union representative stated that she had been appalled at managers attitudes and commented: 'They screw you, so you need some protection!' Finnish union representatives also stated that there were several reasons why so few workers joined the union: first, because many of them often had more than one part-time job; second, some were unwilling to pay the membership fee because they thought they already had the protection of the unions through the collective agreements; and third, most commonly because they did not intend to stay with the company very long.

It's not always high turnover and young workers

However, as we have also seen in Chapter 4, it would be a mistake to think that the McDonald's workforce was only made up of young workers. In Italy, the average age of the workforce is also older than in the UK; Italian McDonald's workers state that this is simply because of the problem of higher unemployment. These older workers cannot get jobs elsewhere and this is particularly acute in the south of Italy. In Germany and Austria, there are large proportions of foreign workers (*Gastarbeiter*), many of Turkish decent in some of the big cities but also a large proportion of economic migrants from the old Eastern bloc countries (*Aussiedler*). This means that the average age of the German, Austrian and Italian McDonald's workforce is older than that in most of the other European countries. In some cases, foreign workers had had some contact with unions in their previous jobs, but this was no longer seen as a possibility while working at McDonald's either because of obvious management hostility or simply because they did not know who to contact. Very few foreign workers in Germany seemed to have any knowledge of what the German union had already achieved for them by way of collective agreements or had no idea that a union had actually negotiated on their behalf. This was particularly acute where there were no union representatives or works councils in the restaurant. For example, only 10% of the hourly paid employees interviewed in the German restaurants where no works council existed (the majority of German restaurants) knew that a union negotiated on their behalf and only 3% knew the name of the union concerned. This comment made by an *Aussiedler* in a German restaurant was typical:

> There are no unions at McDonald's, I don't know why we don't have them here, you hear so little about unions in this industry.

This was despite the fact that a copy of the collective agreement was supposed to be available to every German employee in the form of two booklets covering pay and conditions separately. The back page of both union booklets contains an application form for union membership with the NGG. In restaurants where no works councils were established, the majority of employees did not know about these booklets. Restaurant management often stated that they felt it was 'unnecessary' for the crew to have their own copies of the agreements because the crew could always ask managers if they wanted to know something. However, in restaurants where union-supported works councils were established, employees were much better informed and copies of the agreements were widely available. In sharp contradiction to the statements made by managers and despite the lack of awareness about unions, most workers interviewed in Germany and the UK seemed to have a positive view of trade unions:

> Unions are important, they play an important role in limiting the power of employers and stop employees being exploited.
>
> (UK crew)

> Unions are really too important, it's really a pity that McDonald's are not involved with the unions.
>
> (German crew)

> They are there to serve the rights of the workers which I think is good thing, but I've not thought of joining one.
>
> (UK crew)

> I hope there will always be unions, but there's no information about them here.
>
> (German crew)

Even in the UK, where something like 70% of the workforce is under 21, there is often a core of older workers who tend to stay with the company over the long term, in some cases 5 years or more. First, those who have been 'washed up' in the labour market because of poor qualifications and a lack of other opportunities, and second the 'coasters' that were referred to in Chapter 4. In other countries such as Finland, Spain and Italy, workers tend to stay longer because there is so much high unemployment among younger workers. One Italian floor manager, who had previously been a librarian for 10 years had been made redundant, stated: '...there are no other jobs'. Young Finnish workers reported that it was very difficult to get work elsewhere and that once they had worked at McDonald's other employers would not take them seriously when they applied for other kinds of work:

> There are so many young people without a job it is hard to get other jobs, when you go and they ask if you have any experience and you say 'Oh I worked at McDonald's', they say 'Go back there and make some burgers!'. I've tried I know.

Of course, McDonald's may also offer an opportunity for some to make a real career with the company, especially while it continues to expand at such fast rate. A Norwegian union official described these workers as 'career collaborators'. Overall, the 'acquiescent' nature of the workforce makes it very difficult to organise workers. Those workers who really need the job are not likely to go against managerial will and join the union if they think their job will be threatened. In many cases, workers just do not know about their rights or that a union is there for them, and for many young workers it may not seem relevant or worth the effort or the membership fees.

Explaining variation in union membership levels

How can we explain the different levels of union membership in the different McDonald's operations in Europe? Both Austria and Italy have achieved far higher levels of union membership than the Scandinavian countries that are normally associated with the highest union density rates in Europe. There seems little doubt that the role of the union representative and/or the works council plays an important role. This is not only in terms of raising workers' awareness about their legal rights but also about raising awareness about the role of the trade union. Where unions have been able to establish a union representative and/or some form of works council then union membership levels within those restaurants often increases dramatically; in some cases, from zero to anything up to 50% or more. For example, virtually all of the 2,000 German union members at McDonald's are in restaurants where there are union-supported works councils. However, as we shall see in Chapter 6, establishing works councils or union representatives in McDonald's restaurants is often extremely difficult.

In the Scandinavian countries, the workforces tend to be similar to those in the UK in that they have a high proportion of young workers. As we have seen, unions in these countries have found it very difficult to recruit members and to establish union representatives in the restaurants. This is partly because in many cases workers are employed there for only a short time, partly because young workers may perceive the unions as old fashioned or 'irrelevant' and partly because restaurant management is often hostile to union activity in the restaurants. Although the Swedish HRF union has a union representative working full time on union business in the McDonald's headquarters in Stockholm, the unions do not have union representatives working in every restaurant; in fact, there are very few representatives actually in the restaurants. The Swedish union appears to be placing most of its faith in the full-time union representative operating at the McDonald's head office in Stockholm, other representatives in the restaurants suggest that this is not really adequate. In Denmark, the unions only have one representative working in one restaurant and nobody working at the head office.

With the exception of Germany and Austria, the average age of the workforce in Italy is higher than in most other European countries. In Italy, McDonald's took over a number of existing businesses during its expansion and these units already had unionised workforces. Also, in comparison with Germany, the UK and Ireland, the unions have the right to enter the workplace wherever there are thirty or more employees and have the right to hold meetings on the premises. In Austria, union membership has increased considerably largely because of the recognition agreement signed in the mid-1990s. In Spain, the unions have only been able to recruit a small percentage of the McDonald's workforce, largely because the corporation refuses to recognise the unions and because the works councils have been 'captured' by management-supported candidates (see Chapter 6).

Comparing union membership statistics across different countries is not a straightforward matter as high levels of membership in some countries can be explained by the fact that some unions administer and distribute unemployment benefits. In any case, unionisation rates do not of themselves necessarily indicate the strength or influence of trade unions in the bargaining process. Union membership and collective bargaining are only one part of the equation. Nevertheless, the low rates of union membership at McDonald's do give some indication of the problems that unions face in this type of employment. As we have already suggested, in most European countries legislation provides for worker representation through a combination of works councils and/or union delegates. The next chapter examines how such institutions operate in practice and the problems of establishing them at McDonald's.

6 Co-determination?

What the hell is that?!

> The Americans don't understand works councils, they think works councils
> are trade unions, trade unions are communists and communists must be
> fought. That's the attitude the company brought to Germany. They don't
> understand the Works Constitution Act.
>
> (German franchisee and ex-senior manager)

> Works councils? Oh that's just students playing games, causing trouble, they
> don't work in the McDonald's system.
>
> (German restaurant manager)

American McDonald's managers are probably not the only Americans to be
mystified by the wonders of European legislation on workers' participation
in decision-making. The title of this chapter was taken from a response by
the American General Motors director, David Herman, when he became the
president of Saab motor vehicles and was first confronted with the Swedish
system of co-determination (Brulin, 1995: 207). This chapter examines
McDonald's preferred form of 'employee participation' and the way in which
it has dealt with statutory forms of national-level worker representation in
eight European countries. In practice, this means various forms of statutory
works councils and trade union or employee representatives, which, in theory
at least, allow workers or their representatives to participate in the decision-
making processes of the business. However, before we consider these
institutions in more detail, we begin with a brief analysis of the concept of
worker participation itself.

Understanding 'participation'

It is not within the scope of this book to provide a detailed analysis of the
concept which is in any case dealt with extensively elsewhere (for example,
see Ramsay, 1983; Ackers *et al.*, 1992; Blyton and Turnbull, 1994; Salamon,
1998), but it is necessary to have some understanding of this complex issue.
On the face of it, the notion of worker 'participation' may appear to be a
straightforward matter, e.g. Wall and Lischerson (1977: 38) define

participation as '... influence in decision-making exerted through a process of interaction between workers and managers'. However, there is a danger that this simple definition conflates a number of quite different phenomena and oversimplifies a complex issue. For example, as Salamon (1998) points out, there can be variation in the *depth* of participation, the *form* that participation structures might take, the organisational *levels* on which participation occurs and the *purpose* and *outcomes* of such activity. Indeed, more than any other aspect of employee relations, 'participation' is open to the widest possible interpretation, meaning very different things to different actors and in different societal contexts. Ramsay's (1980) extremely broad classification of forms highlights the problem of definition; as Ackers *et al.* (1992: 271) put it, '... (it) embraces just about everything from workers revolution to managers calling employees by their first names'. To make matters worse, terms such as 'involvement', 'participation' and 'industrial democracy' have sometimes been used interchangeably, despite the considerable difference in the relative power-sharing implications of these different terms (Clegg *et al.*, 1978; Ramsay, 1980).

The *depth* of participatory activity is perhaps best understood as forming a continuum, rather than an absolute, with points on the continuum signifying different levels of employee *involvement* or *influence*. At one end of the continuum, involvement and/or influence over decisions are nil; at the other end, employees have complete control. Somewhere in between are a myriad different forms of 'participation'. For example, the first step along the continuum from *no involvement* would take us to some form of involvement, perhaps where employees *receive information* in the form of newsletters and team briefings. At this stage, the employees still have no active involvement in any decision-making process. As we move further along the continuum, employees or their representatives have the right to exert *advisory power* based on some form of joint consultation. At this point, management will typically discuss issues with employee representatives, seeking comments and suggestions, e.g. quality circles, team working and various forms of joint consultative committees; however, management still retain authority over final decisions.

Without some form of legislation, it is extremely unlikely that workers will move beyond this 'soft on power' stage and attain more say over decisions because this would mean the employer giving up some aspects of managerial prerogative (IDE, 1993). Although some employers may be willing to do this on some issues, it is likely to be only those issues which directly affect production and not issues which affect the terms and conditions of work. Other than through the mechanisms of collective bargaining, the approaches to employee participation in the UK and the USA are still largely based on voluntarism, so most of the forms of participation found in the USA and the UK fit into these first two categories.

However, although many businesses in Europe adopt mechanisms such as teamwork and quality circles, these countries also provide workers with an additional level of participation rights, usually underpinned by legislation and created to encourage democratic decision-making in the workplace. These arrangements can be said to represent a further step along the 'continuum', often referred to as *joint decision-making*. Under 'power-based' joint decision-making, employees or their representatives are able to influence, rather than merely be involved in, the decision-making process. Both Ramsay (1980) and the present author hold the view that it is only at this point that 'true' participation occurs and where 'industrial democracy' begins. Ramsay (1980) suggests that anything on the continuum before this stage is only 'phantom' or 'pseudo' participation.[1] In some cases, these European arrangements have historical roots which go back well into the nineteenth century, and although there is considerable variation in these institutions they often take the form of some kind of works council and/or union or employee representative. Some works councils provide workers with co-determination rights, whereas others offer consultation and information rights; some are based on legislation and others are based on national collective agreements (Streeck, 1995).

Nevertheless, it is also clear that trade unions and employees have also had equivocal and ambiguous responses to participation. For their part, trade unions may see power-centred forms of participation as threatening, in that they may hinder union influence at the workplace or because unions fear they may undermine their bargaining position. At the same time, unions usually view 'soft on power' forms of participation, such as quality circles, as being of little value in terms of representing workers' real interests. In the meantime, employees may only view participation in a positive light if their representatives are seen to be effective, and this usually means that any concerns they raise are actually acted upon by management (Streeck, 1984; Lane, 1989; Blyton and Turnbull, 1994). However, according to two studies carried out by the Industrial Democracy in Europe research group (IDE, 1981, 1993), it is the level of statutory legislation and management attitudes which most strongly determine variations in participation across different countries.

Blyton and Turnbull (1994) argue that the support given by managers for participation stems largely from the principles of 'human relations' management. These are mostly concerned with the connection between communication and consultation with the workforce and with increased worker commitment, job satisfaction, motivation and reduced resistance to change (McGregor, 1960). Managers may also view participation as a means for breaking down worker resistance, affording management the opportunity to correct 'misunderstandings' with the workforce and providing a vehicle to 'get its message across'. It appears that management generally supports the kind of participation where it can tap valuable worker experience concerning the way in which tasks are organised and performed. Various surveys of UK management over a number of years suggest that managers are keen to support forms of participation that are 'soft on power', i.e. those that focus on day-to-day operational issues which did not disrupt the hierarchical structure of managerial authority. UK employers have strongly opposed any extension of union influence, any participation at board level or any extension of participation at a lower level. Indeed, they have tended to view any participation which is seen to impinge on the control function of the firm as unwelcome (Clegg *et al.*, 1978; Poole, 1986; Poole and Mansfield, 1992). Indeed, much the same goes for management in the USA (Lawrence, 1996). In this context, it is perhaps unsurprising that McDonald's views the appropriate method of worker participation as being at the beginning of our continuum, 'soft on power' and 'employee involvement', or what Marchington (1995) identifies as 'downward communication' and 'upward problem-solving'.

'McParticipation'

'Participation' at McDonald's means 'crew meetings', 'RAP sessions', 'grievance procedures', 'notice boards', 'opinion surveys', *McNews* and 'Good ideas'. These forms of participation, which originated in the USA, were evident in all the twelve or more European countries in this study. Some variations were made to adapt for different languages, for example the *McNews* newsletter is called *Big Mäc Nachrichten* in Germany, but the format and content were very similar in all the European countries in this study. Communication is therefore the common theme that runs through all these forms of participation; they are not about giving decision-making power to the workforce, which could interfere with the prerogatives of management.[2] 'Crew meetings' are similar to team briefings, should take place once a month and are intended to allow the company to convey information to the employees. 'Good ideas' is simply a suggestion scheme. Any ideas are passed on to restaurant managers or operations supervisors; its use seems to vary across restaurants and countries. In most countries, it has operated simply as a 'suggestions form' but restaurant employees state that it is rarely if ever used, partly because of lack of interest among crew and partly because of concerns about their anonymity. The corporation has also shown some interest in total quality management (TQM)-style quality circles in the UK; in some cases, 'quality action teams' have brought together crew and managers in restaurants to look at a particular problem, such as service, health and safety or training problems.

If employees have grievances, they are supposed to go to their immediate supervisor and then through the chain of command. In theory, if employees are not satisfied with the response at each level, they can ascend to the next until the problem is resolved. If the matter is still 'unresolved' then it goes to the regional human resource manager and, finally, even to the Vice-President. In practice, employees' complaints rarely go beyond restaurant manager or area supervisor level. Most employees said that they could not imagine ringing someone in head office if they had a complaint. One female UK crew member commented:

> I've heard there is someone at regional office you can phone, but I don't

think anyone would have the nerve…in any case the restaurant manager would go mad if he found out.

The one form of 'McParticipation' that, on paper at least, gives employees some freedom of expression is the RAP session, RAP being an acronym for 'real approach to problems'. Theoretically, it allows employees to complain, make suggestions or discuss anything to do with their jobs. Comments by senior management suggest that RAP sessions are very important: one senior UK human resource manager commented:

> On a local level they are one of the best communication vehicles that we have…along with an open door policy, satisfaction surveys and of course we have regular crew meetings.

However, at restaurant level, management were less than enthusiastic; at best, they seemed to be perceived as an 'early warning' system for potential problems and a means to clamp down on any employee unrest. Sometimes, these sessions are chaired by an area manager, sometimes by a manager from another restaurant or, in the case of a franchise, by the franchisee. They are usually held around 5.00 p.m. or 6.00 p.m. when a shift has ended. They are supposed to be held twice a year or may be held three times a year *if* the restaurant has achieved a good financial turnover. However, in practice, they happen much less often and in some cases hardly at all. Judging from comments made by employees and managers in a number of countries, this is because managers and franchisees would rather not bother. It may be because in the McDonald's system the RAP session is the only real opportunity for employees to criticise management. One UK franchisee stated:

> I don't think they're very constructive, they can go too far and turn into bitching sessions. I have an open door policy anyway, so if someone has problems they can always come to me. It's better to develop a personal relationship with the crew if you want to keep control of things.

Employees' responses frequently centred around complaints that the sessions did not happen at all or as often as they should, that employees were carefully selected and that visiting supervisors or managers from other restaurants tended not to accept criticisms of favoured managers and colleagues. Although in theory any crew member can attend these meetings, in practice most are selected by restaurant management to ensure 'sensible' questions and behaviour. Indeed, union members in Germany, France, Denmark and Italy reported that they were specifically excluded from RAP sessions. In addition, grievances are not always aired because of fears about job security and effects on promotion and the manager's efficiency bonuses. The infrequency of these sessions means that matters raised tend to reflect only the most recent grievances, and longer term problems or problems over previous months tend to be forgotten. Employees in several countries suggest that they generally welcomed the opportunity to raise grievances but that at best the sessions were too few and far between and when they did occur little was achieved. The following comments were typical:

> They're a waste of time, nothing ever changes.

> We've not been able to get management to agree to one for the last two years. In any case I'm not sure that they are all that useful.

> Yes it's good we should have them at least once a year, I believe, but they gave us some excuse that there wasn't enough time for meetings.

In this context, it is quite clear that statutory works councils, which provide employees with rights underpinned in law to information and consultation and in some cases co-determine decisions with management, are quite alien to the McDonald's normal mode of operation. How would the corporation respond when confronted by such mechanisms frequently found in many mainland European countries? The following sections set out to examine the varying forms of statutory participation mechanisms in eight European countries: Germany, Austria, Denmark, Sweden, France, The Netherlands, Spain and Italy. Would the corporation be able to operate independently of such mechanisms or would they prove to be an effective method of providing worker representation in and influence over management decisions?

Germany

The German model of co-determination provides for employee representation on supervisory boards (*Aufsichtsräte*) in larger firms. The 1952/72 Works Constitution Act and the 1976 Co-determination Act govern these institutions for private businesses outside the coal and steel industries. The former legislation deals with supervisory boards of limited liability companies with over 500 employees and with works councils at plant, company or group level. The latter is concerned with employee representatives on the supervisory boards of companies with over 2,000 employees (Lane, 1989; Fürstenberg, 1991; Müller-Jentsch, 1995). With over 50,000 employees, one might expect that McDonald's Germany would have employee representatives sitting on a supervisory board; however, this is not the case. The main reason for this is that McDonald's Germany has retained American registration, it is a wholly owned subsidiary of the American McDonald's Corporation registered in Oak Brook, Illinois. This arrangement is permitted under the German–American Trade Agreement of 1954, which means that the usual obligation for a supervisory board according to either the 1952 or the 1976 Act cannot be imposed. It is probably no coincidence that American law journals are full of warnings for US multinational companies to prepare for the 'horrors' of European regulation (Honig and Dowling, 1994).

However, the issue of the German works council is not quite so straightforward. The 1952/72 Works Constitution Act provides for a works council in all businesses with five or more employees aged 18 years or over. Separate elections are held for blue-collar and white-collar workers. The works council cannot call a strike, but it can sue management for any alleged breach of rights. The council must meet with management every 4 weeks and the law grants the councils a broad range of rights to information, consultation and co-determination. According to Fürstenberg (1991), these rights give employees considerable scope for influence over the management of the business. In addition, in any business or unit with 300 employees, a works council member can be released from his or her normal duties to work full time on works council business. Research carried out on a number of German firms suggests that the works council also has a significant impact on employer decision-making. A study of 2,392 private sector firms, carried out by Sadowski *et al.* (1995), suggests that there is a significantly lower dismissal rate in firms that do have a works council. These authors suggest that employers often refrain from dismissing workers because they anticipate the opposition of the works council. The number of these full-time works councillors increases in proportion to the size of the organisation. This Act also provides for a 'central' works council at company level (Gesamtbetriebsrat – GBR) where there are two or more works councils in the same business. Similarly, where there is a group of companies with works councils, a group-level or concern-level works council (Konzernbetriebsrat – KBR) can be established, but only if this is requested by the works councils of subsidiaries employing at least 75% of the group's workforce. The works councillors represented on the GBR or KBR are also quite likely to be the same representatives on the supervisory board, where this exists (Müller-Jentsch, 1995; Jacobi *et al*, 1998).

At the beginning of October 1999, McDonald's opened its 1,000th restaurant in Germany (employing a workforce of around 51,000); of these 1,000 restaurants, some 65% or more are operated by franchise, leaving approximately 350 company-owned (McOpCo) restaurants (with about 18,000 employees). McDonald's operates some of its 350 'company' restaurants through a number of holding companies, called Anver companies. The typical McDonald's restaurant has between forty-five and 100 employees, so in theory there could be a works council in every McDonald's restaurant in Germany. One might also expect that there would be a company-level works council (GBR) or possibly a concern-level works council (KBR). In 1999, there were between forty and fifty works councils in the 1,000 restaurants, no KBR and, until 4 years ago, no GBR either.

Both the issue of works councils and the establishment and legitimacy of the current GBR are and have been the focus of considerable conflict between McDonald's and the union. Union officials and McDonald's workers allege that over the years the corporation has used some rather extreme measures to stop the establishment of works councils in the restaurants. There were many examples of unfair dismissals and flying squads of managers were sent to restaurants to persuade employees that there was no need for works councils. One famous exponent of this practice was known among works councillors as 'Commando Mueller'. McDonald's also transferred restaurants into different ownership; this had the effect of stopping or delaying the election of works councils. In addition, McDonald's would simply 'buy out' works councillors and their supporters with cash compensation and would nominate management candidates to capture works councils for a management-sponsored agenda.[3]

It appears that McDonald's Germany has a standard procedure for its management to follow if managers suspect that workers are planning to elect a works council. In documentation distributed to McDonald's restaurant managers, 'Practical help in dealing with works councils', it is stated that employees' attempts to establish works councils are a serious problem and a failure of management. It states that the reactions of managers to any such initiative must be carefully handled and that head office in Munich must be immediately informed and must make all the major decisions. The document states (Practical help in dealing with works councils: 8):

> A works council representative from another restaurant visits your restaurant...how do you behave? ...Information about the visit must be sent immediately to headquarters personnel operations...any further measures will not be taken by operations but only by headquarters. You must never talk with union representatives without first having authority from head office...(and)...never give employees the impression that you are against the trade unions or the works council. The incentive to lead someone to do something is much greater than you think.

Indeed, in one case recently reported in the magazine *Stern* (1999), a restaurant manager was allegedly demoted to assistant manager for allowing his workers to elect a works council in his restaurant in 1997. It is also interesting to note that no works councils have been established in the old East German states. Union officials state that McDonald's workers in the new federal states are not familiar with the works council legislation and that because there is still so much unemployment in the East they are much more afraid of upsetting management.

Five restaurants in Dortmund appear to be the current 'thorn in the eye' of the corporation; all five franchise restaurants have works councils and about 200 of the 240 workers employed there are union members. A new franchisee took over the five restaurants at the end of 1997 and, according to NGG officials, has been trying to get rid of the works councils ever since. This franchisee has allegedly made a number of offensive and outspoken comments about the workers involved in these works councils that have been reported in the press (*Stern*, 1999).

If this were not enough, in 1998 there were all sorts of problems with the election of a company-level works council (GBR) at McDonald's. It appeared that two separate GBRs with two different chairmen were both claiming to be the legitimate body to represent McDonald's German workers. Union officials argue that after years of trying to block or nullify the union-supported GBR McDonald's Germany had now decided to establish its 'own' GBR, despite a court ruling suggesting that the corporation had acted illegally and that the GBR election would have to be reheld. After what NGG officials described as more 'underhand' tactics, the corporation managed to get their preferred candidates elected (*Der Spiegel*, 1998). The outcome of the re-election also had implications for the European Works Council (see Chapter 8). Indeed, these kinds of activities appear to be on the increase rather than subsiding. Union officials state that in 1999, in particular, the few existing works councils have been put under enormous pressure from management.

Although the corporation appears to have used a variety of tactics to try to rid itself of works councils, its most effective weapon appears to be the 'buy out' (Royle, 1998). The union has no answer for this tactic; in 1995 alone, union officials state that McDonald's spent close to £250,000 to buy out forty-six works councillors and their supporters, and this was also reported in the press (Langenhuisen, 1995). More recently, according to union officials (and reported in *Stern*, 1999), a works council chairman in Wiesbaden was allegedly offered DM200,000 (almost £70,000) to leave McDonald's. He refused and, according to the same sources, management have since tried to block his works council activities by various means. The *Stern* article also states that the chairman of McDonald's Germany, Raupeter, wrote a letter in September 1999 to the chairman of the employers' association BdS, Thomas Heyll, regarding this stubborn works council. *Stern* (1999) suggests that Heyll is well known for his 'rough stuff' when it comes to dealing with trade unions. In the letter, Raupeter in James Bond-like terms granted the licence to dismiss (*Stern*, 1999: 128):

> With regard to this matter you are authorised to carry out every necessary measure within individual employment contract and works council law.

The conflict over effective worker representation at McDonald's Germany looks as though it is likely to continue. On a more general note, these findings also emphasise the fact that works councils, like any other institution, are to some extent dependent on the action of individuals and the attitudes of the parties involved. Indeed, Kotthoff (1994) in his 20-year study of German works councils makes exactly this point.

Austria

As in Germany, Austrian law distinguishes between collective labour relations at the employer level and at multi-employer level. In the private sector, Austrian works councils are regulated by the Works Constitution Act (Arbeitsverfassungsgesetz – ArbVG). They can be established in any business with at least five permanent employees, provided the workforce wishes it.

The number of works council members increases in proportion to the number of employees in the business. In multiplant companies, each works council is entitled to elect a number of its members to a central works council (Zentralbetriebsrat). Since the 1986 amendment of the Works Constitution Act, employees are also entitled to representation at group level, where there is a group of companies. In a similar manner to German works councils, at each of the above-mentioned levels, Austrian works councils enjoy considerable rights to information and consultation, including the opportunity to conclude a formal plant agreement with management. Their co-determination rights are restricted to a narrow range of social and personnel matters. Management requires works council approval for such things as the introduction of control systems that affect human dignity, performance-related pay, internal transfers and the downgrading of employees in the business. The law specifies which matters can be delegated from sectoral level collective agreements to plant agreements, but collective agreements can also stipulate issues for regulation by plant agreement. According to Traxler (1998), the system of employee representation in Austria resembles the German model, with the main difference being that Austrian works councils have fewer rights.

Despite the fact that there could be a works council in every one of the eighty McDonald's restaurants in Austria, there are none. The McDonald's Austrian workforce appears to be very similar to that found in Germany. It is made up of a large proportion of foreign workers, with the remainder being made up of students over 18 years old and second-income earners such as housewives. Union officials estimate that some 60–70% of McDonald's employees in Austria are foreign workers. This high proportion also reflects trends in wider Austrian society. In June 1990, the Austrian parliament amended the law to increase the proportion of legally allowed foreign workers in the total Austrian workforce to 10%. In addition to the fact that foreign workers are less likely to be aware of their rights regarding representation in works councils, they are also less likely to question managerial authority.

However, there is an additional problem for the establishment of works councils in Austria. Candidates for works council office must be Austrian citizens or citizens of EU member states. For the last 27 years, Austria has been the only European country to restrict employee representation on the basis of citizenship. There has been little, if any, attempt to give foreign workers equal rights; with the exception of some union pressure groups (*'Sesam öffne dich!'*) and smaller unions such as the HGPD, even the big unions and the main union confederation (Österreichischer Gewerkschaftsbund) have done little in practice to support their cause.[4] Moreover, anyone who wishes to be elected to the works council must have worked in the company for at least 6 months. Large proportions of the McDonald's workforce do not enjoy EU citizenship and, as elsewhere, many others do not stay long enough with the corporation. Under these circumstances, it is hardly surprising that no works councils have been established at McDonald's in Austria. This poor outcome for Austrian works councils also has a 'domino effect' as far as the employee representation on the supervisory board is concerned. One-third of seats on the Austrian supervisory board are reserved for employee representatives and they have the same legal status as shareholder members, although their rights are restricted over the election and dismissal of management board members. Although employee representatives are normally appointed by the trade unions, only works council members may be nominated and then only those entitled to vote in works council elections. This automatically excludes union officials who might normally be found sitting on Austrian works councils. As such, there is no employee representation on the supervisory board.

As we have seen in Chapter 5, the relationship between McDonald's and the union has improved, union membership is increasing and the union officials expect that it will continue to do so. However, HGPD officials are not optimistic about the prospects of establishing works councils. High turnover, apathy among students and foreign workers unable to stand for election make it highly unlikely that works councils will be established. There is also a clear distinction between the behaviour of franchises and McDonald's company-owned restaurants towards employees. The corporation has become much more concerned about its public image and has subsequently become more careful about the management of employees in its 'own' restaurants. The relationship with the franchise restaurants is much more like the old relationship with the corporation, and this is significant because they operate 80% of McDonald's restaurants. As there is no provision for worker representatives outside the institution of the works council in Austria, the union's ability to monitor collective agreements is lost. This is a particularly important function where there are large numbers of foreign workers who are often poorly informed about their rights and entitlements.

Denmark

As already suggested, the relationship between McDonald's and the Danish unions has remained cool. Furthermore, the success of acquiring a collective agreement has not translated into effective employee representation in the restaurants in terms of trade union representatives (*tilllidsrepraesenter*), the Danish version of the works council, the co-operation committee (Samenarbedsudvalget) or employee representation on McDonald's board of directors.

As in Germany and Austria, Danish works councils can also be established at either group or company level in larger businesses. In any company with more than fifty workers, employees have the right to elect at least two representatives and up to one-third of the members of the board of directors. Employee representatives exist in about 35% of the companies in Denmark that could have them. The rules for workers participation are not set out in the law but in national-level framework agreements negotiated between the

Danish union confederation (LO) and the Danish employers' federation. The co-operation committee is usually made up of union representatives, other elected employees and an equal number of management representatives. The senior management representative chairs the committee with the deputy chair coming from the employee representatives. These committees can be established in any company where there are thirty-five or more employees or where they are requested by the employer or by a majority of employees. The co-operation committee has information and consultation rights, but it does not have the kind of veto powers associated with Austrian and German works councils and it is explicitly excluded from any role in negotiating collective agreements on pay or other issues dealt with by employers and unions. It is entitled to information on the financial position of the business, the future prospects of the business, including future sales and production issues, employment outlook, major changes or planned reorganisation and the impact of new technology. These information rights can really be seen as consultation rights. This is because the committee should receive this information early enough so that employee representatives can put forward viewpoints, ideas and proposals *before* any decision is made. It is also the body through which both employer and employee representatives can attempt to reach agreement on a number of policy principles, including company personnel policy and human relations, use of personal data, production methods, training and retraining for new technology, equal opportunities and any major business changes (Scheuer, 1998).

Theoretically, there could be between one and three union representatives in every McDonald's Danish restaurant (depending on the number of employees in the restaurant), which means at least eighty union representatives. At the time of writing, there is just one union representative in Denmark, and he is a student. Theoretically, there could also be eighty co-operation committees, one in every McDonald's restaurant in Denmark, with the possibility of a company-level committee. However, there are no co-operation committees at McDonald's Denmark. Similarly, one-third of the board of directors could be employee representatives, but there are none at McDonald's. According to the Danish restaurant workers union (RBF), the main problem in establishing co-operation committees is in getting union representatives and this depends to some extent on gaining an adequate level of union membership. McDonald's Denmark has the same high levels of labour turnover experienced in many other countries, i.e. between 100% and 200%. The lone union representative and union officials at the RBF state that the same kinds of problems exist at McDonald's Denmark as one finds in most other countries. First, management who are opposed in principle to any form of union organisation, and, second, an 'acquiescent workforce'. In Denmark, most of the employees are young workers who do not stay long and who have little knowledge and/or interest in their rights or awareness of union activities.

Furthermore, the union representative reports that he has problems trying to get paid time off to undertake his union duties (something that would normally be negotiated by a co-operation committee) and simply does not have enough time to establish a co-operation committee on his own. In addition, it is difficult enough to get workers to become union representatives, and without union representatives co-operation committees are a non-starter. In these circumstances, it is hardly surprising that there are no co-operation committees and no representation on the board of directors.

The RBF suggests that McDonald's is very adept at persuading workers that there is no need to join the union and are therefore able to keep unions out of the restaurants. The whole point of co-operation committees is for the workforce to have a voice independent of management and for both sides then to discuss and co-operate over issues which concern the workforce. Where there is no will on the side of management to engage in this kind of co-operation, attempts to establish such committees are likely to be an uphill struggle. The absence of co-operation committees and the lack of representation at board level are of some concern to the union. However, it is the low level of membership and the lack of union representatives that is the major issue; without adequate numbers of representatives, establishing committees is a non-starter. The importance of union representatives should not be underestimated. Both the existing representative and the RBF report regular infringements of the collective agreements; however, these infringements are only the 'tip of the iceberg', most simply go unreported because there is no union presence in the majority of restaurants.

Sweden

There is no separate channel to provide a voice for employees outside the traditional union–employer bipartite system as this would not be compatible with the Swedish model, which is based on collective bargaining. There is therefore no elected works council structure as one finds in Germany and in other European countries. Indeed, the current system was established to avoid institutions similar to works councils, of which Swedish unions have tended to be very sceptical.[5] It is the trade unions who provide employee representation for Swedish workers both centrally and at local level. In theory at least, there is no absence of monitoring and enforcement arrangements at the workplace. Co-determination councils, health and safety committees and board representatives ensure that rules are observed. The trade unions' powers in this area are based on the Co-determination at Work Act (MBL) 1977 together with collective agreements that aim to increase union influence over company decisions. The most important of these in the private sector is the 1982 Framework Agreement on Efficiency and Participation (Utveck-lingsavtalet – UVA), which was concluded by SAF, the main employers' organisation, and LO, the workers' organisation. The agreement states that (Brulin: 1995: 199):

...the forms of participation and co-determination shall be adapted to local circumstances at the workplace. The local parties have a joint responsibility for developing suitable participation and co-determination practices.

The agreement also states that there are three possible forms of co-determination and that local agreements must clearly indicate which form of co-determination is chosen. However, Brulin (1995) suggests that in reality very few local agreements have been concluded, although the parties often act as if they have a local agreement. Joint consultative bodies are created for dealing with a particular problem or union representatives are inserted in the ordinary line of management. This appears to be the situation at McDonald's Sweden, where it seems that McDonald's and the Swedish HRF union agreed some time ago to establish a union representative working full time on union matters in the head office of the McDonald's Corporation in Stockholm. Workers are also supposed to be represented by union representatives. Theoretically, this could mean one or more union representative in every restaurant. However, Brulin (1995) suggests that arrangements of this kind are viewed by both parties as bipartite 'participation and information bodies' or 'line negotiations'. However, they have no formal legitimation and the juridical status of these arrangements is therefore unclear.

The Co-determination Act gives all unions and employers or employers' organisations the right to negotiate – but not necessarily to come to an agreement – on any question affecting the employment relationship. In particular, employers are obliged to consult local unions before implementing decisions which involve major changes affecting either employees in general or an individual employee. For other less important matters, unions have the right to demand consultation. If agreement cannot be reached at a local level, the matter can be referred to national level, and employers can be made to pay damages if they fail in their duty of consultation (IDS, 1996). However, the unions, having been informed and consulted in the proper way, must in the end accept an employer's decision. Brulin (1995) also points out that in cases in which employee representation is weak, as may be the case at McDonald's, unions get only minimum information in line with the Act and central agreements. In this situation, the employer does not let the unions take part in the planning and monitoring of change processes. The problem at McDonald's appears to be that there are very few union representatives in the restaurants. One union representative estimated that there were only between five and ten union representatives in the 150 or so restaurants. The danger is that the senior union representative located at headquarters may often be out of touch with what is going on in the restaurants and may also experience problems of role identification. Without representatives in every restaurant, the head office representative must rely on ordinary union members or other employees to bring problems to his/her attention. The low levels of union membership tend to turn this into a vicious circle; without an adequate number of union members, there are likely to be fewer workers willing to take on the role of union representative in the restaurant. In this scenario, there is no need for the corporation to take much active opposition to union representatives. Nevertheless, some union representatives report that some restaurant managements are openly hostile to some of the few union representatives who exist. It may be that the unions themselves feel that the struggle to appoint union representatives in the majority of restaurants in this industry would require too many resources and that more effective outcomes can be achieved by focusing on collective bargaining arrangements. However, without union representatives on the ground, frequent infringements of such agreements are increasingly likely.

France

The French system of employee representation is based on a variety of different structures representing both trade union and employee interests. First, individual trade unions can each establish a trade union section (section syndicale) which can bring its workplace members together. These union sections can be established regardless of the numbers of union members in the business and they have specific rights under the law. Second, in workplaces with over fifty employees, unions have the right to appoint a trade union delegate (*délegué syndical*) who has a role in representing the union and the interests of employees. In addition, two separately elected bodies that have specific rights and duties represent the whole workforce. First, in businesses with at least eleven employees, the workforce is entitled to an employee delegate (*délégués du personnel*). Second, for all companies with more than fifty employees, the workforce is entitled to a works council. Unlike German works councils, the establishment of French works councils does not rely on the instigation of employees. However, in smaller companies with fewer than 200 employees, management can decide that there should be no separate works council and that employee delegates should undertake both roles. Works councils can be established either as a *comité d'entreprise* or as a *comité d'établissement*. Employee delegates and works councils are normally separate, but individuals can be elected to both. Rather like the German model, in large companies with several 'plants' each with their own works council, a company-level works council (*comité central d'entreprise*) should be established. In companies with several plants and more than 2,000 employees, the unions can also have a central trade union delegate. For businesses with several companies, a group-level works council (*comité de groupe*) should be established (IDS, 1996).

French works councils are not employee-only bodies, as in Germany, but they are joint management–employee bodies. A representative of management chairs the French works council, but the secretary is an employee representative. Councils should meet once a month in companies with over

150 employees, but normally only once every 2 months in smaller companies. Trade union delegates often co-exist with works councils (they may be the same individuals); their role is not only to see that existing rules and agreements are applied properly but also to try to improve existing arrangements. Union delegates must be involved in negotiations over pay, training and working time, and these negotiations should take place every year. They should also receive a range of detailed information on actual pay levels in the company or plant as well as other information on the workforce. Works councils are also entitled to be informed about social, economic and financial issues. However, their consultation rights are not so extensive; the employer has to consult the works council in advance if measures are planned which significantly affect the size and structure of the workforce, working time and working conditions. Although the rights of the French works councils are not as substantial as in Germany, they do provide the French unions with the advantage that only they (as 'representative' trade unions) can nominate a list of candidates in the first round of elections. If these candidates get more than half of the votes, they are then elected and the seats are then allocated on a proportional basis. Only if these candidates get less than half of the votes is a second round held in which non-union employees can stand. Works councils are also entitled to use financial experts, who can be called in at the company's expense to examine annual accounts and large-scale redundancy proposals. In companies with more than 300 employees, they can examine financial forecasts and the council can also call in technology experts. Tchobanian (1995) suggests that the 1982 Auroux reforms have put works councils in a central position in the systems of workers' collective action, reaffirming the central role of the unions in worker representation.

The French system of works councillors and employee and union representatives would certainly appear to face multinationals with a considerable number of constraints on its employment relations practices. However, the unions had found it almost impossible to establish either works councils or union delegates at McDonald's. In many cases, their delegates simply disappeared; dismissals were taken to court, but although the union won in most cases it did not improve the situation. McDonald's would pay compensation but workers were not usually reinstated, so it was extremely difficult to retain any union delegates in the company. A similar situation arose with the works councils. By law, the union must notify the company who the candidates for works council election will be; once the company was notified, union candidates 'disappeared'. The unions allege that either they were dismissed or 'bought out' in a similar way as in Germany. An additional problem in establishing union delegates and works councils is the calculation of employee thresholds. Businesses must have over ten *full-time* employees for a union delegate and over fifty *full-time* employees for a works council. Many of the McDonald's workers are of course part time; these workers' hours can be included in the calculation of thresholds but it might take two or three part-timers to make one 'full-time employee'. It may be difficult to obtain accurate and up-to-date information on workers' hours, so together with employer opposition and high labour turnover establishing works councils is problematic.

As we have suggested in Chapter 5, it was the issue of works councils that brought about the 'change' in the McDonald's approach to the unions in 1996. On the morning of 6 July 1994, twelve McDonald's managers were arrested at their place of work and put under judicial investigation. They were accused of impeding union rights and impeding the election of a works council. This conflict concerned twelve franchise restaurants in Lyon, France; the CFDT union argued that because all twelve franchises were run by the same franchisee they should be considered as a single business or 'economic and social unit' (*unité économique et sociale* – UES). Having the restaurants defined as an UES would then have allowed the establishment of a *comité d'entreprise*. McDonald's argued against this and took its case to the French high court (*Tribunal de Grande Instance*). Nevertheless, the court decided in favour of the CFDT. Ten of the twelve were charged with violating the exercise of union rights and interfering with the election of a works council and were forbidden to return to their restaurants. The CFDT also had T-shirts, posters and leaflets made with various cartoons which suggested that McDonald's would suffer if they tried to take on the unions.

Elections for the Lyon works council then went ahead, but came up with some strange results. In the first vote, in which only union representatives could be elected, only thirty-eight from 458 employees actually voted. In the second vote, in which anyone can stand, 260 employees voted, but *only non-union* representatives came out on top. The CFDT allege that workers were told by management that anyone voting for the union would be sacked. The result was that a non-union works council was elected. Although this was a defeat for the unions, the CFDT now decided to focus its activities in Paris, where most of the restaurants are wholly owned and the corporation has a higher public profile. In 1995, further elections for union delegates and works councils were held. The CFDT states that the same kind of voting manipulation also took place here to begin with. However, with the increasing amount of bad publicity, it appeared that this overtly anti-union approach was about to change. In 1995, a new senior human resources manager (HRM) was appointed and McDonald's declared itself to be a driving force in the field of social relations and that it wished to integrate itself into the 'social landscape' (*EIRR*, 1997c: 20). A CFDT official states that on one level the relations with the company have improved since the new HRM took over in 1995. One of the first moves of this new approach was to agree to the establishment of a *comité central d'entreprise* in April 1996. In June 1996, the corporation also concluded a pay agreement with the CFDT for the company-owned restaurants. In October 1996, McDonald's then signed an agreement with the CFDT on the recognition of union rights. This agreement also covers all other trade unions represented in the company. However, like the other agreements, this recognition agreement only covers its McOpCo restaurants.

It is does not include the 90% of restaurants operated as franchises or joint ventures. The CFDT suggests that the pay element of the agreement was not very significant, but that the recognition agreement has had an impact on the union's ability to establish both union delegates and works councils in the company-owned restaurants.

By early 1999, McDonald's had over 720 restaurants in France and around 35,000 employees. The situation in 1999 was that there were five works councils (*comité d'entreprise*) and one central works council (*comité central d'entreprise*) representing the McOpCo restaurants. Since the problems at Lyon in 1994, McDonald's has bought back the franchise restaurants in Lyon and Nice. Four of the five *comité d'entreprise* are union controlled, and in three of these the CFDT has the majority of members. One of the four comité d'entreprise represents managers and some office workers and is organised by the professional and managerial staff federation (*Confédération générale des cadres* – CGC). The fifth is non-union and represents around ten restaurants that are all managed by one franchise operator. This means that out of more than 720 restaurants the approximately eighty or so McOpCo restaurants are represented by two *comité d'entreprise* and a number of *délegué syndical*. In addition, one *comité d'entreprise* represents workers in twenty restaurants operated by a joint venture (90% owned by McDonald's). This means that the approximately 620 remaining franchise and joint venture restaurants have no trade union representation whatsoever. The ten seats in the *comité central d'entreprise* in 1996 contained some non-union members. However, this has changed in the more recent round of works council elections, and they are now made up as follows: CFDT, six; Confédération générale du travail (CGT), one; Force Ouvrière (FO), one; CGC, two. The central or principal union delegate is a CDFT member, he is also secretary of the *comité central d'entreprise* and the EWC employee representative.

Since the Auroux laws that were introduced in 1982 (amended in 1986), there is also the workers' right of expression or *group d'expression*, in which workers have the right to express their views about their working conditions. McDonald's has not instigated any such groups because it says that its workers can already express their views in the McDonald's-style RAP sessions. However, as we have already suggested, RAP sessions appear to offer very little for employees in practice. French law also provides for two or four representatives of the works council (depending on the number of managers employed) to attend board meetings (or supervisory board meetings if these were to exist). These representatives only have a consultative role, but there are none at McDonald's.

However, the recognition of the unions in the company-owned restaurants has had some impact on the establishment of works councils. In accordance with the works council legislation, the employer must provide exclusive use of an office and all equipment necessary for it to function effectively, together with a budget amounting to 0.02% of the total wage bill. In addition, union representatives, works councillors and employee delegates are entitled to paid time off for their activities, depending on their range of responsibilities and the number of employees in the business (IDS, 1996; Goetschy, 1998b). Since the recognition agreement, the principal union delegate has been able to obtain 50% paid time off to carry out his union duties, and the works council representatives/union delegates now have a budget and the use of an office with facsimile and telephone. The more union-positive approach and change of HRM has also had a small but significant outcome in terms of the McDonald's EWC. Despite the fact that EWC employee representatives are normally appointed by the unions, without the recognition agreement it seems unlikely that a union-supported employee representative would have got onto the EWC. The experience of the election of EWC employee representatives in other countries suggests that any election without union involvement would probably have resulted in the election of a 'management-sponsored' representative and probably of a salaried manager not an hourly paid worker (Royle, 1999b).

Nevertheless, in terms of improving the representation of the vast majority of French workers and works councils being able to exercise any real influence over the corporation's decisions, the result has been disappointing. Even in the smaller number of company-owned restaurants, many managers are still outspokenly anti-union and they do not welcome employees asking questions about the calculation of their pay entitlement or their rights to representation. If the restaurant does not have a union delegate, employees are often too 'shy' to question managers about their rights. Union delegates also report that a number of unfair dismissals relating to union activities are still going on and that there are frequent examples where the national collective agreements are not correctly adhered to.

The effectiveness of the existing works councils may also have been undermined by the continuing rivalry that often exists between the different union federations (Goetschy, 1998b). In this case, there were some disagreements between union officials of different union federations and different regional offices in the same federation about who should be appointed as the principal trade union delegate and who should be appointed to the more influential positions on the company-level works council (for example secretary and treasurer). Representatives and union officials suggest that the corporation has also attempted to exploit these differences. In one case, management allegedly spread rumours that one union confederation was doing deals with McDonald's to exclude the other unions. Similar events also took place in Germany, where management allegedly attempted to divide individual works councils (Royle, 1998).

The company-level works council established in 1996 has had only limited practical effect. It has allowed union representatives from different regions to meet face to face and it has also been useful in terms of obtaining a better picture of how the corporation is organised. This is important because it also allows the works councils and unions to appoint additional union representatives at the right level; if they do not do so, the company can simply refuse the appointment, arguing that it is invalid. It can do nothing for the majority of workers employed in franchise operations. McDonald's stated in 1996 that it 'hoped' that the franchisees would adopt similar practices and establish works councils; indeed, it arranged a number of 2-day seminars for franchisees to explain the reasoning behind the corporation's changes (*EIRR*, 1997c). However, in the 3 years since that time, there has been virtually no response from franchisees. In early 1999, there was only one works council representing franchise restaurants and a non-union works council representing just ten or so of the close to 650 franchise restaurants. A CFDT official has recently stated that the new HRM appointed in 1995 may be genuinely trying to improve relations with the unions, but he is very much on his own at McDonald's. The changes introduced in 1996 have yet to achieve concrete improvements for the majority of workers, and with hindsight these changes look increasingly more like a clever public relations exercise than any real desire to be 'integrated into the social landscape'.

The Netherlands

The kinds of problems indicated in the previous chapters, for example not applying collective agreements properly, highlight the importance of establishing union representatives and/or works councils (*Ondernemingsraden*) in every restaurant. Although union representatives are seen as an important mechanism for gaining a foothold in separate plants, it is still the works council which is seen as the most effective institution for employee representation in The Netherlands (Visser, 1998a). The 1971 law on works councils (*Wet op de Ondernemingsraden*) gave works councils a dual role: representing workers' interests and the better functioning of the firm (Visser, 1995). The 1979 Works Councils Act finally removed the employer from the council's chair. Since then, there have been further amendments in 1981, 1990 and, more recently, in March 1998. The 1998 amendments have simplified the existing arrangements. Previously, the legislation had allowed for one type of works council to be created where there were thirty-five or more employees and another works council with more extensive rights where businesses employed more than 100 employees. This distinction has now been done away with and there is now one type of works council to be established in firms with fifty or more employees. In companies with fewer than fifty employees, works councils can still be established, but only on a voluntary basis (IDS Employment Europe, 1998). In effect, the employer must set up some form of employee representation, with more limited rights, if this is the will of the majority of the employees, usually in some form of consultation meetings that must take place at least twice per year. The establishment of Dutch works councils does not depend on the instigation of the workforce, as in Germany, and under Dutch law each independent plant is classified as an undertaking. Since the 1979 amendment, Dutch works councils have been employee-only bodies, with members being elected by the whole workforce

(Visser, 1995). The councils usually meet once per month and the numbers of members vary in size depending on the numbers in the workforce; the council then elects its own chair and one or more deputies. Dutch works councils are not normally involved in collective bargaining and, in fact, the rights enjoyed by works councils are quite similar to those found in Germany. They fall into three categories: information rights, consultation rights and approval rights. In addition, the councils can make proposals to which the employer must respond.

Management is automatically obliged to provide the works council with *information* on a range of financial and economic issues. This includes the structure and organisation of the company, its links with other companies and the structure of management; trends in employment and social policy and the company's own report and accounts (annually); investment plans and prospects (twice a year); and details of long-term corporate plans. The *consultation* rights relate to economic questions, but focus on those matters that directly affect the workforce. For example, plans to sell off all or part of the company, take-over of other companies, changing or ending significant parts of the company's activities, relocations, large-scale recruitment, major investments, technological changes and environmental issues. The *approval* or, as Visser (1995) describes them, co-determination rights cover a range of matters. These include retirement, profit sharing or savings, hours worked and annual leave, salary, wage scales and job classification schemes, the position of young workers, health and safety, recruitment, dismissal and promotion, training, staff assessment, social assistance for employees, consultation at shop floor level and complaints handling. The 1998 amendments further extended these rights to include staff files, systems to check employee presence and sickness and absence rules (IDS, 1996).

Regulations on these issues cannot be introduced, changed or ended without the approval of the works council unless they are covered by a collective agreement. If there is disagreement, the law is designed to ensure that all avenues for conflict avoidance are exhausted. However, employers can appeal to industry-level joint union–management commissions and then the district courts if works council does not give its approval to any measure. These courts allow employers to carry out their proposed action if the works council's refusal is considered to be 'unreasonable' or if the proposed decision 'is based on important organisational, economic, or social considerations' (Visser, 1995; IDS, 1996).

The attitude of McDonald's towards union recognition may have improved, but its attitude towards works councils has not so far been very positive. Union officials state that the corporation's general response has been that works councils would merely represent an unnecessary burden, particularly as they already have their own mechanisms for employee 'communication', i.e. RAP sessions and crew meetings. Without some union presence in the restaurants, the union simply does not know whether the collective agreement is being correctly adhered to or not; equally, where there is a union representative or works council, it is more likely that the collective agreement will be properly implemented. By November 1998, union officials state that there were thirty-one union representatives in Dutch McDonald's restaurants. Although the numbers of representatives has increased considerably since the survey and 'awareness campaign' conducted in 1997–8, the majority of restaurants are still without a 'union presence'.

Perhaps reflecting a traditional tendency in The Netherlands of union weakness in the workplace (Visser, 1998a), the unions have found it extremely difficult to establish works councils under the works council legislation before the 1998 amendments. Although the threshold was technically lower, thirty-five instead of the current fifty, the thirty-five workers had to be full-time employees, i.e. work more than 13 hours per week. This was a particular problem in the fast-food industry, with so many employees working part time. The result under the old legislation was that there were just four works councils representing a small number of restaurants. Furthermore, of these four, only one contained union-supported representatives; this was a works council representing five franchise restaurants run by one franchise operator in The Hague. Of the other three works councils, two represented employees in a small number of franchise restaurants and one represented some company-owned restaurants. All three were non-union. Union officials report that in any case the one union works council was not very effective. The franchise operator simply refused to provide it with meaningful information and adopted a highly paternalistic approach, stating to a union official: '…I work with children, why should I give them information?'

In 1996, the union had tried to persuade the corporation to accept a kind of company-level works council to represent all McDonald's in both franchise and McOpCo restaurants; the corporation disagreed with this and said it might consider two works councils representing franchises and McOpCo restaurants separately. Nothing materialised from these discussions. Union officials state that the reason for this is quite simple: the corporation does not want works councils and wants to control the process of 'communication' itself. It does not want bodies which have specific co-determination and consultation rights enshrined in law, especially where such bodies reveal sensitive financial information.

Although the union was also able to gather statistics on the numbers of employees in every McDonald's restaurant and the hours they worked, it could be argued that the pre-1998 legislation was inadequate in that it was not designed to take into account workers in this 'new' kind of industry. However, union officials are optimistic about the future situation. The new legislation on works councils introduced in April 1998 should make it much easier for the unions to establish more works councils. Nevertheless, there are still practical difficulties. Theoretically, there could be a works council in nearly every restaurant in The Netherlands, but this would involve too many individuals and be somewhat unwieldy. Union officials state that they will try to negotiate with the company to develop a suitable works council structure for the company-owned restaurants first and then move on to work on a suitable structure for the franchises. However, it is the franchises where the majority of workers are employed, and it is these restaurants that are likely to be problematic.

Although the works councils can be imposed under the law, the unions emphasise the importance of having union candidates. McDonald's is likely to reject the union's proposal for one big works council covering all restaurants and it may try to side-step the union by simply encouraging the election of non-union works councils. If this were the case, the works council could be rendered ineffectual, and once again the union would be kept out of the restaurants unless they have a union representative. Union officials hope that the new legislation will help to increase union membership and the numbers of union representatives in the restaurants. Union representatives are therefore essential in establishing an effective structure for works councils, but employer opposition, high labour turnover and workforce characteristics suggest that obtaining adequate numbers of union representatives will be difficult. The Dutch unions have as yet been unable to draw on the significant power resources that are in theory provided by the Dutch works council legislation. McDonald's has as yet been largely untroubled by works councils or any real 'interference' in terms of its employee relations policies in the restaurants; whether this will change in the future remains to be seen.

Spain

Spanish legislation provides for employee delegates (*delegados de personal*) in small firms with ten or more employees; however, employee delegates can be established with as few as six employees where the majority want this. Works councils (*comité de empresa*) can be established in firms with fifty or more employees. The rights and duties of the works councils and the employee delegates are the same. The Spanish works council is an employee-only body, but it is normally elected by two groups, manual and non-manual employees. Neither the works councils nor the employee delegates depend on union involvement, but where unions are well organised they usually play a central role. Unions normally dominate works council elections, nominating some 90% of elected representatives. As in France, the unions are also entitled to establish trade union sections (*secciones sindical*) which are entitled to bring together all the members of a particular union in the workplace. In companies with over 250 employees, members of each union with seats on the works council have a legal right to elect a trade union delegate (Escobar, 1995; Martinez Lucio, 1998).

Spanish works councils have rights to information and consultation. For example, they must be informed of economic and financial matters, such as sales figures and profits. They also have the right to be informed of the type and number of new employment contracts, together with statistics on absenteeism, accidents and illness. In the areas of production transfer, restructuring, changing working hours, payments systems and training, the works council must be informed in advance and be able to comment. The works council also has some protective functions for individual employees. For example, if the employee wishes, the works council has the right to be present when an employment contract is ended and when there are any cases of gross misconduct or punishments. The works council has a duty to monitor whether the employer is complying with the law. However, providing the employer has not broken the law, they cannot prevent management acting as it wishes in the final instance (Escobar, 1995; Martinez Lucio, 1998).

National level collective agreements are still relatively rare in Spain, but in recent years some have been negotiated to deal with key issues in the Spanish labour market. Such agreements have not dealt with pay since the mid-1980s, but Spain does have a statutory minimum wage which is normally uprated each January. Sectoral or company agreements often cover such issues as pay and working time. Indeed, there is a sectoral level agreement for the broader hotel and restaurant industry, but it only covers job classifications, training, discipline and sanctions for non-compliance. In this industry, therefore, improving basic rates of pay is very much dependent on achieving a company-level agreement.

Despite the fact that the Spanish works council does not enjoy any co-determination rights, it is still a key institution in terms of employee representation. Unlike their counterparts in some other European countries, Spanish works councils are often involved in collective bargaining. They can negotiate binding collective agreements covering pay and conditions in their company. In fact, this is what has happened at McDonald's; in two cases, company-level 'agreements' have been agreed with works councils, one covering a group of franchise restaurants in Madrid and one covering the thirty or so McOpCo restaurants in the Madrid area. However, rather than this being a positive factor for the Spanish unions and Spanish workers, it appears to work against them. FECOHT officials suggest that both of these 'agreements' are remarkably similar in that they offer very little to the employees. Neither they nor any other union have been able to get involved in either of these 'agreements'. FECOHT officials suggest that no real negotiations took place and that the works council representatives simply signed an 'agreement' which was presented to them.

FECOHT officials state that there are currently some thirty-three separate works councils established in both franchise and company-owned restaurants, but only in two of these works councils has it been possible for the union to nominate candidates and elect any delegates. Currently, they have just two union delegates, one in a franchise restaurant and one in a company-owned restaurant. Nominations for positions on the works councils are made on the basis of lists for all the members of the works council; they can be drawn up by either unions or groups of individual employees. This is providing that the number of voters supporting a list is three times greater than the number of places to be filled. Those lists that receive less than 5% of the vote are eliminated, any disputes can be referred to the labour court and elections take place every 4 years (IDS, 1996; Escobar, 1995).

Union officials suggest that the reason there is such a tiny proportion of union delegates at McDonald's is because the corporation has been very successful in promoting the election of non-union candidates who will only represent company interests, not the interests of the employees. In many cases, works council representatives at McDonald's Spain are salaried managers. Union officials suggest that McDonald's groups a number of its restaurants together for the purpose of elections, and this ensures that a large works council and not just a delegate has to be elected; typically, this would be five or so restaurants with a total of between 250 and 350 employees. Most workers do not know other workers working in other restaurants and when the list of candidates is presented workers often have no idea who to vote for. The union states that it would be much easier to get union delegates elected in individual restaurants where there may be fewer than fifty workers and no works council is required. The problem for the union is not in attaining the 5% of votes but in being able to nominate union candidates early enough. The result is that the union often has no candidate or that workers do not know his/her identity and McDonald's management usually acquires the majority of votes for the candidates it would prefer. The union suggests that there is no contact or co-ordination between the existing works councils and the union has yet to come across an incident where there has been a disagreement between works council representatives and the corporation.

There is no technical difference between the rights of a union delegate and those of the works council. In firms with more than 250 employees, the unions have the right to appoint union delegates if they have a seat on the works council. McDonald's employs approximately 1,500 employees in its company-owned Spanish restaurants; FECOHT could therefore nominate union delegates because they do have a minimum level of representation and a small number of union members. However, without representation on the works council, such delegates would not have the legal right to time off for union activities. In this situation, union officials state that such nominations would be pointless and would not allow any meaningful union influence.

Spanish law also allows for company-level works councils to be established in firms with more than one plant (*comité intercentros*). However, this can only take place where this is provided for in collective agreements. As the unions have been unable to get involved in the two agreements that do exist, no *comité intercentros* has been established. Even if a company-level works council were established, it is unlikely to be of any real value as a mechanism for employee interest representation with the situation as it stands at present. In sum, the Spanish system of works councils appears to be totally ineffective as far as the representation of employee interests at McDonald's is concerned. The works councils that do exist have effectively been 'captured' by management and the union has been unable to elect adequate numbers of delegates.

Italy

The first form of 'works councils' in Italy dates back to the early 1900s and was known as *commissione interna* or internal commission. These 'councils' were closer to the European tradition in that they were not union bodies but did represent the whole workforce. By the 1970s, the unions regularly criticised these institutions as ineffective and bureaucratic, and other models of representation eventually replaced them. The 1970 Workers' Statute authorised workers from the most representative unions to establish workplace union representation. These bodies were known as RSA (*rappresentanze sindicali aziendali*), but in practice they assumed a variety of forms. The increase in worker mobilisation during the 1970s also led to introduction of another form of representation, the *consiglio di fabbrica* (factory council) or the *consiglio dei delegati* (council of delegates). Although these bodies performed reasonably well, they engendered a good degree of uncertainty and unpredictability (Regalia and Regini, 1998). The whole system was finally reformed in July 1993 with the Tripartite Accord, in which the social partners opted for a single body in all workplaces. These new bodies were given the new name RSU – unified trade union committee (*rappresentanze sindicali unitarie*) – which was chosen to emphasise that this new institution was recognised by the unions. These arrangements are still in place, despite being threatened by smaller left- and right-wing groupings known as *autonomi* (which did not join the confederations) in a referendum held in June 1995 (IDS, 1996; Regalia, 1995; Regalia and Regini, 1998). Italian RSUs are not wholly independent bodies and are not based on the kind of statutory mechanism found in Germany or France. Although the whole workforce elects them, they are predominantly union committees and are based on trade union rights acquired under the 1970 Workers' Statute and confirmed by sectoral level collective agreements.

RSUs are employee-only bodies and can be created in any company employing more than fifteen people. The whole workforce directly elects two-thirds of the 'seats' on the RSU, but only the unions can nominate them. To nominate seats, a union must have signed the July agreement,[6] a union must have signed a national agreement covering that workplace or a union must be properly constituted and be able to present a list of candidates supported by at least 5% of the eligible workforce. For the election to be valid, at least 50% of those able to vote must do so. The remaining one-third of the representatives are elected or appointed by the unions. The trade unions themselves agree the rules governing the operation of the RSU, but it is normally chaired by the leading figure in the largest union in the workplace. However, employers and unions at industry level need to reach agreement before the process can start. The key function of the RSU is to negotiate with the employer at workplace level, and the agreement which establishes them gives them the power to negotiate binding agreements. Most of the issues on which the RSU has to be informed and consulted by the employer depend on the agreement reached either at industry or company level. However, by law, employers must inform and consult RSU representatives on matters such as health and safety, the use of public funds for industrial restructuring, large-scale redundancies and business transfers (IDS, 1996; Regalia and Regini, 1998).

In early 1999, McDonald's had 220 restaurants in Italy; by the end of 1999, they had over 250. About 80% of McDonald's restaurants are franchises (about 176 in spring 1999). On average, McDonald's management estimates that they have between fifty and sixty employees in each restaurant; in early 1999, they had around 8,500 employees, but this was closer to 10,000 by the end of 1999. In a typical RSU in a McDonald's restaurant, there would be three representatives. In larger firms, there can be larger numbers of representatives. For example, six representatives in firms with over 200 employees, three more for every 300 additional employees and after 3,000 employees three extra seats for every 500 additional employees. According to union officials at FISASCAT (the union of hotel, restaurant and service workers affiliated to CISL), there are approximately 100 RSUs in the 220 restaurants in Italy. The unions have not been able to establish RSUs in every McDonald's restaurant. Italian McDonald's workers suggest that this is mostly due to a combination of restaurant management resistance to union activities, concerns about unemployment and the relatively high level of labour turnover among students which tends to lead to a lack of interest in union activities.

Just as in other countries, the union delegates/works councils are an important mechanism for increasing union membership in Italy and the bulk of the union membership is mostly in the restaurants where RSUs have been established. Most are located around the cities of Rome, Bologna, Genoa and Milan. At local level, RSUs can negotiate with management to bargain for improvements in such issues as working time organisation and working conditions, over and above the minimum standards agreed at national level. In fact, one such agreement has been reached with local McDonald's management in Rome over working hours for part-time workers. Representatives are elected for 3 years, they enjoy legal protection from unfair dismissal and anti-union behaviour is unlawful. However, despite these protections, both workers and RSU representatives state that they often suffer from regular harassment precisely because they are union members and in some cases have been threatened with dismissal; this appears to be more extreme in franchise restaurants. Union delegates report that they are constantly under pressure from management, and especially so shortly before visits of senior management to the restaurant. In some cases, union representatives were demoted shortly before a senior management visit took place. In addition, they claim that management will not give union representatives adequate notice of their shifts, some reporting that they do not know what hours they will be required to work until the day beforehand. In fact, various infringements regarding union rights and health and safety matters have gone to the labour courts, have usually resulted in court rulings in favour of the unions and have been reported in the Italian press (*L'Unita*, 1998). Once again, the bulk of these problems appears to be in the franchise restaurants, where 80% of workers are employed.

The Italian system also provides for a form of company-level works council called a *coordinamento*. These company-level councils can be established where there are several companies in a group or where there are several workplaces in a single company. RSUs send delegates to the *coordinamento* and this body then meets with the national trade union secretariat to discuss the main concerns of the employees in that company. These discussions would then feed into national-level collective bargaining. Where a company-level agreement is in place, the *coordinamento* could also take part in negotiations with the national union secretariat and the employer. There is also a *coordinamento* at McDonald's, but its effectiveness has so far been limited because McDonald's has repeatedly delayed union proposals to negotiate a company-level collective agreement. McDonald's has also specifically ruled out an agreement that would cover both the company-owned and the franchise restaurants, where the majority of workers are employed. Indeed, the European Works Council delegate would normally be elected from the *coordinamento*, but McDonald's has ignored this procedure despite a specific request from the unions (Royle, 2001).

Re-regulating statutory worker representation

In Chapter 5, it was suggested that, where possible, McDonald's has gone to some extreme lengths to do without collective bargaining arrangements, but where this is not possible it then tries to control the bargaining process. In some countries, neither of these options has been possible, and in the long run it appears that McDonald's has learnt that there may be some distinct advantages to taking part in collective agreements. However, the day-to-day 'interference' of works councils and union representatives in its restaurants appears to be quite a different and is apparently perceived as a much more threatening matter. Of course, some systems of worker representation may be perceived as more 'threatening' than others: some may be easier to avoid,[7] some are weaker and have no co-determination rights, some are more easily 'activated' and some may entail more severe sanctions for management obstruction. In most countries, works councils are also an important mechanism in increasing trade union membership, raising notions of 'solidarity' and awareness of trade union activities. Hege and Dufour (1995) argue, for example, that French and German works councils are much more effective when they have close links with strong unions. Where is there is no or little union organisation, such workplace institutions tend to have little effect and they tend to lose legitimacy in the eyes of employees, frequently being relegated to purely social activities.

Even in the countries where McDonald's appears to have a more positive relationship with the trade unions (Sweden, The Netherlands and, more recently, Austria), there is a suspicion that worker representation appears to have been sidelined in favour of less troublesome collective bargaining arrangements. The Dutch unions remain optimistic that the new works council legislation introduced in 1998 will soon enable them to establish an adequate structure of works councils, although there appears to be no great evidence of this at the time of writing. The relationship between McDonald's and the unions in Austria and The Netherlands has improved in recent years, e.g. McDonald's is no longer overtly opposing the principle of union membership in Austria. It may be that the unions in these countries do not want to jeopardise these more positive relations by pushing the issue of works councils too hard. This may be especially so in Austria, where a large proportion of McDonald's workers cannot in any case take part in works council elections because of a continuing legal anomaly. Whether this will change if the legal situation changes remains to be seen. Although there are not enough union representatives at restaurant-level in Sweden to ensure that collective agreements are adhered to, it would appear that the Swedish unions are satisfied with the outcomes of their bargaining arrangements and the mechanisms that they have put in place. They may be less interested in pursuing a more effective structure of worker representation, perhaps because it is either perceived as impractical or too costly in terms of union resources. The relatively low level of union membership in all the Scandinavian countries could also be an important factor in this equation. Obtaining larger numbers of union representatives is extremely difficult if union membership is very low. Unions may also decide that pushing for more restaurant-level representation will only antagonise McDonald's and will disturb existing understandings and ultimately bargaining relationships at sectoral level. Indeed, this may be a general weakness of sector-level bargaining.

Like most of the other European countries, relations in Denmark have remained on a more antagonistic footing: there are no co-operation committees in Denmark and there is only one workplace union representative for all of eighty or so restaurants. The unions are principally concerned with the low levels of union membership, which they feel must improve in order to find individuals willing to become restaurant-level union representatives. Without adequate numbers of union representatives, co-operation committees are a non-starter, and in any case union officials argue that even if such committees were created McDonald's has no intention of 'co-operating' or allowing employees to co-determine anything with management.

In other countries where works councils and other forms of worker representation are more of a practical reality, they are much more of a contentious issue. In France, it seems that despite management statements to the contrary works councils and union representatives are still being opposed in the restaurants. Those that have been established almost exclusively represent the small number of company-owned restaurants and not the vast majority of franchises. The 'company-level' works council has so far made no real impact on the corporation. In Germany, Spain and Italy, the relationship with the unions is either non-existent or is still largely confrontational. In Spain, it appears that legislative loopholes have meant that where works councils have been established they have been captured for a managerially sponsored agenda and there is no relationship or dialogue with the unions. The conflicts over works councils in Germany is probably the most high profile and longest running; it has been going on for nearly 30 years and shows no signs of abating. McDonald's appears to be absolutely determined to fight the establishment of union-supported works councils at all costs. In Italy, there are continuing problems with the alleged harassment of union representatives and there have been a number of recent strikes, resulting in some restaurants being closed at weekends. Italian legislation makes it more difficult for McDonald's to avoid union delegates and works councils altogether, but works councils are not established everywhere and mostly they are concentrated in and around the northern cities and Rome. The company-level works council (*coordinamento*) has not had a significant impact on the corporation so far because McDonald's has continued to stall over union proposals for a company-level agreement, to which the *coordinamento* would normally have a major input. However, the legislation does allow unions to enter restaurants and establish RSUs where there is enough support from the workforce.

In general, the absence of works councils and union representatives means that there is no effective mechanism in place to ensure that the collective agreements are properly adhered to, and without them it is very difficult to monitor health and safety issues and day-to-day working conditions. In addition, even the 'weaker' works council models, if well organised, have the potential to interfere in management decision-making both at workplace and, perhaps more significantly, at boardroom level. By its very nature, the McDonald's system does not allow for co-determination or co-operative decision-making because it functions on the basis that the 'decisions' have already been made.

The post-Fordist concept of a 'new era' in which employers will promote meaningful participation in order to seek a mutual accommodation of interests at the point of production never did consider the fast-food industry (Hyman, 1988). McDonald's seems to provide particular problems for worker representation. Its 'success' in this regard appears, in part, to rely on the passive acquiescence of the workforce in employer decisions, with its view of participation taking the form of, at best, a paternalistic consultation regime. As already suggested in Chapter 4, the distinctive nature of the workforce characteristics and mode of work organisation in the industry foster this 'acquiescence'. Of course, the McDonald's organisational structure and its high proportion of franchise operations further exacerbate this. In practice, it is extremely difficult to establish one central or company works council to cover the entire McDonald's workforce in any country. It also makes it difficult to establish plant-level works councils for every restaurant. As indicated in Chapter 3, the 'separation' between McDonald's and its franchisees is a legal not an economic distinction. The distinction allows McDonald's to have effective control over virtually all aspects of its franchise operations while at the same time allowing it to distance itself from the employee relations practices of individual franchise operators. Franchise operations also allow for an extremely paternalistic form of management, one that allows the close monitoring of individual employees and one that undoubtedly helps franchisees, and indirectly the corporation, to hinder the establishment of works councils or union representatives.

With the trend towards more decentralisation of collective bargaining in most European countries (Ferner and Hyman, 1998), the works council is often seen as the institution on which more responsibility will fall (Tchobanian, 1995). This analysis suggests that the existing legislation underpinning works councils in most countries may not be adequate for this task. Indeed, the clear message that emerges from this analysis is that tighter and more comprehensive bargaining arrangements may be essential if a better outcome for workers is to be provided. Some may argue that statutory works councils are not therefore worth bothering with, but this is not the conclusion drawn here. Industrial relations systems based on voluntarism, as in the UK, the USA and to some extent Ireland, are unlikely to provide workers with adequate representation. Left to their own devices, companies can provide or withdraw even minimal levels of 'participation', depending on how it suits them. Despite the ever present management rhetoric of the need for 'empowered' and co-operative employees, the reality is a continuing reluctance to inform, consult and especially co-determine decisions with employees. If national governments are serious about protecting workers rights and developing more co-operative relations then perhaps it is time to re-regulate existing institutions to allow them to function more effectively. Rather than pursuing more deregulation, policy-makers may need to provide existing national systems with a broader remit of powers in order to take account of decentralising trends and new forms of employment. In fact, the main German trade union federation is lobbying for precisely these kinds of changes to be made to the Works Constitution Act, which is currently under review by the German government. We now try to assess the broader impact of both trade union organisation and national-level mechanisms of worker representation by examining the outcomes for workers in terms of the impact on pay and conditions.

7 For a few dollars more

Comparing pay and conditions

> We sold them a dream and paid them as little as possible.
> (Ray Kroc, in Vidal, 1997: 40)

The US economic model is usually seen as the driving force behind and as proof of the success of liberal economics. The USA is much less regulated than most European markets and trade unions are weak, allowing the market mechanism to function 'closer to perfection'. One of the ways in which the alleged 'efficiency' of more deregulated markets is measured is to compare the purchasing power parity of average net wages. For example, the Union Bank of Switzerland regularly compares average net wages with a basket of goods to indicate the purchasing power of different national currencies. Time and time again, the USA, paragon of the free market, comes out on top with high purchasing power and high average wages. However, the problem with this approach is that it does not take into account how evenly such wages are distributed across society. It tells us nothing about the way in which wealth is divided between those at the top of the scale and those at the bottom. However, 'liberalism' as engendered by the USA does not concern itself with the notion of equality, only the 'freedom' of the individual. But, in modern consumer society, being a 'free individual' may have little meaning for those with only limited financial resources. 'Collectivist'-orientated systems may compromise some individual freedom in order to promote equality, with trade unions and statutory mechanisms of worker representation limiting the worst excesses of the market and making business more accountable to other stakeholders in society.

However, in the current global economic climate, driven by liberal economics, such constraints are seen as aberrations. The goal is the relentless drive for 'efficiencies', higher profit margins and the removal of regulation. In this climate, workers have the freedom to be insecure and have their wages and conditions constantly threatened by market forces. Of course, highly skilled workers are always likely to be able to demand better wages, conditions and job security. But how many workers will be in this fortunate situation? As already suggested, most of the new jobs being created today are in the service sector and most are in low-skilled and often precarious work. It is in this context that a comparison of pay and conditions at McDonald's is pertinent. This chapter assesses and compares such pay and conditions in the more 'deregulated' countries of the USA and the UK with the more 'regulated' countries of mainland Europe. Do the more unionised and regulated systems of mainland Europe provide workers with better pay and conditions than those found in the USA and the UK? What does such an analysis tell us about variations in the inequalities of wage dispersion across these societies?

As we have already seen, the ability of trade unions to organise and gain recognition for collective bargaining at McDonald's varies considerably in different European countries. A major factor in the success (or otherwise) of the unions in bringing McDonald's to the negotiating table appears to be largely attributable to the effectiveness of supportive labour legislation and the willingness of workers and other unions to act in 'solidarity' in each country. Some national systems that, on paper at least, appear to offer considerable obstacles to multinationals may in practice be unable to provide unions with recognition and/or an effective mechanism to take part in determining the wages and conditions of employees. We focus mostly on the issue of basic starting pay, rates for unsociable hours, periods of notice for redundancy and holiday entitlements in a few of the countries in the study. We also compare workers' starting pay with the earnings of top executives at McDonald's. Finally, we provide a brief analysis of particular problem areas and try to evaluate the advantages and disadvantages of the various collective agreements in place.

It appears that, with one main exception (Sweden), in virtually every country in Europe McDonald's began by trying to carry out the same kind of labour relations practices that it had in the USA. Although McDonald's has automatically been caught by national- or sectoral-level collective agreements in several European countries, even a relatively superficial examination of these sectoral level agreements indicates that there are considerable differences in the impact of these agreements in terms of the pay and conditions that they provide. Some sectoral agreements only provide a basic platform of rights that may or may not include pay and conditions; some provide good pay and conditions whereas others only provide very low pay and basic conditions. In some cases, where only basic pay and conditions are imposed by sectoral level agreements, McDonald's has been unwilling to improve on these arrangements by negotiating a company-level agreement, and in some cases has refused to join the relevant employers' federation. In other cases, where McDonald's has finally agreed to negotiate a company-level agreement, it normally only covers those employed in company-owned (McOpCo) restaurants. Although it has only been possible to undertake a limited examination of the pay and conditions in different European countries, even this limited analysis suggests that there is considerable variation in outcomes. However, before we go on to examine and compare pay rates and other conditions of work, we briefly explain McDonald's 'normal' approach to pay determination. The McDonald's approach to remuneration was developed in the USA and is one that is normally unfettered by much legislation or the need to recognise unions. As we saw in Chapter 5, this is also reflected in the UK and in Ireland, where similar circumstances prevail. In its 'pure' form, the McDonald's approach does not automatically provide additional pay for length of service seniority but for good performance. The next section therefore briefly examines the McDonald's system of performance pay.

McDonald's 'performance' pay system

In theory, McDonald's workers can increase their basic pay through good performance. In the UK, 'outstanding' workers can achieve an extra 15 pence increase per hour, every 4 or 6 months, providing they can achieve an almost perfect 93.5% rating on their 4- or 6-month performance review sheet. In practice, this means that virtually every operation checklist (OCL; see Figure 3.1) which is completed for them by a superior has to give them this high rating in order to secure a sufficiently high average. Similarly, a 10 pence increase is paid for 89% and over, and a 5 pence increase for 76% and over. Very few employees will receive the 15 or 10 pence increase very often, and because turnover is so high many employees have left before these increases might even apply.

In addition, the OCL, on which the whole system depends, is often either completed much later than it should be or is not completed at all. In this scenario, much depends on the relationship between the employee and the employer. This is particularly marked in franchise operations, where it is likely to be the franchisee who will make the final decisions about pay increases because he or she is the one footing the bill. Indeed, in a number of franchise operations in this study, franchisees often choose not to bother with OCLs at all and made decisions about increases in pay on the basis of suggestions from their managers and 'training squad'. According to the McDonald's UK Crew Handbook, the guideline for attaining a 93.5% performance is 'performance is always of exceptional quality'. An 87% performance is 'employee performance consistently exceeds job requirements and expectations'. Many employees complained that the system was unfair and highly subjective or, as one German employee put it, *Nasenpolitik*; in other words, if your face fits, then you get a rise. In practice, only a small minority of employees earmarked for promotion to training squad or above are likely to be awarded the increases.

The performance pay system is also associated with the 'five star' training system commonly found in the UK, Ireland and the USA. Crew members receive a star on their uniform when they have mastered certain stations or attitudinal tests, for example the 'smiley badge', in accordance with an adequate mark on their OCL. Crew can therefore be described in some countries as a 'one star', 'two star' or 'five star'. It appears that most countries still have this performance pay system in place, but in practice it is not always in use and not always with the 'stars'. For example, in the early days of its operations in Germany, McDonald's used to implement its 'five star' badge system. However, German union officials suggest that the introduction of the collective agreement there in 1989 with pay groupings and a pay rise according to experience meant that the small rises based on stars quickly lost their relevance for most workers. The German personnel director suggested that they dropped the stars because they were seen as 'too American' and unsuitable for Germany. Interestingly, British management also criticised the star system as 'too American'. However, as one UK employee pointed out, there is no collective agreement in the UK to undermine its 'value'. In summary, performance pay is simply irrelevant for many of McDonald's workers because labour turnover is so high, because appraisals are not carried out at sufficiently frequent intervals or because collective agreements reduce the attraction of such potential small pay rises. Most of the following analysis therefore focuses on the issue of basic starting pay and some of the other conditions of employment at McDonald's.

Comparing basic pay

In the USA, McDonald's workers usually start at the federal or state minimum wage, whichever is the higher. Since September 1997, the federal minimum wage has been $5.15 (£3.23) per hour and, in 1999, this is the rate that McDonald's pays in New York. The most generous state minimum wage is in Washington, where it was $5.70 (£3.57) in 1999. However, workers under 20 years (who, as already mentioned, make up the vast majority of McDonald's workers) can be paid a lower rate of $4.25 (£2.66) for the first 90 days of their employment, providing their employment at that rate does not displace the jobs of other workers. In addition, there is also the opportunity to employ full-time students at a lower rate of $4.37 (£2.74) per hour, but only on the basis of a maximum 8-hour day/20-hour week during term time. However, the currently low levels of unemployment in the USA suggest that there may not be very many workers willing to work at these lower minimum rates. As McDonald's usually pays just at or above the minimum wage in the USA, a large proportion of McDonald's US workers starts on or just above £3.23 per hour. Nevertheless, in states or areas where unemployment is higher, large numbers of employees could be employed at either just £2.66 or £2.74 per hour.

In comparison, the rates of pay in the UK are more generous, but then tax rates and social security deductions are probably somewhat higher in the UK. Before the recent imposition of the minimum wage, those working in the regions who were less than 18 years old started on £3.25 per hour and those who were more than 18 years old started on £3.75 per hour. In January 1998, McDonald's UK increased its rates of pay for the first time in several years, and this was almost certainly in anticipation of the minimum wage legislation which came into force on 1 April 1999. When first introduced, the national minimum wage provided a minimum rate of £3.60 per hour for those aged 21 years and over and £3.00 for those aged between 18 and 21 years.[1] There is no minimum wage for those who are under 18 years old. In the UK, McDonald's has three separate pay 'scales' for inner London, for outer London and for the provinces, and it has both under-18 and over-18 starting rates. In fact, McDonald's increased its UK pay rates again by a flat rate of 10 pence on 28 March 1999 to bring the over-18 starting rate to £3.60 outside London. Something like 70% of McDonald's UK employees are under 21, and approximately 30% are under 18.

The fact that there is no minimum wage for under-18s and only a £3 minimum for those aged 18–21 years makes the minimum wage legislation look rather disappointing. After all, in this kind of job, 16- and 17-year-old employees work just as hard as those aged 18 or 21, and yet they still receive only £3.35 outside London. As we have already seen, there are some opportunities for workers to earn more if they 'perform' well, but for the vast majority it is the basic starting wage that is most relevant. Nevertheless, even a minimum wage of £3.60 for older workers is likely to have a positive impact on overall wage levels. Statistics from a Low Pay Network Survey suggest that when the UK system of 'wages councils' was abolished in 1993 employers quickly reduced overall pay rates (Quiney, 1994). McDonald's UK also took advantage of this situation by removing paid time off for public holidays. The issue of low pay is nothing new in the broader hospitality sector. It has often tended to be lower than in other industries. In 1992, in the UK, it was 65% of the average for all industries (Quiney, 1994). That McDonald's UK pay is low was also confirmed in the McLibel trial, according to Vidal (1997: 312) the judge determined that '… the British McDonald's operation pays low wages and it depresses wages for other workers in the industry'.

The first German collective agreement introduced in 1989 did have a considerable impact on both pay and conditions, providing better terms for payment in lieu, overtime and sick pay, minimum guaranteed hours and the washing of uniforms. In addition, pay levels at the lowest rate increased from DM7.10 (£2.30) to DM9.85 (£3.19) per hour.[2] A comparison of German and UK pay rates for the years 1994, 1998 and 1999 is given in Table 7.1. Of course, comparing pay rates by exchange rate in this manner is not really satisfactory because such figures do not take into account fluctuations in exchange rates, cost of living and taxation systems, but it does provide a rough guide. Since the increases in 1989, the German unions have been unable to persuade McDonald's to improve its pay significantly.

McDonald's German pay levels may look higher than those in the UK, but when one compares German pay with pay in jobs in similar food-processing industries (see Table 7.1) then pay at McDonald's Germany is just as low. Indeed, if one takes into account the higher German income tax rates, the lower starting rate introduced during the 1997 collective bargaining round suggests that German pay may be even lower than in the UK in real terms.

Table 7.1 Comparison of hourly pay rates in Germany and the UK (£)

McDonald's UK	Under 18 years	Over 18 years	Promotion to training squad
1994	2.65	2.90	3.25
1998	3.25	3.50	3.60
1999	3.35	3.60	3.75

McDonald's Germany	N/A	Less than 12 months (TG1)	More than 12 months (TG2)	More than 33 months (TG3)
1994	a	3.66	3.79	4.04
1998	a	3.84	3.94	4.22
1999 West	a	3.97, 3.57[b]	4.10	4.36
1999 East	a	3.41	3.50	3.50/3.75[c]

West German industries (1994)	First 12 months	After 12 months	After 24 months
Bread and baking	4.66	4.66	5.96
Fruit and vegetable processing	4.00	4.66	5.75
Coal-mining			
Cleaner	6.60		
Kitchen assistant	6.87		
Doorman	7.16		

Sources for industries other than the fast-food industry: *Statistisches Bundesamt* (1994).

Notes

TG, Tariff (pay) group according to collective agreement.

a No separate rate for under-18s at McDonald's because there are hardly any employed there.

b Restaurant managers have been able to employ people at this lower rate since the 1997 collective agreement if they can find adequate numbers of employees who are willing to accept it (see text).

c In East Germany, workers can only receive TG3 if they are promoted to training squad. The UK figures are based on pay rates in the regions outside London.

NGG officials state that in order to obtain the McDonald's signature on the 1997 collective agreement they had to accept the employers' association (BdS) demand for the possibility of a lower introductory pay rate of £3.57 (DM11.04). In return, other employers, such as Burger King, agreed to other employment benefits for their employees, but McDonald's offered none.

All the companies in the BdS would now be allowed to engage workers at this lower rate for the first 18 months of employment. There was to be no restriction attached to this lower rate; it would only be a question of finding employees willing to work for this level of pay. Where it is applied, it effectively reduces wage levels to those prevailing in 1994. As yet, there are no precise figures available to indicate the proportion of the McDonald's German workforce being paid at this lower rate. Both works councillors and union officials estimate that only a small number of workers are actually employed at this rate; most are likely to be either foreign workers or school and university students and there are none where there is a union-supported works council established.

The increasing number of foreign workers looking for work in Germany suggests that these employers may indeed find enough workers willing to accept the lower rate. Indeed, the imposition of the lower pay rate may also have been encouraged by the recent establishment of ZIHOGA,[3] an institution apparently created for the training of workers in the hospitality industry. Together with the Federal Employment Service[4] (*Bundesanstalt für Arbeit*), ZIHOGA have provided McDonald's with around 250 employees per year directly hired from Poland, Rumania and Bulgaria. A recent article (*Stern*, 1999) suggests that there are some cases in which foreign workers have signed contracts to work for McDonald's at the higher starting rate of £3.97 (DM12.27) in their homeland, but on arrival in Germany had to sign a new contract at the lower rate of £3.57. Of course, compared with the rate in East Germany, this lower rate is still favourable, and compared with the situation in Bulgaria or Rumania it looks even more favourable.

Comparing pay by exchange rate only is clearly unsatisfactory, especially as it is generally accepted that at more than DM3 to £1 the pound is overvalued; a more realistic rate would probably be closer to DM2.70. In any case, it is difficult to find an entirely satisfactory way of comparing wages across different countries, so what has been attempted here is a bit of 'burgereconomics'. The 'Big Mac' is now so ubiquitous that it has been adopted as a benchmark good, in other words an international measure of purchasing power. The 'Big Mac Index', compiled by the Union Bank of Switzerland (UBS), has been used by *The Economist* since 1986, with the McDonald's hamburger 'Big Mac' being used to calculate the relative values of international currencies. *The Economist* suggests that 'burgereconomics' is an extremely reliable method of valuing currencies in relation to the dollar; as *The Economist* (1993a: 79) puts it, 'The McDonald's Big Mac...is the perfect universal commodity'. Indeed, as the UBS (1997) survey points out, differences in purchasing power are particularly graphic when they are expressed as the

Table 7.2 McDonald's gross wages (1999) compared with the average gross wage (1998)

Country[a]	Average gross wage (1998)[b] (£)	McDonald's gross starting wage (1999) (£)	McDonald's gross wage as a percentage of the average wage
Norway	8.50	7.32	86.1
Denmark	9.69	7.30	75.3
Sweden	6.77	4.52	66.7
France	6.14	3.87	63.0
The Netherlands	8.40	4.70	55.9
Italy	7.25	4.04	55.7
Spain	5.65	2.86	50.6
Belgium	9.19	4.57	49.7
Finland	7.04	3.47	49.2
Ireland	6.66	3.21	48.2
Austria	6.85	3.28	47.8
UK	8.05	3.75	46.5
Germany	8.95	3.97	44.3
USA[c]	8.79	3.23	36.7

Notes

a Countries ordered in relation to the relative value of the McDonald's wage compared with the average wage.

b Average wage figures provided by the Organisation for Economic Co-operation and Development (OECD). The OECD figures have been recalculated from dollars to pounds and the wage figures have all been recalculated from original currencies. Exchange rates have been calculated at rates provided by the *Financial Times* on 1 December 1999. £1 is equal to: Austria, Sch21.76; Belgium, BFr63.8; Denmark, DKr11.77; Finland, Fmk9.40; France, FFr10.38; Germany, DM3.09; Ireland, I£1.24; Italy, L3063; The Netherlands, G3.48; Norway, NKr12.84; Spain, Pta263.2; USA, $1.59.

c McDonald's US figures are based on typical pay in New York City, one of the wealthiest cities in the USA. However, pay can vary considerably across different states, reflecting variations in the tightness of labour markets. For example, in Maryland and Michigan, where unemployment has been lower than in New York City, pay has tended to be higher in recent years.

price of a benchmark good in terms of the average hourly net wage. In Table 7.2, we begin by comparing the gross wage at McDonald's with the average gross wage as calculated by the OECD for 1998. The figures presented for McDonald's wages represent the typical starting wage for a worker aged 18 years or over. In Table 7.2, we also indicate the relative value of the McDonald's gross wage as a percentage of the average gross wage. In Table 7.3, we then calculate the disposable income or net wage proportion of the gross average wage and the gross McDonald's wage by deducting tax and social security contributions, again on figures provided by the OECD.

These figures are then used to calculate the value of the McDonald's net wage as a percentage of average net wage and these percentages are presented in the line graph in Figure 7.1. In this calculation, and with the exception of Austria and Germany, the values of the McDonald's wages in the UK, the USA and Ireland are the lowest of all fourteen countries presented here.

Excluding Germany and Austria, one could argue that as a proportion of the average wage the McDonald's net wage is lowest in countries where no collective bargaining arrangements exist. How can we account for the presence of Austria and Germany in the bottom half of the table? From the analysis in the earlier sections and chapters of this book, it seems likely that the lower wages can be accounted for in terms of workforce characteristics. Both Austrian and German McDonald's workforces rely on large percentages of foreign workers who, often being marginalised in the labour market, are much more likely to be willing to work for lower wages. This is especially so in Germany, where unions have also had to accept the possibility of an even lower wage than the one used in the calculations here.

In Table 7.4, we use the net wage figures to calculate how many minutes' of work would be required to purchase a Big Mac on both the McDonald's net wage and the average net wage. The final column indicates how many additional minutes' work it would take for a McDonald's worker to earn enough to buy a Big Mac compared with the time it would take on the average net wage. Unfortunately, at the time of writing, the latest figures available from the OECD on average wages were for 1998 and not for 1999. Nevertheless, the figures provide a fairly accurate contrast of the relative values of the disposable income in each country and of the value of the McDonald's wage compared with the average wage. Had the 1999 average wage figures been available then the relative value of the McDonald's wage would clearly have been smaller, if only in terms of inflation.

The analysis clearly indicates that workers in Denmark and Norway do best in terms of pay; indeed, the McDonald's pay in Norway is remarkably close to the average wage. What is most striking, however, is the fact that McDonald's US workers come worst off; the disparity between the US average wage and the US starting wage at McDonald's is huge. An American earning the average wage needs to work less than 19 minutes to earn enough to pay for a Big Mac, but working at McDonald's 1 year later an American McDonald's worker would have to work for nearly an hour, i.e. over two and a half times as long. This is graphically illustrated in Figure 7.2.

Table 7.3 McDonald's net wage compared with the average net wage

Country	Tax etc. (%)[a]	Average net wage (1998) (£)[b]	McDonald's net wage (1999) (£)[b]	Percentage[c]
Norway	30	5.75	5.12	89.0
Denmark	43	5.52	4.16	75.3
Sweden	34	4.47	2.98	66.6
France	27	4.48	2.82	62.9
The Netherlands	34	5.54	3.10	55.9
Italy	29	5.15	2.86	55.5
Spain	20	4.52	2.28	50.4
Belgium	42	5.33	2.65	49.7
Finland	35	4.58	2.25	49.1
Ireland	25	4.99	2.40	48.0
Austria	29	4.86	2.33	47.9
UK	25	6.03	2.70	44.7
Germany	42	5.19	2.30	44.3
USA	26	6.50	2.39	36.7

Notes

a Figures used for calculating the net wage; these figures, provided by the Organisation for Economic Co-operation and Development (OECD) for 1998, represent the percentage of tax and social security contributions payable in each country.

b Net wage after tax and social security contributions.

c McDonald's net wage as a percentage of the average net wage.

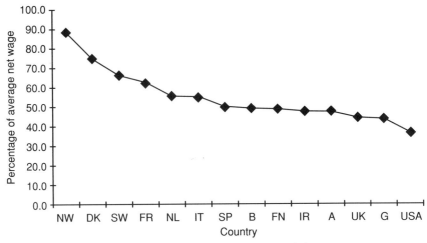

Figure 7.1 McDonald's net wage (1999) as a percentage of the average net wage (1998)

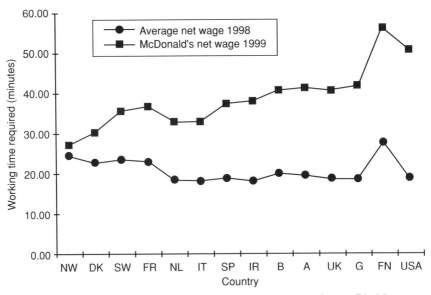

Figure 7.2 A comparison of the working time required to purchase a Big Mac on the McDonald's net wage and on the average net wage

A similar but less extreme disparity is also evident between the purchasing power of the average net German wage and the German McDonald's wage, which suggests that German McDonald's workers have to work twice as long as the German worker on the average wage to purchase a Big Mac. Finland moves close to the bottom of the table in terms of purchasing power, and this

Table 7.4 Relative purchasing power of the McDonald's disposable wage[a]

Country[b]	Cost of Big Mac (£)	Working time required on average net wage (1998) (minutes)	Working time required on McDonald's net wage (1999) (minutes)	Additional working time required on McDonald's net wage (minutes)
Norway	2.34	24.45	27.45	3.00
Denmark	2.10	22.80	30.30	7.50
Sweden	1.77	23.75	35.70	11.95
France	1.73	23.20	36.80	13.60
The Netherlands	1.70	18.45	32.95	14.50
Italy 1.57	18.30	33.00	14.70	
Spain	1.42	18.85	37.40	18.55
Ireland	1.52	18.30	38.00	19.70
Belgium	1.80	20.30	40.80	20.50
Austria	1.60	19.75	41.25	21.50
UK 1.90	18.90	40.60	21.70	
Germany	1.60	18.50	41.80	23.30
Finland	2.12	27.80	56.55	28.75
USA 2.03	18.75	51.00	32.25	

Notes

a McDonald's wages are based on the starting pay for a worker aged 18 years or over.

b Countries ordered in terms of the additional minutes required to purchase a Big Mac on the McDonald's disposable wage compared with average disposable wage. Figures for the 'Big Mac' are based on a sample of restaurants in the capital or major city of each country; the US figure is based on a sample of New York restaurants.

may reflect the high level of youth unemployment in that country. One final point of interest here is the relatively low level of pay in Sweden compared with that in Denmark and Norway. One might have expected that Swedish pay would be closer to that in Norway and Denmark because both of the OECD figures suggest that average pay in Sweden is above that in Denmark and similar to that in Norway. Could it be that another reason for the low level of conflict in Sweden is partly a result of the somewhat lower wages paid to McDonald's Swedish workers?

Overtime and additional rates for unsociable hours

According to the Fair Labor Standards Act, first introduced in the Wagner Act of 1935, any hours worked over 40 hours per week in the USA should be paid at an additional rate of 50%. However, as already suggested, few hourly paid workers ever work more than 40 hours per week in the USA. Although overtime payments are therefore theoretically possible in the USA, they are likely to be very rare in practice. In the UK, the crew handbook specifically states that, because additional rates of pay are provided for unsociable hours, overtime is not normally applicable; in fact, in practice, it is rarely paid.

The first German collective agreement stipulated that the rate for overtime should be increased from 15% to 25% of the hourly wage. In Germany, the agreement states that overtime rates should be paid if workers exceeded 173 hours in any one month or more than 8 hours per day for part-time workers. However, the German agreement specifically states that overtime should be avoided, so although overtime is technically possible in practice it is also rare at McDonald's Germany. Nevertheless, in other countries where collective agreements have in one way or another been imposed on McDonald's, overtime payments are usually stipulated and paid in practice if it occurs. In The Netherlands, overtime is paid if workers exceed 494 hours in any 3-month period, with a maximum of 45 hours in 1 week and 10 hours in one day, with stricter restrictions for the under-18s. The Dutch agreement stipulates that overtime should be granted as time off in lieu; however, if this is not possible, workers receive an extra 50% of the hourly rate. In Finland, overtime is payable when an individual works more than 120 hours in any 3-week period. However, according to crew members and union representatives in a number of countries, the problem is that even when overtime is due it is not always paid when it should be or, when it is paid, it is not always calculated correctly. As suggested in Chapter 4, this issue is of particular concern where there are large numbers of foreign workers (such as in Germany and Austria) who are not aware of their rights. Once again, there may be considerable differences between what should happen according to the agreement and what actually happens in practice.

The additional rates paid for unsociable hours may be a better indicator of real pay and conditions rather than agreed overtime rates. There is a good deal of variation in countries with regard to the provision of these additional rates. In the UK, before 1990, and notably before the abolition of the wages council in 1993, there were three rates of pay for working unsociable hours at McDonald's. These were a normal rate from 7.00 a.m. to 7.00 p.m., an 'evening rate' between 7.00 p.m. and 11.00 p.m. and a 'premium rate' between 11.00 p.m. and 7.00 a.m. Employees used to receive an extra 25 pence per hour for 'evening rate' and a further 25 pence per hour for 'premium rate', making a total of a 50 pence per hour increase for very late working. However, this arrangement has since been done away with and now there are just two rates of pay, one for 'normal' working hours and a second increased rate for unsociable hours. The starting period for extra pay is now even later, there is no extra rate for evening work before midnight and workers only receive the extra 50 pence per hour between 12.00 a.m. and 6.00 a.m. Surprisingly, the German collective agreements do not provide an additional rate for unsociable hours because of the 'nature of the business' – the collective agreement is supposed to take this into account in the 'additional' pay it provides. However, when one compares basic wages and the additional rates paid in some other countries, the German wage rate looks rather low.

In the Scandinavian countries, collective agreements tend to provide generous additional rates of pay for non-standard hours. In Denmark, for example, in addition to the basic Danish kroner (DKr)86 (£7.30) per hour, workers receive an extra DKr9.15 (£0.78) per hour for any hours worked during Monday to Friday between 6.00 p.m. and midnight. In addition, they receive an extra DKr9.15 per hour from 2.00 p.m. to midnight on Saturdays and for working Sundays they receive an extra DKr15.07 (£1.28) per hour. They also receive an extra DKr15.07 for any late night work between midnight and 6.00 a.m. Similarly, workers in Sweden receive an extra Swedish kronor (SKr)11.50 (£0.85) for evening work between 8.00 p.m. and midnight, an extra SKr11.50 on Saturdays between 4.00 p.m. and midnight, an extra SKr13.50 (£1.00) per hour for late night working between midnight and 6.00 a.m. and an extra SKr11.50 on Sundays. The considerable variations in these additional rates are highlighted in Table 7.5.

As suggested in Chapter 5, these payments were arrived at in different ways; in Sweden, McDonald's was unable to avoid the imposition of a sectoral level agreement, whereas in Denmark the collective agreement was only arrived at after years of conflict. Danish union officials make the point that the improvement in conditions was a direct result of their continued pressure to bring McDonald's to the negotiating table. By the time the collective agreement was finally signed, McDonald's had already improved the conditions of its workers. Each time the unions criticised McDonald's in the press, the corporation responded by improving conditions in an attempt to deflate criticism and make the union's case for recognition more difficult. When, for example, the RBF union criticised the corporation for not paying an extra rate for night work and weekends, the company responded by providing such payments. Nevertheless, as also suggested in Chapter 5, McDonald's has been trying to roll back the basic pay and conditions in the

Table 7.5 Additional rates for unsociable hours

	Basic pay rate	Evening (weekday)	Late night (after midnight)	Saturday (afternoon/evening)	Sunday
UK (inner London)	4.00	0.00	0.50	0.00	0.00
Germany	3.97	0.00	0.00	0.00	0.00
The Netherlands	4.70	0.00	0.00	0.00	2.22
Denmark	7.30	0.78	1.28	0.78	1.28
Sweden	4.52	0.85	1.00	0.78	0.78

Note
To receive the Sunday bonus, Dutch workers must have been employed for at least 2 weeks and must work for a minimum of 4 hours per week.

first 'landmark' agreement ever since. Danish union officials argue that without the struggle that went on for seven years conditions would reflect those in the UK. In other words, McDonald's would still be paying around the minimum wage of DKr70 (£5.95) and there would only be minimal or no allowances for working Sundays, public holidays and unsociable hours.

'For a fistful of dollars': executive pay

Although comparing basic pay across the different European countries is interesting, it is also interesting to put this level of pay into perspective with that earned by the McDonald's top executives. The 1996 Notice of the McDonald's Corporation Annual Shareholders' Meeting to be held on 23 May 1996 at McDonald's Office Campus (corner of Kroc Drive and Ronald Lane, Oak Brook, Illinois) provides a number of interesting insights into the levels of compensation paid to top executives. On page 10, the report states that the McDonald's compensation committee:

> ...believes that a significant and increasing portion of executive compensation should be at risk, that good performance should be rewarded and that the financial interests of executives should be aligned with shareholders through stock ownership. ...annual cash compensation for our executives, as for all our employees, consists of base salary plus a variable at-risk incentive under the Target Incentive Plan (TIP)

The TIP is the bonus paid for performance; however, using the term 'at risk' to describe these bonuses when basic salaries are so high and the bonuses themselves are only likely to be reduced and not eradicated seems somewhat ingenuous. The bonuses paid to the top executives from 1993 to 1995 averaged around $500,000, with the chief executive's bonus increasing each year from $800,000 to over $1,050,000 in 1995. Furthermore, to suggest that this kind of 'at-risk' bonus was applicable to *all our employees* seems even more ludicrous when one compares a (maximum) 15 pence per hour increase for the ordinary worker with what Michael Quinlan, the Chairman and CEO of the McDonald's Corporation until 1998, received in 1995. His performance pay amounted to around £315 per hour awarded for every hour of a 40-hour week over 52 weeks per year. Indeed, even the basic 'not at-risk' salary is extremely generous compared with an ordinary worker's basic pay.

The total compensation paid to Quinlan in 1994 was $2,115,930, and rose to $2,463,862 in 1995. In 1994, basic starting pay for the under-18s in the UK was £2.65 and for the over-18s was £2.90 per hour. On this rate of pay, even a worker achieving the maximum performance increase of 15 pence per hour twice after two 4-monthly reviews and working 40 hours per week for 52 weeks per year could not expect to earn more than £306 in total performance pay. This scenario is in any case unlikely as most employees do not work a full 40-hour week and may only be working for a few weeks or months at any one time. Based on a 40-hour week, the CEO was earning something like £635 ($1,017) per hour in 1994 and £740 ($1,184) per hour in 1995. The contrast with the typical starting wage in the USA in 1994 is particularly stark. In 1994, a US worker could expect to start on the equivalent of around £2.50 ($4.00) per hour. Table 7.6 compares the amounts of basic pay and possible performance bonus for ordinary US and UK workers with the actual basic pay, performance bonus and other annual compensation but *excluding* stock options paid to McDonald's top executives from 1994 to 1995.

In addition to the annual salary, bonuses and other compensation, the top executives also own huge amounts of stock. The executive officer group beneficially owned 7.8 million shares of Common Stock on 1 February 1996. Even executive or 'outside' directors of the McDonald's Corporation in the USA were earning $35,000 per annum plus additional payments of $2,000 for each board meeting (in 1995, amounting to $14,000) and a further $1,000 for each committee meeting attended as well as various stock options. According to Vidal (1997: 218), Paul Preston, McDonald's UK President, while in the witness-box during the McLibel trial stated:

> No, he didn't think that a pay rise (for workers) of 5 pence per hour in two years (less than 1 per cent a year) was 'low'.

According to Vidal (1997: 218), even lesser executives such as the senior management in the UK had salaries of over £75,000 per year in 1993 (about £36 per hour), while in the same year starting pay outside London was just £3.00 for the over-18s and £2.65 for the under-18s. In fact, McDonald's in the UK had in the past always set its wages just a few pence above the recommended rate set by the abolished wages council and, as we have seen, roughly in line with the new minimum wage.

Probation period and notice for dismissal

Table 7.7 suggests that, with the exception of Spain where union-negotiated collective agreements are established, McDonald's workers get a much better deal in terms of notice for dismissal, especially during the probation period. These periods vary somewhat, e.g. the probation period in the UK is usually 3 weeks, in Finland it is 2 months, in Spain 1 month and in Belgium the probation period is the whole of the first year (however, it is the same for every company in Belgium). It can be extended to more than 1 month in Sweden, but in most cases the probation period is 1 month. In the UK, management can sack an employee at any time with no notice during the first month. In Spain, McDonald's workers can also be sacked without notice at any time in the first month. In Germany, management must give 3 days' notice during the 3 weeks of probation.

UK workers only seem to benefit slightly more than their German counterparts when they have been employed for more than 5 years and benefit

Table 7.6 Workers' and top executives' pay 1994–5

Name (position)	Year	Basic salary	Bonus	Other payments	Total ($)	Average hourly rate (£)[a]
Michael Quinlan (Chairman and CEO)	1994	$1,050,925	$1,050,000	$362,937	$2,463,862	£740.34
	1995	$998,875	$950,000	$167,055	$2,115,930	£635.79
Edward Rensi (President, CEO McDonald's USA)	1994	$752,375	$495,422	$225,675	$1,473,472	£442.75
	1995	$711,375	$485,462	$469,638	$1,666,475	£500.74
James Cantalupo (President, CEO McDonald's International)	1994	$732,675	$547,934	$192,531	$1,473,140	£442.65
	1995	$684,025	$499,194	$124,100	$1,307,319	£392.82
Jack Greenburg (Vice Chairman, Chief Financial Officer)	1994	$714,250	$520,792	$216,516	$1,451,558	£436.16
	1995	$668,875	$473,478	$121,337	$1,263,690	£379.71
McDonald's US worker[b]	1994	$8,320	$306	N/A	$8,626	£2.60
McDonald's UK worker[c]	1994	$9,651	$490	N/A	$10,141	£3.05

Notes

a Hourly rates are based on a 40-hour week with the US dollars converted at $1.6 to the pound.

b In 1994, many McDonald's US workers started on the US minimum wage of $4.00 per hour. Figures assume that the worker has worked for 40 hours per week for 52 weeks and that the performance bonus is calculated at the US equivalent of 15 pence per hour.

c Assuming that the UK worker is over 18 years, working 40 hours per week for 52 weeks and successfully achieving the maximum performance pay rise of 15 pence twice in 1 year (after two 4-monthly reviews).

Table 7.7 Periods of notice for redundancy in 1999 (days)

	Length of service (months)				(years)									
	0–1ᵃ	1–2	2–6	6+	1+	2+	3–5	5+	6+	8+	10+	12+	15+	20+
UK	0	14	14	14	14	14	21	35	35	35	70	90	90	90
Germany	3	14	14	14	14	21	21	28	28	28	30	30	90	90
Belgium	7	7	7	7	28	28	28	28	28	28	56	56	56	84
France	8	8	8	30	30	60	60	60	60	60	60	60	60	60
Finland	0	30	30	30	30	30	30	60	60	60	90	90	120	120
Sweden	14	14	30	30	30	60	60	90	120	150	180	180	180	180

Note
a Probation period; figures indicate the length of notice required during this period.

significantly more only after 12 years. Clearly, this will not apply to the majority of McDonald's employees in the UK. The most significant period for dismissal notice is the first few months, and in a smaller number of cases it is the first few years. However, as we have seen in Chapter 4, a large proportion of the McDonald's German workers are foreign workers and they do tend to stay much longer with the corporation because of fewer job opportunities. It is interesting to note, therefore, that German workers fare worse in terms of dismissal notice than their counterparts in France, Sweden and the UK if they do stay with the corporation over the long term.

Holiday entitlements

Until the introduction of the European Working Time Directive, McDonald's employees in the UK appeared to have a raw deal compared with their European partners. Table 7.8 provides the details of paid leave entitlement in 1994 and 1999.

For the first 6 months, employees have no entitlement to paid leave and after that they only receive 14 days on a pro rata basis. To receive 2 days' paid leave, therefore, the UK worker had to work for 7 months. The working time directive has improved the situation for some McDonald's workers in the UK. From 23 November 1998, all UK employees (with the exception of some agricultural workers) will be entitled to 3 weeks' holiday per year and after 23 November 1999 to 4 weeks' holiday. However, this entitlement does not arise until a worker has been employed continuously for 13 weeks during the whole or part of each of those weeks. Reflecting its concerns about job creation, the UK government has stated that the 3-month qualifying period is necessary to minimise the potential threat to employment in seasonal and temporary jobs such as tourism and agriculture (LRD, 1998).

As most McDonald's employees work part time and for shorter lengths of time than in many other industries, the leave entitlement in the early days of employment is significant. Under Swedish law, all Swedish employees have the right to 25 days' holiday regardless of length of service and they are also allowed take 4 weeks' holiday between the 15 May and 15 September if no other company-level agreement is in place. Indeed, similar arrangements are in place in Denmark and Norway. In addition to these entitlements, Swedish employees also receive 1 full day's paid leave on a number of occasions, e.g. on their own wedding day, on their 50th birthday, when they are ill and visit a doctor or dentist, when a close relative dies, when they go to a funeral of a close relative or when a close relative suddenly becomes seriously ill. Officials at the hotel and restaurant workers' union afffiliated to the FGBT in Belgium state that 20 days is the legal minimum set out by legislation; in practice, most larger employers have company-level collective agreements which usually provide 5 or 6 weeks' holiday, not the 4 weeks' holiday given at McDonald's. Of course, most employees are part time not full time. In most countries, part-time employees working fewer than 5 days per week receive a

Table 7.8 Paid holiday (days) for full-time (35+ hours) hourly paid employees (1994 and 1999)

	Length of service (months)							(years)						
	1	3	6	7	9	11	12	1–2	3–4	5–6	7	12.5	25	40
UK														
1994	0	0	0	2	7	11	20	20	20	22	22	22	22	22
1999	0	0	10	11	15	18	20	20	20	22	22	22	22	22
Germany														
1994	2	6	12	14	18	22	24	24	26	28	30	30	30	30
1999	2	6	12	14	18	23	25	25	27	29	30	30	30	30
Belgium														
1999	1	4	10	11	15	18	20	20	20	20	20	20	20	20
Finland														
1999	2	6	12	14	18	22	24	30	30	30	30	30	30	30
The Netherlands														
1999	2	6	12	14	18	23	25	25	25	25	25	26	28	30
Sweden														
1999	2	6	12	14	18	23	25	25	25	25	25	25	25	25

proportion of the total depending on the number of average days or hours they work over the year. So, for example, holiday entitlement for a Swedish employee working 3 days per week would be calculated as 3 divided by 5 multiplied by 25, i.e. 15 days' holiday per year.

In Germany, leave can be carried forward into following years, but only in exceptional circumstances, whereas in the UK leave cannot be carried forward under any circumstances. In Germany and The Netherlands, crew receive one-twelfth of the yearly entitlement for every completed month; 14 and 15 days of employment counts as a full month for holiday entitlement in each of those countries respectively. So an individual who worked for McDonald's in The Netherlands and Germany for just 3 weeks would be entitled to 2 days' paid leave. Indeed, in most of the mainland European countries, collective agreements also provide for additional holiday pay on top of the number of days of paid holiday. For example, in Germany, workers receive an additional DM700 (£226) in years 1 and 2 of their employment, DM800 (£259) in years 3 and 4, DM900 (£291) in years 5 and 6 and DM1,000 (£324) for 7 years' service onwards. Before the changes brought about by the European Working Time Directive, the McDonald's German holiday entitlement was much better than that of McDonald's UK; however, when one compares McDonald's German holiday entitlement with average German holiday entitlement, it does not look quite so positive. In 1998, only 1% of the German (East and West) workforce received just 20–25 days' holiday, 20% received 25–30 days' holiday and 80% received 30 days or more (*EIRR*, 1999a).

Conclusion and discussion

The usual approach by McDonald's to pay determination is one based on basic pay and additional pay for good performance. However, as suggested for many McDonald's workers, performance pay rises will be a rare occurrence. First, because the high rates of labour turnover at McDonald's make it irrelevant; second, because the decisions to award such rises are based on subjective judgements, often dependent on a good personal relationship with managers or franchisees; and finally, in many cases the prerequisite performance appraisal is often infrequent or does not take place at all. Our examination of basic starting pay therefore seems a more logical point to begin to understand the reality of wage levels for most workers at McDonald's. This analysis suggests that in most cases where collective agreements have either been imposed or established McDonald's workers have definitely benefited from improvements in pay. This analysis suggests that a strong union presence and stringent systems of regulation reduce inequality by improving the pay and conditions of low-skilled and low-paid workers. It also suggests that a society such as the USA, which is dominated by the liberal economic agenda, will be a much more unequal society, with those working in low-skilled jobs having to survive on a very small proportion of the wealth that they have helped to create. This is clearly indicated in this study where there is a great disparity between McDonald's US wages and the average US wage.

The analysis also highlights that, among the varied systems of Europe where pay and conditions are generally better than in the USA, there are considerable variations which appear to depend very much on the stringency of labour regulation and the strength of trade union organisation. The analysis suggests that the difference between the purchasing power of the McDonald's wage levels in countries such as Denmark and Norway and such as the UK and the USA is particularly great. A comparative study of trends in wage determination by Almond and Rubery (1998) suggests that Anglo-Saxon countries with decentralised industrial relations systems have 19–25% of the full-time workforce in low pay compared with less than 6% in some Scandinavian countries. It seems likely that this disparity will be more extreme for part-time workers (who make up the majority of McDonald's employees) because the regulation of such work tends to be looser in decentralised systems. Dex *et al.* (1999) in their study of low pay also suggest that the USA and, to a lesser extent, the UK have more pay inequality at the lower end of the earnings distribution, with the sort of labour markets that more greatly penalise uneducated workers. Despite the improvements brought by collective agreements, basic pay levels are very low in Germany and Austria and Finland. Indeed, the initial improvements brought about by the early German collective agreements appear to have been steadily undermined in recent years. How can we account for this anomaly? Almond and Rubery (1998) suggest that there is a considerable degree of earnings inequality in Austria, but they also find that there is a lower inequality of earnings in Germany. The problem with this kind of quantitative survey is that it does not reveal the idiosyncrasies of particular labour market sectors. The answer may lie in a closer examination of labour markets and the requirement for certain types of labour in some sectors. The high levels of youth unemployment in Finland mean that there is no shortage of young workers willing to work for low wages at McDonald's. In Finland, if McDonald's managers determine that the employee has had no previous work experience (and of course most have not) then they are classed as 'trainees'. So, for example, for the first 300 hours worked at McDonald's in Finland, workers receive only 80% of the full starting pay. For many part-timers, who only do 15–20 hours per week, this means that they will not go on to full starting pay for 5 months. Some may never get on to full starting pay because they leave after a few weeks or months. In other words, instead of receiving Finnish markka (Fmk)40.72 per hour, they only receive Fmk32.58 per hour in Helsinki; outside Helsinki, rates are even lower. Similarly, as suggested in Chapter 4, in Germany and Austria around 60% of the McDonald's workforces are made up of foreign workers. In these countries, there is also no shortage of workers willing to work for lower wages.

In most cases where sectoral agreements apply, franchisees are automatically covered. However, in many cases, these sectoral agreements, although providing basic conditions, do not provide the better kind of conditions that one might normally have associated with this kind of powerful multinational. The McDonald's pay may not be the lowest in the sector; but McDonald's is not a small employer but a huge and highly profitable multinational. When one compares the extremely high rates of remuneration paid to senior management and those at the top of the corporation with the rates of pay for the ordinary restaurant worker, surely they could afford to pay somewhat more. It could be argued that this is indeed possible because it is already happening in some of the Scandinavian countries such as Denmark and Norway.

In other countries, workers are somewhere in between the USA and the Scandinavian countries. For example, in Spain, Italy and Belgium, the unions are still hoping to negotiate a company-level agreement to bring pay and conditions more in line with the norms for larger companies. In fact, in Spain, although company collective agreements have been concluded to cover McDonald's employees in its company-owned restaurants (indeed, one agreement also exists covering employees in one group of franchise restaurants), these 'agreements' have been concluded by company-friendly works councils and not the trade unions. Unsurprisingly, Spanish union officials have stated that these agreements have achieved little for employees, but they do acknowledge that employees working in most Spanish franchises are paid even less.

The broader terms and conditions of work at McDonald's appear to be similar in the UK, Ireland and the USA, and generally much better in mainland European countries. In terms of holiday entitlements, it is quite clear that the European Working Time Directive has had a positive impact on the holiday entitlement of McDonald's UK and Irish employees. Having said that, the 3-month qualifying period (determined by the UK government's interpretation of the directive) means that many of McDonald's employees will still lose out compared with their European counterparts. In other areas, such as the hours actually worked by salaried restaurant management, it has had no effect; managers have simply been asked to sign away their rights under the directive so that long unpaid hours still continue. It is probably in terms of the general conditions of work where most McDonald's workers in mainland Europe have benefited from the national collective agreements. This is particularly marked in terms of additional rates of pay for unsociable hours, special leave, sick pay, holiday entitlements, scheduling of hours and other issues such as washing of uniforms.

Although the collective agreements have generally achieved a great deal for McDonald's workers on paper, it is another matter making sure that the employer actually complies with the letter of the agreement. Union officials and workers frequently report that restaurant management, particularly those in franchise operations, continue to 'side-step' aspects of the collective agreements. In a number of countries, McDonald's has employed new starters, classified them as 'trainees' and given them a lower rate of pay than that stipulated in the collective agreements. Similarly, some workers are being paid at a lower rate of pay than that to which they are actually entitled under agreements. This has been particularly common in Germany and Italy, but there have also been examples in The Netherlands. Once again, it is often the franchisees who appear to be the worst culprits. For example, after 33 months' employment, McDonald's German employees should be paid in tariff group 3, but NGG officials report that many are still being paid in the lower tariff group 2. Workers and union officials have also reported a number of instances in Germany, Italy and Denmark where employees were not paid for the hours that they were being trained as crew trainers or floor managers in the restaurant.

A further problem that occurred in several countries was that young workers were frequently asked to attend meetings or to come in to work late at night and work for nothing. This is common practice in North America, Ireland and the UK. In Finland, the management called it 'Mac tonight'; in Denmark, it was presented as a 'clean-up' competition. Management would 'invite' the workers to what they described as a 'party', where there would be lots of 'fun'. In fact, the workers would be expected to clean the whole restaurant from top to bottom. Sometimes, this would occur when a senior manager was due to visit the restaurant or sometimes when the corporation announced it was going to have its 'cleanest restaurant competition'. The winners would be awarded a real party sometime afterwards. This first came to the attention of the Danish unions well after the first collective agreement was in force. The Danish unions had recently acquired a union representative working in one of the restaurants and it was he who 'blew the whistle'. The union representative first protested to his own restaurant management. They told him that they were allowed to do this, but he nevertheless reported it to local union officials. Working for nothing in this way is strictly outlawed under the Danish collective agreement. The union sent a letter to the McDonald's head office and the corporation was obliged to stop the planned 'clean-up' operation. If they had not, they would have run into trouble with their own employers' association, who could have been fined by the courts. However, the problem for the unions is that without union representatives or works councils in every restaurant the same practices could well be continuing without their knowledge. Another example of the importance of worker representation in monitoring collective agreements arose from a casual discussion with one German franchisee. In this particular restaurant, there was no works council and the franchisee expressed some pride in the fact that he washed his employees' uniforms. The franchisee pointed out that none of his contemporaries in the region did this for their employees. He said that these other franchise operators had explained to him that he could get his employees to pay for their own cleaning of uniforms and that he was wasting his money. However, according to the German collective agreement, the employer must bear the cost of cleaning of uniforms. Most employees are simply unaware of their rights, and when there is no works council or union representative they are very much dependent on the goodwill of a management under enormous pressure to keep labour costs to a minimum.

Despite these problems, collective agreements are essential; without such agreement, the unions would have no redress to stop many of the corporation's activities, such as the 'working for free' syndrome. In the absence of either stringent sectoral level agreements or negotiated company-level agreements, the McDonald's employment practices might begin to undermine existing agreements and the pay and conditions in other companies in the same sector. The Italian unions allege that McDonald's Italy are deliberately using stalling tactics to delay the negotiation of a company-level agreement and that over the longer term this may well destabilise the existing pay and conditions at their main competitor Autogrill. Union officials suggest that this may be an attempt to undermine or destabilise basic conditions in the whole Italian fast-food sector.

The important monitoring role of worker representation mechanisms is also evident in the area of health and safety. There is not enough scope within this book to address this issue adequately; in fact, it was not specifically included as part of the research project. However, health and safety is an important issue often mentioned by employees during the course of the study and is often a key aspect of works council or union representative functions. Despite the fairly stringent European and national level legislation in this area, health and safety issues were constantly raised as a major grievance among workers in many countries in this study. Although McDonald's senior management has often stated that health and safety in its restaurants is high on its list of priorities, there seems little doubt that competing pressures to maintain high sales volumes inevitably conflicts with this kind of issue. Indeed, there appear to be no end of health and safety horror stories that have emerged over the years at McDonald's in a number of countries. In Canada, for example, workers have complained of dangerous equipment and receiving electric shocks from kitchen equipment (Featherstone, 1998). In one case in the UK in October 1992, Mark Hopkins, a McDonald's employee, was killed when he received an electric shock from a fat-filtering machine at a McDonald's restaurant in Manchester. According to Vidal (1997: 229) in the McLibel court case, a McDonald's memorandum dated February 1992 clearly admitted that there had been several instances of McDonald's restaurant staff receiving severe shocks from faulty items of electrical equipment. After an inquiry into the death, McDonald's was later ordered to install safety devices to its electrical equipment in its wash-up areas. Vidal also quotes a confidential 1992 Health and Safety Executive report that made twenty-three recommendations for improvements. It stated:

> The application of McDonald's hustle policy [i.e. getting staff to work at speed] in many restaurants was, in effect, putting the service of the customer before the safety of employees.

Finnish workers complained that health and safety was often sidelined in restaurants when restaurant management felt under pressure to increase sales. In one instance, some workers were burnt when they could not shut a fire down in the kitchen that was caused by a gas leak; the fire department was called and the entire restaurant was closed. Italian workers also complained of inadequate ventilation in the kitchen areas and dangerous wet floors that had claimed many 'victims'. The Italian union confederations have repeatedly requested that workers should be provided with appropriate footwear, but as yet the corporation has not responded. Monitoring health and safety and the correct application of collective agreements is clearly a job for the works council, the union representative or indeed the health and safety representative or committee in the restaurant, as the case may be. However, when these statutory mechanisms are absent, such matters are left to the whims of management.

Despite sometimes being considered a back door for other European legislation, such as the working time directive, European health and safety legislation itself has not come in for so much criticism. However, this is not the case in other areas. For example, EU proposals to provide workers with statutory mechanisms for rights to consultation and information have frequently met with hostility. The next chapter deals specifically with this issue by examining the way in which McDonald's has responded to the EU's attempts to provide workers with rights to consultation and information in multinational corporations: the European Works Council Directive.

8 Where's the beef?

The European Works Council

> ...the (EWC) will concentrate on supra-national issues...which may have
> significant implications for McDonald's restaurants in the European Union.
> (McDonald's European Works Council Agreement)

This chapter examines the McDonald's voluntary European Works Council
(EWC) agreement established under Article 13. A good deal of analysis
already focuses on whether the EWC directive can be seen to be a move
towards a more democratic form of decision-making and its broader impact
on European industrial relations (Rehfeldt, 1995; Streeck and Vitols, 1995;
Ramsay, 1997; Marginson *et al.*, 1998). However, this chapter shows how even
the more limited aims of the EWC directive can be frustrated by a non-union
employer. The seventeen countries in the European Economic Area (EEA)
are subject to the directive, not just those in the EU. The essential
requirement of the directive is the establishment of a European committee,
or an information and consultation procedure in every 'community-scale'
undertaking. In practice, this means every undertaking with at least 150
employees in two EEA states and 1,000 employees in the EEA states in total.
A form of procedure or council should be established where at least 150
employees or their representatives from at least two countries request this.

Up until the end of 1997 this did not include the UK. However, the election
of the Labour government in May prompted a change in UK policy, with the
Treaty of Amsterdam formally ending the UK's 'opt-out' of the Social Chapter.
On 15 December 1997 the EWC directive was extended to include the UK,
and this came into force on 15 January 2000 (EIRR, 1997f; 2000a; IDS Focus,
1997). Despite the late inclusion of the UK within the directive, a large
number of UK-based companies had already created their own EWCs. These
companies have allowed UK employee representatives to take part in
meetings, as have, in some cases, foreign companies allowed UK
representatives to participate in their EWCs (Barrie and Milne, 1996). UK
companies which were newly caught within its scope had 2 years (until January
2000) in order to negotiate 'Article 13-type' voluntary agreements; in fact,
they will be agreements based on Article 3 of the Extension Directive. There

are estimated to be some 200 such companies based in the UK, many of which will be Japanese and American (EIRR, 2000a).

The directive also covers the European operations of companies with headquarters outside the EEA whose employment within the seventeen countries meets the size thresholds mentioned above (Rivest, 1996). McDonald's was already present in most European countries and was automatically caught by the directive. How has it dealt with the EWC directive in practice and how have employees and trade unions responded?

In particular, the following analysis raises a number of questions about the efficacy of the existing EWC legislation. For example, who is defined as an 'employee representative'? How are employee representatives elected in practice? What role do existing substructures play in the establishment of the EWC and its operation? Can employee representatives effectively co-ordinate their roles in the absence of significant unionisation? What sanctions are available if employers frustrate the aims of the directive?

The EWC directive

It is not within the scope of this book to discuss the progress and history of the EWC directive in any great detail; in any case, this has already been covered extensively elsewhere (see for example Hall, 1992, 1994; Cressey, 1993; Gold and Hall, 1994; Streeck, 1994; Streeck and Vitols, 1995). However, it will be necessary to provide a short analysis of the particular features of voluntary agreements and the directive's subsidiary requirements. The directive provided for a transitory period of just over 2 years, during which voluntary EWC agreements[1] could be established under Article 13. The deadline for such agreements was 22 September 1996. After that date, the social actors had 3 years to reach an agreement; if no agreement was reached after that time, the 'subsidiary requirements' of the directive automatically came into force. In other words, a standard model would then be imposed on the social actors.

The standard model is defined as an EWC with at least three, and at most thirty, members, including at least one employee representative from every EU member state in which the company has its operations. The EWC has to meet at least once per year with European central management to exchange information and consult on such issues as economic, financial, structural and social developments affecting employees in more than one country. In addition, when there are exceptional circumstances, for example in the event of relocations, closures or collective redundancies, there should, as soon as possible, be an extra *ad hoc* meeting where employee representatives must be consulted. Before the official meeting, employee representatives have the right to a 'pre-meeting' without the presence of management. This is the only legally guaranteed opportunity for the employee representatives to meet independently of management for a common exchange of views and development of policy. However, managerial prerogative is not affected, employee representatives will have no right to block management decisions.

The Article 13 arrangements prescribe only a limited and relatively vague model, leaving most of the concrete arrangements for the bargaining process between the social actors in each multinational and meaning that social actors within each multinational corporation are completely free to negotiate over the kind of EWC they want. This is what Streeck (1991) and Streeck and Vitols (1995) have referred to as a 'menu' approach to European legislation. In practice, this means that the specific framework of each EWC will be based on a complex bargaining process reflecting the relative bargaining power of employee representatives, unions and employers. Barrie and Milne (1996) suggest that by establishing voluntary EWCs multinationals have been able to interpret the directive flexibly, framing the rules to suit themselves rather than having the standard model imposed on them. For example, some Japanese multinationals (Sony, Honda and Matsushita) which were initially strongly opposed to the idea of an EWC later come forward with their own proposals to keep the process under management influence (Schulten, 1996).

Establishing the McDonald's EWC

McDonald's was also one of those companies which decided to opt for an Article 13 agreement. European management established it, but US managers and an American international human resource consultant were also involved from the beginning. One UK manager stated that McDonald's European and USA management heads had been considering what to do about the EWC directive since early in 1994. Besides specific meetings to discuss the EWC, the matter was also discussed at a number of other meetings at which European heads were discussing other matters.

The composition of the EWC is along the lines of the so-called French model, an employee–management joint committee and not an employee-only model. Two-thirds of all Article 13 agreements have adopted this model. However, this model is particularly predominant among US companies (96% of US companies) and arguably among those sectors which tend to have less union strength, i.e. food, drink, tobacco and financial services. Metalworking, paper and transport, which usually have stronger union organisation, are the sectors where employee-only EWCs tend to be found (Marginson *et al.*, 1998). The original agreement stipulates that the management side will consist of top European managers and representatives of the personnel department and that one of these will act as 'president'.

However, it is the way in which the McDonald's EWC 'agreement' was established which is of more interest. A German 'employee representative' first signed the McDonald's voluntary agreement on 21 November 1995; it was to be called the 'European Communications Group'. Employee representatives from each of the other thirteen countries[2] were supposed to have signed the 'agreement' in accordance with the 'normal procedure' in each country. From the beginning, this 'agreement' did not have the support of the European trade unions. The German hotel and restaurant union NGG was particularly disturbed that this agreement had been signed by the then chairman of the recently established German company-level works council (Gesamtbetriebsrat – GBR) and his deputy.

The GBR chairman was a law student and floor manager with McDonald's, and at the time the GBR was established he was a union member and had the support of the NGG union. A number of other works council representatives had already expressed concerns about his true loyalties during interviews in the summer of 1995. The NGG had specifically stipulated that in no circumstances should any EWC agreement be signed without their approval and the approval of other European unions. NGG officials state that not only was their advice deliberately ignored but also the chairman had effectively 'sold out' to the corporation. On 23 November 1995, 2 days after he had signed the EWC agreement, the GBR chairman left McDonald's employment with an *ex gratia* payment estimated to be around £30,000 (Langenhuisen, 1995; Royle, 1998). NGG officials were not entirely surprised by these events; one stated:

> A functioning GBR would have been unpleasant for McDonald's because it would have been able to look at the internal balance and wage payments of the firm.

The whole issue of works councils has been the focus of a long-running battle between the NGG and McDonald's Germany. The NGG had made several previous attempts to establish and then gain recognition from McDonald's for its GBR (Royle, 1998). When the NGG did finally establish a GBR, McDonald's either refused to recognise it or would not enter into meaningful negotiations with its representatives, sometimes refusing them information, delaying or refusing to arrange meetings and refusing payment to representatives for their time off for GBR activities (Royle, 1998).

However, it appears that when McDonald's needed an appropriate person to sign the EWC agreement it did, on this one occasion, recognise the GBR. The chairman was not the only individual to receive an *ex gratia* payment; in fact, forty-six other McDonald's employees, all supporters or members of German works councils, received payments. At a stroke, this removed eight key restaurant-level works councils and the GBR (Langenhuisen, 1995). The union is particularly concerned about this buy-out 'strategy', in which some individuals exploit their position and the corporation's willingness to pay for the 'removal' of works councils (Royle, 1998). The fact that the GBR was removed and its chairman left the company immediately after signing the agreement made no difference as far as the EWC 'agreement' was concerned. It was on the basis of this agreement that the EWC was founded.

Management respondents state that this agreement was put to all the appropriate employee representatives in each European country and was signed by them. However, despite several requests from individual European trade unions and by the ECF (the European organisation of the IUF – International Union of Food, Agricultural, Hotel, Restaurant, Catering,

Tobacco and Allied Workers' Associations), they have not received a copy of the document signed by all European employee representatives. Probably more significant is that the ECF's requests to take part in discussions regarding the establishment of the EWC were declined by McDonald's. Only the corporation seems to know who signed the original agreement on behalf of the European employees. In addition, despite the fact that a number of European trade unions do have trade union members in McDonald's restaurants, no trade union had been given the opportunity to take part in establishing the original agreement.

One further issue regarding the original EWC agreement is that of the selection of a 'representative agent'. As McDonald's is a US corporation, its central management is supposed to designate the management in a specific member state in which it operates to negotiate on its behalf. This also has the function of determining which national law is applicable in interpreting its agreement. If the company does not designate someone to negotiate the agreement on its behalf then the responsibility automatically falls to management where the largest number of people are employed. With the UK having opted out before 1997, Germany is the biggest market in the EU. The fact that the EWC agreement began with the signature of the German GBR chairman does suggest the involvement of the McDonald's German management. However, according to a UK manager with specific knowledge of EWC developments, the corporation made a conscious decision that they would not designate a representative agent to negotiate the agreement. How were the 'negotiations' carried out? The unions suggest that the answer to this is simple: there were no meaningful negotiations. We now turn to the issue of the election of representatives, but first we need to clarify who should be considered to be an 'employee' representative under the terms of the directive.

Who is an 'employee' representative?

In understanding the issue of employee representatives in the EWC, an important distinction needs to be drawn regarding the employee hierarchy at McDonald's. Employees in the restaurants can be split into two broad groups: the more senior full-time salaried managers and the generally (but not exclusively) part-time hourly paid employees. This structure is pretty much the same the world over, although in some European countries national and sectoral level collective agreements sometimes blur the distinction between hourly and monthly paid employees. Each restaurant usually has a restaurant manager and two or three assistant managers. These managers are salaried employees and can usually be relied upon to identify with the corporation's goals. Some enter this group either as trainees or they work their way up through promotion. The remainder of the restaurant employees are usually part-time and/or hourly paid workers, i.e. floor/shift managers, training squad/crew trainers and ordinary crew, who make up 95% of the total McDonald's workforce.

Part of the problem for the EWC directive is that the term 'employee' is not precisely defined in the directive; all it states (Section 1, Article 2) is that '"employee representatives" means the employee representatives provided for by national law and or practice'. If one takes the definition normally used in the member states (Gabaglio, 1998: 11), it is defined as:

> ...any working person dependent on their income who does not occupy a management position. A person with decision-making power over the budget and personnel is not an employee.

This definition would suggest that the McDonald's salaried managers, especially restaurant and assistant managers, who do have decision-making control over personnel and to some extent budgets should not be nominated as employee representatives. The majority of seventeen 'employee' representatives are still assistant restaurant managers or above. For example, the Irish employee representative was a salaried accounts manager. In fact, at the second meeting, only one 'employee' representative was a part-time or 'hourly paid' employee and this was the representative from France. It is perhaps no coincidence that McDonald's prefers to call 'employee' representatives 'country delegates'.

The second problem in deciding 'who is an employee' is complicated by the McDonald's use of franchise operations, joint ventures and holding companies. In legal terms, these operations are frequently deemed to be separate businesses. This means that the employees of franchise operations, holding companies and joint ventures cannot be bundled together with the rest of the McDonald's employees. In most cases, the EWC directive does not cover these employees. On average, over 65% of McDonald's European restaurants are operated as franchise restaurants. For example, in Italy, France and The Netherlands, 80%, 85% and 90% of restaurants are operated as franchises respectively. In Germany, 65% of restaurants are franchises, with another 25% or more operated as holding companies. Although franchises are legally separate companies, in practice they are tightly controlled by the corporation and franchisees enjoy very little freedom of decision-making (see Chapter 3; Royle, 1997). Indeed, such control appears to be an increasing feature of many large organisations with a variety of different structures (Prechel, 1994). Franchisees are unlikely to be operating in two EU countries and are unlikely to be large enough to meet the thresholds. In other words, the McDonald's EWC can only represent McDonald's employees actually employed in 'company-owned' restaurants. This means that the EWC does not represent the majority of European workers employed in McDonald's restaurants. In this sense, franchise employees are not 'employees' of the multinational as far as the directive is concerned. When asked who the 'employee' representatives were, one UK manager replied:

> There were all levels of employees representing the employees, we didn't have a standard selection method...it's not something we would want to

split down and say there was this, this, and this level, they were employee representatives who were duly selected from each country.

Can the McDonald's EWC really be seen to be 'representative' of the whole European workforce when, first, the majority of the McDonald's employees are excluded altogether from any part in the election process and, second, although salaried managers may well be 'employees' in one sense can they really represent the interests of the vast majority of hourly paid and/or part-time workers? This then leads on to our next question. How are 'employee' representatives actually elected in practice?

Electing the 'employee' representatives

One of the major concerns raised by the trade unions about the McDonald's EWC is the election of employee representatives. The original agreement seems to suggest that 'electing' representatives is a matter for the corporation. It states:

> The (EWC) shall consist of representatives of all the workers employed by McDonald's Corporation and its subsidiaries...it being understood that theses workers have a common interest in the success and future of the company. The appointment of representatives shall be governed by the various McDonald's **companies** in each country.

This kind of approach seemed to be confirmed by a UK manager, who stated:

> The European Human Resource Management group had to decide how we would get the (employee) representatives, because in some countries it was a more significant task than in others.

The subsidiary requirements of the directive state that:

> The EWC shall be composed of employees...elected or appointed from their number by the employees' representatives or, in the absence thereof, by the entire body of employees. The election or appointment of members...shall be carried out in accordance with national legislation and/or practice.

In countries where the legislation is weak, such as the UK and Ireland, then the directive is not very helpful. According to a UK manager, the Irish accounts manager was elected because at the time of his election in 1996 there were no non-management employees working for McDonald's company-owned restaurants in Ireland. The twenty-five or more McDonald's restaurants in Ireland at that time were franchise operations and so the 1,500 or more Irish hourly paid employees could neither be nominated nor take part in the EWC 'election'. The accounts manager put himself forward for nomination and was duly elected by a number of other managers.

Until December 1997, the EWC directive did not apply to UK employees. However, a UK manager stated that the existing agreement would simply be amended to include the UK representatives when the directive was extended to cover the UK. Rather than select their employee representatives as they had when they had the status of observers, there would be a kind of competition among the 'best employees'. UK employees would be informed of the EWC's agenda in the company newsletter and individuals would be asked to nominate themselves as candidates. Their nomination would require the votes of two hourly paid employees *and two salaried managers*. If too many employees applied, the employee and manager 'of the year' would help to decide who should be nominated. Nominees would then have their details published in the company newsletter and all employees in company-owned restaurants could vote. As the UK was likely to be allowed two employee representatives, management stated that they thought that at least one should be a salaried manager.

One might expect that in other countries with legislatively underpinned systems of works councils and other similar institutions that the workforces would be better organised and that trade unions would be involved in the process? Especially as such works councils usually have strong union representation in most European countries (Ramsay, 1997). However, this has not been the case. In the majority of European countries where McDonald's operates, the trade unions have been unable to get involved in the election process. By the time of the second meeting, only two of the fifteen employee representatives were union-supported representatives. These were the French representative, who is also the principal French union delegate (*délégué syndical*), and the principal Swedish union delegate. When asked whether any of the employee representatives were union representatives, a UK manager commented:

> There certainly were union representatives at the meeting, well I believe they were. But people didn't say, 'oh that person is a union member', that would not have been appropriate in that situation, and I don't think it is appropriate for me to know that. It wouldn't have made any difference to the meeting, it wouldn't have changed the way we did things.

In Italy, the three trade union confederations submitted written proposals to McDonald's not only for a company-level collective agreement but also to request specifically that the Italian EWC representative should be an elected union member from the McDonald's Italian works council (*coordinamento*). Despite the fact that some 20% of Italian McDonald's workers are union members, the unions never received a reply regarding this request. Most Italian workers have no idea who their representative is or how he/she was elected. The unions state that the representative is a non-union manager.

The same kind of story emerges from most of the other European countries. In addition to those in the UK, Ireland and Italy, the Austrian, Belgian, Danish, Dutch, Norwegian and Spanish unions all complained that they were not given an opportunity to get involved in the election process. It appears that in most cases only the corporation knows for sure how these other representatives were elected. However, the German unions knew exactly how the German EWC representative had been elected.

Electing the German EWC representative

In Germany, the company-level works council (Gesamtbetriebsrat – GBR) chairman or group-level (Konzernbetriebsrat – KBR) works council chairman normally takes a seat on the EWC. However, at the first meeting in September 1996, the German employee representative on the EWC was not even a plant-level works council chairman, nor was he supported by the trade union. By the time of the second meeting in 1997, a new company-level works council (GBR) had been established with the support of the trade union. Under normal circumstances, this new chairman would also be the EWC representative; however, his position had been 'usurped' in July 1997, 2 months before the second EWC meeting took place. This struggle was reported in *Der Spiegel* (1998) and the German national newspapers (for example, see Edmunts, 1998). There appeared to be two GBRs with two different chairmen claiming to represent the McDonald's German workers. NGG officials state that after years of trying to block or nullify the union-supported GBR the corporation allegedly decided to establish its 'own' GBR.

In July 1997, in what the NGG describes as a 'Putsch', representatives of twenty newly elected works councils, which were not supported by the union, effectively 'took over' the GBR meeting. These new works councils were all elected in company-owned restaurants; according to the NGG, they were led by a salaried assistant manager. With the support of the 'twenty', this manager had the majority of votes at the meeting. A motion was put forward to dissolve the existing union-supported GBR and its chairman and to elect a new GBR. Despite the protests of the other works council representatives, a vote was then held and the salaried manager was elected as the new chairman of the new GBR.

The NGG and the other works councillors took the case to the labour court in April 1998. McDonald's denied that it had tried to influence the election in favour of the salaried manager. However, the court argued that the re-election was a clear violation of the Works Constitution Act. *Der Spiegel* (1998: 140) states that the surprise deselection of the union-supported chairman was 'obviously planned'. The court also noted that McDonald's had been responsible for the separate travel and accommodation arrangements for the two separate groups of works councillors. The court made a settlement: the union-supported chairman could not be reinstated and both sides agreed before the court that the GBR elections would have to be reheld on 23 July

1998. This decision reflected the formal nature of the legislation on German works councils. The institution of the works council has to be seen to be totally democratic and must therefore allow all parties to take part in elections. In the few months before the new election, the corporation carried out a media blitz with a full-page spread of their candidate in a number of high-circulation magazines, e.g. *Stern*, *Focus*, *Brigitte*, *Impulse* and others. The salaried manager was pictured smiling and clasping a McDonald's 'M' to his chest together with the caption 'I am McDonald's' and there was a statement which suggested that as GBR chairman he would represent the interests of all the McDonald's workers.

NGG officials state that, in addition, the corporation sent individual letters to all employees eligible to vote in the July 1998 election and that these letters allegedly painted the union candidate in a negative light. The salaried manager candidate was relieved from his normal duties on full salary in order to work full time on the campaign and his 'works council' activities. McDonald's did not, however, relieve the union-supported candidate, an hourly paid employee, from his work duties. Although the McDonald's candidate was given a company car to conduct his campaigning, the union candidate allegedly even had trouble claiming his public transport travel expenses from McDonald's.

In the 2 weeks before the 1998 election, McDonald's transferred the ownership of three restaurants with union-supported works councils into McDonald's holding companies, the so-called Anver Restaurants. The effect was that the union-supported works council representatives in these restaurants were no longer able to take part in the GBR election. McDonald's stated that the restaurants had been 'sold' because they were not very profitable. Both union officials and works councillors in these restaurants dispute this. In terms of the GBR election, however, it meant that the union-supported candidate now had little chance of re-election.

The McDonald's candidate and another salaried manager won the second election and became the chairman and deputy of the new GBR. The original GBR chairman was relegated to a place on the finance committee (*Wirtschaftsausschuß*). The result also appears to legitimise the salaried manager's position as the EWC employee representative. However, most of the McDonald's German workforce could not take part in the election of their GBR/EWC employee representative. This is either because they were employed in Anver holding companies or franchise restaurants or simply because they did not have a works council in their company-owned restaurant. Although these kinds of employer tactics may raise eyebrows in mainland Europe, there is plenty of evidence to suggest that they are common practice in the USA (Friedman *et al.*, 1994; Towers, 1997).

EWC meetings and agendas

The first meeting took place on 9 September 1996; it lasted for a day and a half and was held in Vienna. It involved discussion times, formal presentations on 'best practice' and 'break-out sessions'. The latter involved 'employee' representatives being sent off into different rooms with 'facilitators' (McDonald's managers) to brainstorm issues such as the image of McDonald's as an employer, training and development, communications, career opportunities, food safety, McDonald's in the community and new products. It also included a strong social and informal element, beginning on the evening of 9 September, with as one manager put it:

> ...a warm-up session, a fairly light hearted type of social event...with the formal meeting all day Tuesday 10 September, ...there was a lot of informal communication going on because we built in some good leisure time, we went down-town to Vienna and we had a very nice dinner, so there was a lot of opportunity for people to chat and talk about what was happening in their countries.

The preamble in Appendix 1 of the original McDonald's EWC agreement suggests that the EWC is a means of communication for improving the business, not a mechanism for providing workers' rights. It states:

> ...it is vital for us to guarantee transnational communication in areas such as customer service, quality, training and teamwork... (the EWC) will concentrate on supra-national issues arising in these areas which may have significant implications for McDonald's restaurants in the European Union.

The original EWC agreement also suggests that it is the management that will make the decisions about the agenda for meetings. It states:

> The personnel department shall draw up the agenda for meetings. The topics to be discussed by the European Communications Group shall exclusively concern issues of general interest such as customer service, quality, people, training, teamwork, new working methods and new processes, respect for the environment, products, organisational structures, the performance of all the companies in Europe, the evolution of business within the EU and any major changes affecting companies in more than one member state.

This philosophy was also confirmed by a UK manager with specific involvement in the EWC, who commented:

> Each country operates McDonald's as an autonomous unit, but because we had to have this co-operation, we had to co-ordinate it. So European HR group have had, prior to the first EWC, two major meetings to organise and decide on topics, to decide who would be doing what, allocate

who would be responsible for the agenda...who would be doing presentations.

The second meeting: amending the agreement

At the second EWC meeting held on 11 and 12 September 1997 in the Hotel Princess Sofia, Barcelona, Spain, the McDonald's European Communications Group was renamed the 'European Communications Council'. This meeting was of considerable significance because management used it to amend the constitution of the original agreement. A management respondent stated that '...there was a need to introduce some more rules and procedures'. This may be because the original agreement would not bear too much scrutiny. The unions suggest that the original 'agreement' was not an agreement at all. Amending the agreement, adding some more precise rules and getting 'employee representatives' to sign it during a meeting would be a way to give it more legitimacy. The amendments themselves are of interest, but what is also interesting is the way in which the changes were introduced. The issue was treated as just another item on the agenda.

According to the minutes of the second meeting, it began with a welcome from a Spanish regional manager, then some very basic information on financial results and a few facts and figures on new restaurants. The meeting was then turned into a number of 'quality circles', with manager and employee representatives asked to provide solutions for better construction, environmental issues and operations. Later, the meeting was once more split into three groups, and management gave each group a topic for discussion. One theme was 'safety and security in the workplace', a second was 'employer opportunities' and a third was 'rules and regulations'.

Management had sent out copies of their proposed new rules to the representatives 2 weeks before the meeting. This was not a great deal of time for the employee representatives to organise a coherent strategy. Nevertheless, the French and Swedish union-supported representatives tried separately to amend these rules. They suggested that there be a limit of one management representative per country, that the employee representatives should have some say in determining the agenda of meetings and that only restaurant employees should be considered as 'employee representatives'. The first and second suggestions were accepted, and management proposed that the agenda setting be carried out among one employee representative, an elected Vice-Chairman and the Chairman. However, the third suggestion was rejected outright.

The human resources manager (HRM) for McDonald's France, who had led the 'rules' group, then called on all the delegates to vote to accept formally the new 'rules and regulations'. They also suggested that the delegates should elect the Vice-Chairman to sign the rules and regulations protocol on behalf of all the employee representatives. The meeting then adjourned for lunch. After lunch, the vote on 'rules and regulations' was taken. The Chairman proposed that the vote to accept the new rules should be carried out by a show of hands. The result was unanimous, with the fifteen 'employee' representatives and two UK observers all voting to accept. The protocol was signed by the Chairman on behalf of management and the French HRM then suggested that the employee representatives vote for their Vice-Chairperson and that a mandate should be given to him/her to sign the agreement on their behalf, once again by a show of hands. Again, there was a unanimous vote. Then there was the vote for the Vice-Chairperson, but this time the employee representatives were allowed a secret written vote. The Swedish employee representative was elected as Vice-Chairperson and it was to this individual that the whole responsibility of signing the new EWC agreement fell. The Swedish representative signed the agreement.

The Swedish representative had only recently been made the full-time union representative. Previously, she had been a student and had worked part-time as crew and then later as a part-time floor manager. The existing full-time union representative asked her if she would be interested in taking over the position. She decided to accept and moved into an office at McDonald's headquarters in Stockholm. She was released from her normal duties to work full time on union matters with responsibility for fifty restaurants around Stockholm, and she was promoted to the equivalent of an assistant restaurant manager. She had been advised by her union before the meeting not to sign any documentation without first consulting a union official. When she was asked why she had signed the document against the advice of her union, she stated:

> I didn't feel comfortable about not signing the agreement, it would have seemed like I wasn't acting in good faith and we did manage to get some improvements.

ECF officials found it difficult to understand why such an agreement had been signed because it looked as though it had ended all hopes of gaining a better agreement for the McDonald's European workers. This may suggest that employee representatives were under considerable pressure. A Swedish union official has also stated that there was some misunderstanding because their representative had signed the agreement only on behalf of Swedish employees. Nevertheless, this is not how McDonald's portrays the events. Acquiring a signature of a union-supported representative at the meeting appears to give the second agreement legitimacy. Both the French and Swedish unions seem to take a philosophical view of the EWC; although they state that it is not a good agreement, it is at least a starting point. Most of the other unions, and particularly the ECF, are not so sanguine. The Swedish representative admitted that she was not happy about the 'representativeness' of the 'employee' representatives and raised the issue with the EWC chairman. However, the response from the chairman was that although the chairman agreed that the EWC was unrepresentative it would be 'difficult' to change.

The amended agreement

The rules and procedures developed in the second EWC meeting do slightly improve the position on the employees' side. First, it states that there should be a maximum of one management representative for each country; in the first two meetings, there were a number of additional senior managers present. Second, as already mentioned, the agenda for future meetings should be prepared and agreed by the Chairman and the Vice-Chairman. However, the second agreement also stipulates that management approval is required for amendments to the agreement, admission of outside experts and any decision that may result in extra costs for McDonald's. In other words, management has complete authority on almost any major issue. As far as the dissemination of information is concerned, there appears to be no real change. This is also a significant issue because, as Marginson *et al.* (1998) suggest, feedback is vital; if the role and significance of the EWC is not clear to the entire workforce then its role becomes marginal and it is unlikely to have any influence. Employee representatives, in particular, need to be able to disseminate the outcomes of their work on the EWC. The first agreement states that:

> ...information concerning topics discussed at meetings shall be communicated to workers...using appropriate means of communication. The personnel department shall be responsible for this.

The second agreement makes no direct statement regarding dissemination of information to the workforce as a whole, but does state that:

> Confidential information may be given to ECC members...but that...any such information will be regarded as confidential when the Chairman declares it. It is then the responsibility of each member to...ensure it is not disclosed.

If representatives are unable to feed back information without management authority then it seems that there is no way that the role and actions of the McDonald's EWC can be disseminated to the McDonald's European employees in an objective manner. There may be occasional references to some kind of European communications body in McDonald's newsletters, but there is unlikely to be any critical evaluation of issues affecting worker's interests. Most of the part-time and hourly paid employees working in European restaurants in this study appear to have little idea that the EWC exists and even less idea of what it does, what it is supposed to be doing for them and who is representing them.

The third meeting

No further changes to the constitution of the agreement appear to have been made during the third meeting, which took place in September 1998. As usual, delegates were accommodated in a good hotel; this time it was the Athens Hilton. The topics on the agenda were information on the financial results of the corporation, an update on European development, the Euro, retention in a competitive environment, recruitment, improving McDonald's 'positive' image through the media, the environment, quality of service, improving the employee experience, McDonald's 'intranet', health and safety and examples of 'best practice' from each country. As usual, again, all representatives were asked to bring something gastronomically symbolic of their country as an 'excellent way to begin the cultural sharing process'.

However, there was one significant change from the second meeting. The Finnish representative had changed from a non-union representative to a union-supported representative. Now, the union-supported representatives have three seats on the EWC. For the first two meetings, just as in the majority of other European countries, McDonald's Finland had a non-union salaried manager as employee representative, arguably because the unions had been unable to get involved in the election process. By 1998, the Finnish Hotel and restaurant Workers Union (HRHL) had acquired some new trade union members and even a few 'shop stewards' in the McDonald's restaurants. Together with these new union representatives, the HRHL began to work out a plan to try to gain more effective influence in the company. The union contacted the health and safety authorities in order to make McDonald's comply with 'real' elections for health and safety representatives. According to the collective agreement in force, trade unions must be involved in the election of this representative. As a result, elections for health and safety representatives had to be held with the involvement of the trade unions.

Both McDonald's and the union campaigned in the election that took place in June 1998. McDonald's tried to allow salaried managers to vote in the election in the hope that this would sway the vote in favour of their non-union candidate. Eventually, the election took place and the union candidate was elected as national health and safety representative, and he also became the EWC representative. He was voted in very narrowly by a majority of just ten votes. One problem still remains, however, in that he can only represent the thirty or so McOpCo restaurants in Finland and not the majority of workers in the fifty-five franchise restaurants. In this situation, the national substructures were able to play a role in providing a platform for union involvement. However, with the relatively high levels of labour turnover associated with this kind of industry, the 'union' presence on the EWC is always going to be vulnerable.

Co-ordinating an employee-side strategy? Pre-meetings

An analysis of nearly 400 voluntary EWCs (Marginson *et al.*, 1998) states that 85% of EWCs have the right to hold preparatory meetings without management being present. Marginson *et al.* (1998) point out that such meetings can be most valuable for the side of the employees. In particular, they provide an opportunity for the employee members to achieve consensus or to work out a common strategy before meeting with management. The subsidiary requirements state that:

> Before any meeting with central management the European Works Council...shall be entitled to meet without the management concerned being present.

The amended McDonald's agreement merely states that any extraordinary meetings can only be called by joint agreement of the Chairman and Vice-Chairman, in other words such preparatory meetings must have management authorisation. This matter was also raised by the Swedish employee representative, but the response from management was that it would be 'too costly'. Hardly the kind of response that one might consider to be in keeping with the spirit of the directive. Gaining a regular pre-meeting would be an important achievement, but it would not solve all the employee representation problems. The French union-backed representative pointed out that, even if they did have a separate meeting of 'employee representatives', trying to develop a coherent strategy with employee representatives who were assistant managers or above would be a pointless exercise. Such representatives were much more likely to have their own careers and the organisation's goals in mind, not the rights of part-time and hourly paid workers.

Despite the extra support of a third union-supported representative and the changes in the agreement made at the second meeting, the 'three' employee representatives stated that they were unable to influence the content of the meeting or effect any changes, particularly because the meetings were already heavily 'structured' by management. There was also the continuing 'Babylon effect': the 'three' could not really communicate adequately without a translator provided by McDonald's management, although the Finnish and Swedish representatives could communicate to some extent in Swedish.

Inadequate sanctions?

There seems little doubt that the sanctions available to impose on companies who do not comply with the spirit of the directive are quite inadequate. In fact, the current proposals to provide European legislation on some form of national level of information and consultation imply a recognition of the deficiencies of the EWC directive in this regard (*EIRR*, 1997e). In practice, one needs to look no further than Renault's high-profile decision to close its Vilvoorde plant in Belgium. Renault was said to have blatantly ignored both the spirit and provisions of the EWC directive when it ignored the consultation rights of its 'European group committee', which had been established by voluntary agreement (*EIRR*, 1997b). Renault was fined approximately £1,600 by the French courts, which was not the kind of sanction likely to cause the company any serious reconsideration of its decision. Despite displaying a considerable degree of solidarity, the multinational workforce was unable to stop Renault from closing the plant. It was this high-profile case that led the European Trade Union Confederation (ETUC) to call for the EWC directive to be 'beefed up' (*EIRR*, 1997b, 1997d).

The EWC as an unrepresentative and ineffective 'talking shop'

As far as the corporation is concerned, the EWC appears to mean 'business as usual'. In this light, the EWC is just another institution to be captured for management; another method of 'getting the message across'. It is certainly not perceived as being about providing employees with rights. It is also clear that it is not the only American multinational that perhaps sees the EWC as an unwelcome interference, the EWC at PepsiCo being a case in point (Overell, 1996). Also, there have been a number of other EWCs in which companies have attempted to marginalise trade union representation, e.g. Marks and Spencer, BP, Unilever and Honda (LRD, 1995; Barnett, 1996). Schulten (1996) and Marginson *et al.* (1998) are of a similar view: EWCs are likely to fall into two categories. First, those where there is some form of independent co-operation on the employee side and the EWC is an *active institution*. The second is where the EWC is merely a formal *symbol* or *procedure*, in which there is little or no influence over management decisions. This latter kind of EWC is clearly evident in this study, and it appears to fall somewhat short of the 'best practice' envisaged in the subsidiary requirements.

There are several reasons for this view. First, the majority of employee representatives are not really 'employees' in the sense that one might have assumed was intended by the directive, but are actually salaried managers. As such, it is questionable whether they can really claim to represent the interests of the predominantly part-time and/or hourly paid employees who make up over 90% of the workforce. A key feature of US legislation is that the definitions of employee, supervisor and manager are clearly defined in the 1935 Wagner Act and1947 Taft Hartley ACt (Towers, 1997). Having said that, these definitions have given rise to legal actions and there is some fear that these distinctions are being diluted by changes in working practices, which may progressively undermine the rights of employees (Gould, 1994). Having said that, these definitions have given rise to legal actions, and there is some fear that these distinctions are being diluted by changes in working practices that may progressively undermine the rights of employees (Gould, 1994). However, the issue of defining precisely who the employee representative should be is only part of the problem: where election processes are not open and transparent to all employees and to anyone outside the company there is always the danger that management will be able to colonise the 'employee representatives' in the way in which they appear to have done here.

A second issue is that of pre-meetings for employees. McDonald's has effectively disallowed them; in their 'agreement', such pre-meetings require the consent of management and have so far been ruled out on the grounds of 'cost'. Without such meetings, how are the employee representatives expected to develop a meaningful employee-side strategy? Third, despite the supposed joint agenda setting, in practice the structure and organisation of meetings are strongly influenced by management. Fourth, there is the low or non-inclusion of trade union-backed members as employee representatives, and in some cases dubious election processes; of particular interest here is the extent to which McDonald's has been be able to take advantage of legal loopholes in national European labour legislation. Fifth, international sectoral trade union organisations have been kept out of the process, and outside 'experts' can only be brought in with the permission of management. A sixth issue is the ability of the employees' side to be able to feed back meaningful information on their EWC activities effectively to the majority of hourly paid and part-time employees.

Finally, there is the additional question of franchise operations and holding companies: something like 65% of McDonald's 200,000 European workers have no representation whatsoever. The franchise arrangement appears to be something that has not been adequately addressed in the directive's provisions. In theory, employees could challenge the agreement in the European labour courts, requesting a special negotiating body to be set up under Article 5. If the corporation refused, the case could then go to the courts, but is such a challenge likely to be mounted? The nature of industry and workforce characteristics (Royle, 1999c) suggests that a challenge is not very likely.

In accordance with Article 15 of the directive, in September 1999 member states and the social partners began a review of its operation. In accordance with this procedure, the ETUC set out a 'wish list' of items that it would like to see included in any amendment of the directive, for example reducing the employee thresholds and tighter definition of 'consultation' (see EIRR, 2000b). There is one brief mention of franchises under the issue of joint ventures, where they are referred to as 'contracts of domination'. The ETUC states that there is scope within the directive to address this issue. Much of the emphasis on the interpretation of the directive has centred on the definition of 'ownership'. However, the ETUC argues that this is too narrow and that the focus should be on the issue of the 'controlling undertaking', which is covered under Article 3.1 of the directive. The key issue in respect of franchises would be to prove in each case that one organisation had a 'dominant' influence over another, by virtue, for example, of ownership, financial participation or the rules which govern it. Part of the problem is that the law applicable in order to determine whether an undertaking is a 'controlling undertaking' has to be the law of the member state which governs that undertaking. Hence, the issue of non-EU multinationals choosing a representative agent becomes more critical.

At the time of writing, the EWC directive was still under review by the social partners. The only outcome of the review so far has been a report by the European Commission, published in April 2000. However, the report was rather limited and made no recommendations for any revision to the directive confining its comments to an analysis of national implementing measures and other practical problems. In fact, Portugal was very late in transposing the directive and so far it has only been partly transposed in Italy. Nevertheless, the Commission does raise the concept of 'controlling undertaking' as something requiring further clarification. A legal solution, however, may not get past the practical difficulties, and even if the necessary changes were made it could be that the unions would have to find employees willing to take their case to court separately for each franchise operator in turn.

Even if the issue of the franchise is addressed and a number of amendments favourable to employees are made, there remain a considerable number of practical problems for effective interest representation. The individual competence of employees to be able to deal with a powerful management group and the ability to develop a cohesive employee-side strategy are considerable obstacles. First, the frequent problem of a lack of education, knowledge and expertise and, second, a need for training in language and negotiating skills (Miller and Stirling, 1998). Finding individuals willing to commit themselves over the long term with the necessary maturity to be able to confront management in an effective manner at this level may be an added difficulty in the fast-food industry.

The aim of the EWC directive is to ensure that management consults and provides information to the workforce on a wide range of issues. Although it is not directly intended to provide collective bargaining at a European level, management perhaps fears that it will interfere with their decision-making process or that there may be some capacity to reinforce collective bargaining through improved intelligence of company operations and international labour networking. However, there is very little 'beef' in the directive as it stands at present. The substantive requirements of the directive are not very extensive and it is clear that the Article 13 arrangements provided are particularly weak. There seems little doubt that this voluntarist approach to regulation allows an exit for employers (Streeck and Vitols, 1995). Paradoxically, therefore, even if the directive is 'beefed up', it is still likely to remain a symbolic rather than a practical threat to managerial prerogative in many cases.

This analysis suggests that there is a good case for the EWC directive to be tightened up to make it more difficult to manipulate or evade. The only other alternative would be for national-level collective bargaining arrangements to be strengthened; however, the current economic climate, driven by economic liberalism, makes this rather unlikely at present.

9　Conclusion

Every age accepts the doctrines evolved to deal with a previous one and neglects the message most relevant to its own time.

(Samuel Brittan, 1972)

We began by suggesting that the activities of the McDonald's Corporation in Europe could be seen as a contest between two opposing forces – McDonald's, representing the driving force for economic liberalism, and the industrial relations systems of Europe, still based on collectivist aspirations. Has McDonald's been able to operate independently of the societal frameworks in most European countries and if so to what extent? How effective are national and supranational regulatory systems in protecting employment rights in practice? What are the implications for the more collectivist-orientated systems of national industrial relations in the mainland European states and for the wider issue of multinational regulation in the contemporary global economy? Before we can answer these questions, we provide a review the key findings presented in each chapter.

Reviewing the findings

In Chapter 2, we began with an examination of the way in which the McDonald's corporation was founded, the details of its expansion and some of the problems it encountered. The corporation has remained surprisingly faithful to the original system laid down by the McDonald brothers and then 'fine tuned' by Ray Kroc. This chapter also suggests that despite the early problems associated with international expansion the corporation found that it was better to stick to the original system and to avoid changes if at all possible. McDonald's appears to make a virtue of standardising not only its product range and its manufacturing processes, but also, by and large, its management practices, regardless of cultural differences across societies. Indeed, this is explicit in Love's (1995) official biography of the corporation. Love (1995) suggests that the standardisation of its management practices even extended to its management in Japan, which, as other authors have pointed out, is usually seen as having a very different approach to management from that found in the West (Morgan, 1986). Would a more thorough analysis of its management and employee relations in Europe also support this notion? McDonald's work, organisational and operational practices may seem similar from the view of an outside observer, but, as we suggested in Chapter 1, multinationals have to operate within a considerable variety of international contexts. On paper at least, mainland European industrial systems provide multinationals with considerable constraints in the management of their workforces.

Chapter 3 examined the implications of the widespread reliance of McDonald's on a system of franchise operations for its domestic and international expansion. How can McDonald's maintain the uniformity of its operations when it depends on so many 'independent' operators? In fact, the analysis suggests that the corporation retains very tight control over its franchise operations through careful recruitment, training and socialisation and through strict legal and financial controls. Advances in technology are increasingly allowing corporations to monitor data on unit labour costs, product sales and productivity (Marginson *et al.*, 1988). McDonald's is no different; franchisees are unable to conceal low performance. The corporation is currently installing new tills and other information technology that will allow the management at headquarters to receive full details on every item sold in every restaurant instantaneously (*Financial Times*, 1999b). Senior management can 'punish' or reward franchisees by cancelling their licence or allowing or disallowing additional restaurants in a similar way to which other multinationals might reward or punish production sites by allowing or withdrawing investment (Marginson and Sisson, 1994). Franchisees must be highly committed and operate exactly in accordance with the corporation's policy. Rather than being fully independent and autonomous operators, we argue that they are *de facto* subsidiaries of the corporation. In other words, the separation between McDonald's and its franchise is a legal rather than an economic distinction. Franchises provide McDonald's with capital, they share risks and provide local knowledge of markets and social institutional arrangements. In fact, the study suggests that franchise operators are also particularly good at keeping labour costs down and removing wastage. Franchises and the small unit nature of the restaurants allow for close monitoring of all aspects of the business. McDonald's receives a percentage of the franchisee's profits and also leases the restaurant to the franchisee. Providing that the franchisee does not damage the brand through bad publicity, McDonald's can directly benefit from franchisees who go beyond the corporation's own 'limits' in terms of labour cost savings. McDonald's is therefore able to maintain very tight controls over the uniformity of the standards and procedures of its operations across different societal cultures *because of*, as much as in spite of, its high percentage of franchise operations. It is probably no coincidence that Marginson and Sisson (1994) suggest that forms of strategic control over formally independent organisations, such as franchising, is increasing.

Chapter 4 examined the organisation and the nature of the work in the restaurants, the employment relationship and the characteristics of the workforce in different countries. The detailed study of the German and UK operations and additional evidence from other European countries suggests that virtually the same kind of restaurant hierarchy and organisation is in use in every country. Although there appeared to be some differences in the numbers of workers employed in restaurants in different countries and differences also in labour turnover, this could be explained by a broadly similar employment 'strategy'.

In most European countries, as in the USA and elsewhere, the average age of the McDonald's workforce is young. In the UK, for example, approximately two-thirds of the workforce are under 21. However, in Italy, Germany and Austria, the average age of the workforce is much older. In Germany and Austria, very few under-18s are employed, largely because their employment is strictly regulated by national legislation. In addition, a large proportion of these workforces consists of foreign workers, particularly *Aussiedler* economic migrants from Eastern Europe. In Italy, the high levels of unemployment, especially in the south of the country, mean that older workers cannot find employment elsewhere. In the USA, where there has been a shortfall in youth workers as a result of lower unemployment, youth workers are being replaced by the old and the disabled.

The findings suggest that all of these workers have something in common; they are unlikely to resist or effectively oppose managerial control. In effect, McDonald's is able to take advantage of the weak and marginalised sectors of the labour market, what we have termed *recruited acquiescence*: in other words, young workers who lack the previous experience, maturity and confidence to challenge managerial authority and foreign workers who are very concerned about keeping their jobs. Furthermore, employees in all 'categories' may have no long-term interest in the company, in which case contesting management prerogative may simply 'not be worth the trouble'. Many of the foreign workers in Germany and Austria have a lot of previous work experience and come from a wide variety of backgrounds, and many have qualifications from their country of origin. However, these workers are effectively marginalised in the labour market and find it difficult to find other work elsewhere for several reasons: first, because of problems with language; second, because of problems with the recognition of their qualifications; third, because these labour markets are extremely competitive in terms of qualifications; and, fourth, because the number of foreign and other migrant workers in Germany and to some extent Austria is increasing and unemployment remains relatively high.

The work offered by McDonald's may have some positive elements, but workers are often choosing employment at McDonald's in the context of having few other attractive options. Almost regardless of what people think of the work itself, working at McDonald's could be said to offer advantages for some employees who want flexible hours and are engaged in other activities and responsibilities. For example, this would apply predominantly to students and those still at school and to second-income earners such as married women with or without children. Second, some students see working at McDonald's not only as providing some money but also as providing some useful work experience. For those marginalised in the labour market who have few chances of a job elsewhere, McDonald's offers much needed work.

However, the employees' dependence on McDonald's and/or their tendency to see their employment as a short-term strategy makes them vulnerable to management manipulation. Those with minimum interest simply leave if they do not like it, and this is clearly reflected in high labour turnover. In Germany, Austria, Finland and the south of Italy, in particular, labour turnover is much lower than in other countries where other job opportunities are simply not available. In the UK, several respondents noted the presence of 'coasters'. These include young employees or other workers who have little confidence in their own abilities, those who are uncertain about what to do with their lives and those with little experience of any other kind of work. McDonald's may be attractive for these kinds of workers. 'Coasters' may start off with no intention of staying long, but, as one respondent put it, they get 'sucked in'. Perhaps they are attracted by the combination of fairly secure employment, familiar 'family' surroundings created by a highly paternalistic approach to management and lots of employees of similar age or temperament. This may help to explain how the corporation sometimes retains individuals who could probably obtain better paid and more skilled work elsewhere. As Maguire (1986) puts it, it is 'recruiting as means of control'. As already suggested, however, whether this is a deliberate 'strategy' or something else is not clear (Mintzberg, 1994).

The employment relationship at McDonald's is managed by a complete spectrum of controls, from simple, direct and bureaucratic controls to the management of subjectivity. At one end of the spectrum, restaurant managers are disciplined to accept tough work schedules and must prove themselves 'up to the challenge' of punishing schedules. Long hours and loyalty are locked in, with young managers being persuaded not only to accept as the norm many hours of unpaid work but also to gain a perverse satisfaction from surviving these tough and uncompromising work routines. In addition, young managers who may or may not get similar 'opportunities' elsewhere in the labour market are romanced by offers of promotion and career development. At the other end of the spectrum, more direct methods are used to maintain control. In some cases, foreign workers in Germany are constantly on call and are totally dependent on McDonald's not only for their wages but also for their work permits and accommodation. However, this still leaves unanswered the question of how the corporation has managed to sustain the uniformity of its employee relations practices despite major differences across societal cultures.

Bartlett and Ghoshall (1989) suggest that companies try to 'socialise' workforces through careful recruitment, development and acculturation of key decision-makers. The international transfer of managers undoubtedly plays some role here and is something widely promoted by McDonald's. When operations are being established in a new country, senior management and franchisees are often trained in North America or at other centres where a 'hamburger university' is well established. Recruitment is likely to be a second method, which, once again, raises the issue of 'recruited acquiescence'. This issue is to some extent reflected in other studies. Winfield (1994), for example, argues that the selection techniques used in Japanese subsidiaries are aimed at creating a workforce which has low ego needs, a high tolerance of frustration, a deferential attitude towards the wishes of the leader and, in the case of Nissan, a lack of previous work experience. At the managerial level, senior and ex-senior McDonald's franchisees and managers displayed remarkably similar responses regarding the appropriate (no unions needed here) management style in a number of European countries. This tends to support the assertion by Evans and Lorange (1989) that globally orientated companies are able to take advantage of natural variation within populations to recruit local managers whose personalities match their own cultural values rather than being, for example, 'typically' German, Italian, Danish or British.

If direct controls are seen as adequate and appropriate for the majority of part-time and hourly paid workers, managers are also likely to face 'cultural' controls through the maintenance of corporate culture. A strong corporate culture is one which is uncontaminated by rival 'ends' or values to which the discretion of employees might be otherwise 'misdirected', such as trade union involvement (Willmott, 1993). Under the guise of giving more autonomy to the individual, Ouimet (1991) and Willmott (1993) suggest that sometimes corporate culture threatens to promote a new hypermodern neo-authoritarianism. Far from lifting or diluting control over management, corporate culture promotes its extension through the design of value systems and the management of the *symbolic and emotional* aspects of organisational membership. This would suggest that in addition to bureaucratic rules and hierarchies McDonald's promotes its own values and symbols in a way which systematises and legitimises a mode of control that seeks to shape and regulate the practical consciousness. While this is unlikely to be relevant for the hourly paid worker, it is extremely pertinent for restaurant management. New trainee managers who join the company have their own values and basic assumptions; these may pose a problem for the organisation if they are in conflict with the key assumptions of the corporation. Willmott (1993) suggests that individuals may only internalise the corporation's key assumptions if they feel that they are morally acceptable. However, whether they internalise such values or not may be irrelevant in practice and may be of less interest to senior managers (Anthony, 1994). What matters is that managers are seen to support the view that it is the norm to regularly work many hours of unpaid overtime and that it is preferable to operate without trade unions. In this sense, corporate culture can be seen to play a key role in maintaining uniformity of action in certain key areas.

Any management strategy that seeks to exploit labour power is likely to be contested in some way, even if only by manifesting itself in labour turnover or in some form of discontent. However, whatever residual discontent that exists other than through labour turnover has few outlets for organised resistance at McDonald's. Even when employees have been able to organise themselves and have been able to draw on the power resources in the legislation supporting unions and worker representation (as Chapters 5 and 6 indicated), it is still an uphill struggle.

For example, in Chapter 5, we examined the issue of union organisation and the impact that the national collective bargaining frameworks have had on the corporation's operations in Europe. We began by examining McDonald's non-union legacy from North America and briefly provided some examples from other countries around the world such as Russia, Australia, Mexico and Lithuania. We then turned to the main focus of the book, i.e. the countries of Western Europe. In general, we argued that the non-union legacy of McDonald's is still very much intact. With the exception of Sweden, McDonald's has been in conflict with trade unions and national legislative arrangements to some degree or other in every European country in this study. Although relations may have improved in some countries over time, McDonald's is still trying to impose its American-based system, only making adaptations to host country systems where this is absolutely unavoidable.

In The Netherlands, for example, relations with the unions improved in the mid-1980s, some 10 years after its operations began. In Austria, relations improved in 1994, some 17 years after it began operations there. In most other European countries, a relationship between the unions and McDonald's simply either does not exist or is antagonistic. Sweden is the only European country in which McDonald's appears to have enjoyed positive relations with the unions from the beginning. However, this may be the result of the extremely hostile reaction of wider Swedish society when McDonald's first entered the market, which manifested itself in physical attacks on the restaurant. Although the Swedish entrepreneur who opened the first restaurants there in 1973 was a big fan of American business methods, he quickly came to the conclusion that to confront the Swedish unions would be extremely damaging for the corporation. McDonald's did not attempt to open restaurants in another Scandinavian country for nearly 10 years. When it finally did try again, in Denmark, it began by trying to impose its American-style practices of employment relations and immediately ran into all sorts of problems. After 10 years of conflict, which eventually culminated in strikes, boycotts, union sympathy actions in other sectors and in Finland and the threat of further support from the Swedish unions, McDonald's finally agreed to negotiate a collective agreement. However, relations are still antagonistic in Denmark, and a similar pattern emerges elsewhere. In Germany, it was 15 years before McDonald's would negotiate collective agreements and relations have not improved significantly. In recent years McDonald's has threatened to pull out of agreements and tried to push through changes which undermine existing agreements. In France, McDonald's appeared to be adopting a more union-friendly approach when after 15 years of conflict it agreed to sign a union recognition agreement. However, this agreement appears to have been little more than a clever public relations exercise. It has not had much impact as it only applies to 10% or so of McDonald's French restaurants. In addition, there are continuing problems with the infringement of collective agreements.

The kinds of conflicts that have erupted in each country may reflect in part the type of industrial relations systems that have been encountered. In a number of countries, sectoral collective bargaining agreements automatically apply to companies when they start up business. However, the 'stringency' of these collective bargaining arrangements varies considerably from one country to another. Some are highly intrusive, stipulating basic pay, general conditions of work and the rights of works councils and/or union delegates. In others, for example Spain, they specifically exempt pay and detail only limited aspects of working conditions and other issues such as training and education (although there is a statutory minimum wage in Spain). It is worth noting once more that, despite 16 years of operation in Spain, the Spanish unions have been unable to gain recognition or to develop any kind of relationship with McDonald's.

The more positive relations in The Netherlands may be the result of the all-encompassing nature of the sectoral agreements that automatically apply to all businesses. However, as Visser (1998b) argues, Dutch unions have typically been organised at industry level in a way in which union activity at plant (restaurant) level is neglected, leading to a power balance in favour of employers. This argument is also supported by the fact that works councils and union delegates, who would normally ensure that such collective agreements were correctly applied, are virtually non-existent in the McDonald's Dutch restaurants. A very similar situation is evident in Austria; although the unions have been allowed to enter restaurants and recruit union members since 1994, there are no works councils. Where unions have been strongly supporting the rights of workers to establish works councils and union delegates, for example in Germany and Italy, considerable additional conflict has occurred.

This perhaps suggests that in The Netherlands, Sweden and Austria the unions are generally satisfied with what has been achieved in collective agreements and are less interested in supporting the establishment of union delegates, works councils and supervisory boards. Unions may consider that trying to promote worker representation would require too many resources in what is admittedly a difficult environment. Of course, for various reasons, union attitudes towards worker representation have at times been somewhat ambiguous in a number of countries. While not wanting to underestimate the considerable number of practical difficulties in establishing works councils and union representatives (which were only too evident in Chapter 6), the lack of such institutions in some countries may be partly a reflection of union ambivalence. Ironically, as we argued in the final sections of Chapter 5, without adequate worker representation at plant level trade union efforts may be undermined, increasing the likelihood that the employer may not comply with agreements and vital aspects of health and safety.

The reconceptualisation of mobilisation theory put forward by Kelly (1998) also helps us to clarify some of these issues. It seems likely that worker representation mechanisms will often be the focus for transforming perceived injustices into a collective definition of interests and possibly collective action. In addition, such institutions often bring unions into the workplace, further encouraging collective interest definition. Although an increase in union membership itself does not necessarily provide a mechanism for collective action in the workplace, worker representation mechanisms may increase workers' awareness of the rights established under collective agreements and provide a more active mechanism for the definition and mobilisation of collective interests. It is not difficult to argue, therefore, that it is this issue which has created a good deal of the recent conflict in the McDonald's European operations.

In Chapter 6, it was argued that the corporation's own interpretation of worker 'participation' could at best be described as a paternalistic consultation regime that offers workers very little effective influence over decisions that affect them. In most cases, this is because the McDonald's system leaves little room for other voices because decisions have already been made. When there is no legislation in place to establish information, consultation or co-determination, other than through collective bargaining, as in the USA, Canada, the UK and Ireland for example, then 'McParticipation' is the order of the day. Theoretically, McDonald's should face a quite different situation in most mainland European countries. These countries provide workers and unions with specific rights to worker representation, which on paper at least cannot be ignored and which directly contradict the corporation's normal mode of operation. However, in practice, what we find is that McDonald's has been able to take advantage of weaknesses in national legislation, which in most cases have either eradicated or interfered with the establishment of such democratic mechanisms.

In addition to works councils, several countries also provide statutory worker representation at board level on some form of supervisory board. In Germany, for example, two pieces of legislation provide two different models of board-level representation, depending on the size of the company. However, a legislative loophole has allowed McDonald's to avoid the imposition of a supervisory board in Germany. In other European countries, the establishment of worker representation on a supervisory board often requires the establishment of a works councils. If there are no works councils established then it is either impossible or very difficult to establish a supervisory board. Although worker representation on a supervisory board would in theory have been, possible in most of the McDonald's European operations none has been established in practice.

However, works councils have proved more troublesome. It appears that

McDonald's has had to resort to a range of sophisticated tactics to hinder the establishment of works councils, most of which have been successful. Trade unions have been struggling to establish any significant numbers of works councils in the restaurants or to establish higher level works council structures in McDonald's national organisations. In France, McDonald's appeared to soften in 1996 when it agreed to the establishment of works councils. However, in practice, the few works councils that have been established since that time are very small in number and only represent a few of the 10% of company-operated restaurants and not the vast majority of franchise operations. In addition, attempts to establish an effective company-level works council have so far failed. At the time of writing, the trade unions have only been able to establish and retain about forty works councils in over 1,000 restaurants in Germany. The unions' repeated attempts to increase the small number of works councils in the restaurants have been met by an amazing level of hostility. In practice, it appears that McDonald's has become particularly adept at finding weaknesses in German legislation that will allow it to avoid works councils. Indeed, there is some evidence that a number of MNCs have also developed a number of 'avoidance strategies' (Royle, 1998). Works councils have been the focus of an enormous amount of conflict between McDonald's and the unions for the best part of the last 30 years in Germany, and this conflict looks set to continue. Where works councils have been established in Spain, they have been captured by management, and, in stark contrast to Spanish norms, the unions have been unable to get involved in the process. In Italy, the unions have been able to establish some 100 works councils in the 220 or so McDonald's restaurants, but they have been unable to influence management at senior level because management has so far refused to conduct any meaningful negotiations with the union and workplace union representatives. In other countries, it has simply been impossible to establish works councils or union delegates because of a combination of employer hostility and employee disinterest and/or various legislative loopholes. The combination of franchise operations, joint ventures and holding companies that operate the McDonald's restaurants in several European countries has also thwarted and/or complicated attempts to establish company-level or group-level works councils to represent workers at senior management level. Franchises also play a significant role in opposing the establishment of works councils at restaurant level and McDonald's is able to use the law to separate itself from its franchises and disclaim any responsibility.

In Chapter 7, we examined the practical outcomes of collective agreements and compared the pay and conditions of McDonald's workers in different European countries. We pointed out that in its original format the McDonald's system of pay determination is grounded on basic pay with possible rises for good performance. However, we also pointed out that in practice few workers would receive significant pay increases through this system. We therefore focused on the issue of basic starting pay and provided an analysis of the basic starting pay in the USA and thirteen European countries. This analysis suggested that in most cases where collective agreements have been either imposed or established McDonald's workers have generally benefited from improvements in pay. However, there appear to be considerable variations in the level of improvement in different European countries. The purchasing power of the McDonald's wage levels in countries such as Denmark, Norway, The Netherlands and Sweden is much higher than that in the UK and the USA. The chapter also compared McDonald's wages and the average wage in each country. In the case of the USA, the disparity between the average wage and the McDonald's US wage in some states is particularly stark. However, the analysis also suggests that pay levels are determined by differences in the tightness of the labour markets, e.g. basic pay levels are very low in Germany, Austria and Finland despite the improvements brought about by collective agreements. Indeed, the initial improvements brought about by the early German collective agreements appear to have been steadily undermined in recent years. The high levels of youth unemployment in Finland and the employment of large numbers of foreign workers in German and Austrian McDonald's restaurants help to account for this. The comparison of top executives' pay with that of ordinary restaurant workers merely emphasised the very low levels of wages paid to workers at McDonald's. The chapter also provided an analysis of some of the broader terms and conditions of work, including agreements on such things as overtime payments, additional rates for unsociable hours, notice for dismissal and holiday and special leave entitlements where these apply. It is in this area in particular that mainland European workers fare much better than their counterparts in Ireland, the UK and the USA, precisely because industry trade unions have been unable to gain union recognition and because sectoral level collective agreements do not apply in these three countries. Overall, mainland European McDonald's workers have benefited from stronger collective bargaining arrangements. However, even here, there are still considerable problems with ensuring that the employer correctly adheres to agreements; this is particularly marked where franchise operations are involved. As we have already suggested, this underlines the importance of establishing union representatives or works councils in the restaurants not only in terms of monitoring pay and conditions but also in terms of health and safety issues.

In Chapter 8, we examined the effectiveness of one piece of European legislation, i.e. that of the European Works Council (EWC) directive. The McDonald's 'European Communications Group' highlights some of the inherent weaknesses in much of the menu-driven European social legislation of this kind. First, it showed that large numbers of Euro-companies such as McDonald's had taken the opportunity to set up a voluntary agreement which would give them much greater freedom in determining the form and purpose of their EWCs. Consequently, even the limited participation rights envisaged in the directive have been effectively bypassed. Both the manner in which the McDonald's EWC was established and the way in which it operates is clouded by controversy and could hardly be said to be adhering to the spirit of the directive. Now that it is up and running, it appears to be little more than a talking shop for a managerially sponsored agenda. For example, management has effectively banned employee pre-meetings and dominates the agenda of meetings. In a rather dubious manner, management has woven a web of obscurity around the election processes for employee representatives and has kept both national and the European trade union organisations out of the process in all but three of the fifteen countries represented. Furthermore, the vast majority (some 65%) of McDonald's workers employed in franchise operations are not covered by the directive whatsoever and have no representation in the EWC. In a number of other cases where multinationals are not really meeting the spirit of the directive, there have been calls to have the directive beefed up. The issue of franchising has been raised by the ETUC under the current review of the directive by the social partners. The ETUC has argued that the focus should be on the issue of the 'controlling undertaking' not 'ownership'. However, even if the ETUC can improve the legislation, there are still considerable practical problems in trying to include franchise employees in the scope of the directive.

Like any other legislation, the way in which EU social policy legislation finally makes its way onto the statute book tends to be a long and tortuous process fraught with difficulty. Both employers and their associations have, for example, continually and often successfully lobbied national governments and the European Commission to dilute proposed labour legislation and arguably to promote the cause of economic liberalism. Furthermore, under the guise of job creation and 'social responsibility', McDonald's has been actively lobbying national governments around the world to allow it to become involved in various aspects of national education programmes. With this in mind, the next section examines the way in which McDonald's carries out such lobbying activity in practice and provides some examples of the outcomes to date.

Promoting the cause of economic liberalism?

Multinationals lobby national and supranational bodies not only as individual corporations but also in co-operation with others. In 1995, McDonald's was influential in establishing a European-level federation for the fast-food industry, the European Modern Restaurant Association (EMRA). EMRA's main aim is to lobby the European Commission and to monitor the impact of proposed EU legislation. EMRA does not have a permanent office, but its spokesperson can be contacted at the same telephone number as the McDonald's head office in Brussels. 'Euro-groups' of this kind are intended to allow member corporations to lobby EU bodies more effectively (McLaughlin and Greenwood, 1995). Indeed, one of EMRA's most important duties is to monitor potential developments in EU social policy and provide a platform on which to express its concerns. However, major multinational corporations continue to be extremely powerful as independent entities. As McLaughlin *et al.* (1993: 200) suggest:

> ...where the (European) Commission is sceptical of a (Euro) group view, it will often test that position by seeking the opinions of individual companies.

It has also been suggested that in the EU business interests are in a much better position than other social partners to lobby effectively because they have the financial resources to locate individuals and documents (McLaughlin and Greenwood, 1995). These trends have also been strongly identified in research carried out on the activities of large corporations in the USA (Wilson, 1990). Establishing the German fast-food employers' federation (BdS) and finally taking the presidency of the French fast-food employers' association (SNARR) may also represent McDonald's increasing ability to lobby national governments and their agencies. McDonald's arguably has a long history in lobbying the political process. Ray Kroc got McDonald's into a lot of serious controversy with his personal contribution of $250,000 to the 1972 campaign to re-elect Richard Nixon. The ensuing Watergate scandal and negative publicity suggested that Kroc's donation may have been connected to an attempt to prevent an increase in the minimum wage, which, as Love admits, '... covers a small army of young workers at McDonald's restaurants'. Love (1995: 357) also states:

> McDonald's franchisees were amongst hundreds of business people lobbying against an increase, as well as for a law exempting part-time students from the minimum wage. The controversial student exemption legislation proposal was quickly dubbed 'the McDonald's Bill'.

The US Congress eventually passed a limited exemption which has undoubtedly had a negative effect on the wages of young McDonald's workers in the USA. Although it is not yet clear whether or to what extent McDonald's lobbying activities have had an impact on European- or national-level labour legislation, it certainly has had considerable success in influencing the shape of national education systems. For example, the annual report of the IUF (1998) states that in the state of Victoria in Australia McDonald's has succeeded in getting the secondary education authorities to agree to a vocational programme preparing students for the food retail trades, in spite of opposition by trade unions and other interest groups. McDonald's determines the content of the programmes, selects participants who are its own employees and uses McDonald's staff members as instructors. This could well be seen as unwarranted interference in national education systems as McDonald's is not in business to provide individuals with an education who might ultimately question its own corporate values.

During the first round of interviews conducted in 1994, the McDonald's

German personnel director made it clear that one of the company's long-term aims was to have its training recognised within the national German vocational training system. He stated that for several years this had met strong resistance from educational bodies and the trade unions. At that time, union officials said that McDonald's would never get recognition for their training from the authorities because there were simply not enough recognisable skills in the jobs at McDonald's to qualify as a German national apprenticeship, which is held in high regard. However, this underestimated the corporation's determination and lobbying power. By 1998, McDonald's finally succeeded in having its apprenticeship scheme recognised as part of the national vocational and training system. The new apprenticeship is called *Fachmann* (or *Fachfrau*) *für Systemgastronomie*. The result is that McDonald's can now employ some young workers on a lower apprenticeship wage and can claim to be part of the highly respected German vocational education system. The corporation has also been trying to persuade national authorities in a number of other countries to accept its training in a similar manner. It has not yet succeeded in every country, but like a Schwarzenegger-style 'Terminator' it absolutely will not stop until it gets its way. This kind of MNC lobbying activity is symptomatic of broader global processes which are increasingly challenging the political economy of both national and regional trading blocs, something we now consider in more detail.

Economic liberalism, European industrial relations and convergence

Europe is facing considerable pressure to reduce its regulation and labour costs. The rise of new international competitors and the availability of a large pool of relatively skilled and very cheap labour in countries such as Poland, Hungary and the Czech Republic arguably weaken the position of unions and employees in the West. Since the post-war period, most European countries have competed on quality rather than on low costs; this is particularly notable in Germany, which still has some of the highest labour costs in Europe. However, Ferner and Hyman (1998) suggest that competing on 'quality' alone is no longer an alternative; success will depend on the ability to combine quality with lower costs. Despite being highly regulated, Germany is often put forward as one of the most adaptable industrial relations systems in the European economy. However, mounting demands from German employers for more flexibility, the pressures of increasing global competition, German re-unification and economic policy adaptations to meet the criteria for European Monetary Union have led some commentators to suggest that the German model can no longer cope (*The Economist*, 1996b; Sauga *et al.*, 1996). The liberal economic climate is increasingly putting pressure on European companies and countries to become more 'Anglo-Saxon' and to do away with 'burdensome' regulation (Streeck, 1997; Hassel and Schulten, 1998; Flecker and Schulten, 1999; Morgan, 1999). The furore created over the hostile bid by Vodaphone for the German engineering company Mannesmann is a case in point. When Tony Blair came out in support of the takeover, he was, in effect, supporting economic liberalism. Matthew Taylor – head of one of the Blairite think-tanks, the Institute for Public Policy Research – stated that (Morgan, 1999: 4):

> ...the Prime Minister was espousing the wrong kind of capitalism...Blair's support for Vodaphone would have been more palatable had he not come across as saying 'let's go for productivity and efficiency and to hell with the social consequences'.

Hyman (1994) suggests that it is the differences in the robustness and adaptability of differing industrial relations systems that have had different consequences in different countries. Assessing the impact of the above-mentioned pressures on different industrial relations systems is difficult, not least because a term such as 'flexibility', for example, has been interpreted in different ways in different countries. Nevertheless, referring to Streeck (1992), Hyman (1994) suggests that throughout Europe the same general scenarios are emerging. Existing regulatory regimes forged in an earlier period of inter- and intraclass compromises, when nation-states still enjoyed considerable political capacities, are increasingly being exhausted by the pressures of international finance and multinational firms. Whether a nation-state's regulatory regime is broken down very quickly or is gradually worn down only depends on that system's underlying strength or weakness. As Hyman (1994: 10) puts it:

> The completion of the single European market, sweeping away many institutional restraints on the impact of transnational economic forces further undermines the capacity of nation-states to pursue autarchic policies. No national industrial relations system has escaped the operation of these forces.

Hyman's argument may be unnecessarily pessimistic, but the current indicators suggest that any substantial defence of collectivist principles is not yet on the agenda. The aspirations of more left-wing-orientated commentators in the UK have undoubtedly been disappointed by much of New Labour's policy to date. The 1999 Employment Relations Act, for example, may be more important symbolically rather than in terms of having a significant impact on the slide towards economic liberalism. Indeed, there is a strong sense that the liberal economic orthodoxy is limiting UK government policy. The new Act may lead to as many cases of union derecognition as recognition, and as far as the fast-food industry is concerned it is unlikely to have much impact in the UK. In addition, the current government seems to take the view that by bringing 'business' into more and more aspects of social life it will somehow make government more effective.

One need not look much further than the railways, air traffic control and the overhaul of the civil service for examples of this.

On a European level, Teague (1993: 175) is also rather pessimistic and sees the most likely outcome for employee relations as being increasingly decentralised, reflecting experience in the USA. He suggests that under a decentralised labour market system enterprises will be more or less free to choose employee relations' policies without interference from external labour market institutions. For collective regulation to remain viable under these circumstances, Hyman (1994) suggests that it must become international in application. However, as already suggested, international codes of conduct are unlikely to develop into anything stronger in the current climate, and, as Teague points out, European-level legislation is unlikely to fill this gap adequately (Teague, 1993: 170):

> ...while...EC Social policy...will probably make heavy intrusions into areas such as health and safety and perhaps equal opportunities, its presence in areas like arbitration and reconciliation systems will be virtually non-existent.

This conclusion is also reflected in the suggestion by Streeck (1991) that economic liberalism constrains the available options. In other words, we are likely to see an incremental erosion of socially regulated employment regimes, weakened by the creeping intrusion of more voluntary and flexible industrial relations regimes. Streeck (1992) suggests that, being less mobile, the only way in which both governments and labour can respond to regime competition is by offering capital or other inducements not to emigrate. These inducements are likely to include promises of no extra regulation in labour markets, which may include assurances of friendly, i.e. less demanding, behaviour. Streeck and Vitols (1995) also emphasise this point when they state that EU law remains weak, with a preference for 'soft' rather than 'hard' law and 'private' rather than 'public' order. This is something clearly evident in our analysis of the McDonald's EWC in Chapter 8.

In broader theoretical terms, the analysis presented in this book therefore raises questions about the importance of national systems in regulating employment relations. Both Locke (1995) and Marginson and Sisson (1994, 1998) suggest that multinationals may increasingly begin to question their involvement in national systems of industrial relations and may develop their own organisation-based employment systems. In similar ways they suggest that countries where multinationals operate are becoming less distinct in terms of their employment practices. This is because there are considerable pressures for multinationals to standardise their human resources management procedures internationally in order to maintain internal consistency and to transmit 'best practice' to all their subsidiaries. They also make the point that there is considerable diversity within national systems. Indeed, the findings presented here suggest that, although national and EU regulation still have an impact on employment regulation in the fast-food industry, the full impact of such systems is being mediated and undermined by the strategic imperative of powerful company-based employment practices. This suggests an increasing divergence within national systems but an increasing convergence across national borders, driven by leading multinationals which set the agenda for certain sectors.[1]

This suggests that one should not rely too heavily on the 'divergence', 'societal effect' and 'national business systems' explanations of the sort put forward, for example, by Whitley (1991) and Whitley and Kristensen (1996). This is not to suggest that societal effects are not important, but this analysis does highlight the limitations of this approach.

The unequal struggle?: collectivism versus the 'McRegulation' of society

We began by suggesting that McDonald's experiences in Europe are representative of a struggle between the forces of economic liberalism, as represented by a major multinational with a seemingly global presence on the one hand and a more collectivist agenda associated with the labour legislation governing industrial relations in the European context on the other hand. To date, the orthodoxy of economic liberalism appears to be hegemonic in creating an international business environment in which multinationals are allowed to roam the globe in search of bigger profits, inadequately 'fettered' by existing regulation. This study suggests that even national and supranational European arrangements are insufficient in terms of protecting existing employment rights. In the context of an increasing globalisation of capital flows and the growing influence of bodies such as the WTO, multinationals probably have greater power and influence in the world economy than at any time in the past. As suggested in Chapter 1, attempting to regulate multinationals through voluntary codes of conduct is unlikely to prove effective in practice. However, other than national legislation and some arguably weak initiatives from the EU, there appears to be little else at present.

Most recently, there has been considerable debate in both Europe and the USA about the extent to which the WTO should be responsible for addressing issues of workers' rights and labour conditions. Although this study has focused on Europe, those most vulnerable to labour abuses may not be in the developed Western countries at all, nor do the negative effects of unregulated global trade only affect workers directly employed by multinational corporations. The IUF recently reported that a Hong Kong company, Keyhinge Industrial Co., supplying McDonald's with the 'Disney' toys that it gives away in its 'happymeals', was employing workers in appalling conditions and paying extremely low wages. In February 1997, the IUF reported that twenty-five workers at the Hong Kong factory collapsed and three were hospitalised as a result of acetone poisoning. A week after this incident occurred, Keyhinge management illegally fired 200 workers at the factory. McDonald's is said to have investigated the factory and declared that problems were resolved. However, the IUF reported that only a week after this statement seven more workers were hospitalised after exposure to the hazardous chemicals acetone and toluene. The Hong Kong supplier also has factories that make toys for McDonald's in China and Vietnam. The IUF states that in these countries conditions are even worse: workers are treated like bonded labour and are expected to work 15-hour days and 7-day weeks in dangerous conditions. Indeed, in January 1992, twenty-three Chinese workers at the Chi Wah (Keyhinge) toy factory were hospitalised and three later died because of acute benzene poisoning.

Other than trying to gain publicity for these events, the international unions appear to be powerless to stop these kinds of activities. It is hardly surprising that Western companies find it difficult to compete on prices when new competitors adopt these kind of employment practices. It also highlights the way in which multinationals can avail themselves of lowest cost labour, yet at the same time distance themselves from the way in which their supplies are produced. Those who argue that the WTO should promote a set of core labour standards to which all member countries would have to adhere often meet resistance from developing country governments, which argue that such measures would make them less competitive by increasing their cost of labour. However, constructive efforts to mitigate the negative consequences of a global economy regulated only by the market logic of liberal economic orthodoxy must recognise that poorer countries are trapped in a dangerous 'race to the bottom' in terms of attracting foreign investment from companies seeking an environment that offers low labour costs and minimal regulation.

This book has suggested that such pressures may also be operating even in Western Europe. Although the worst excesses of the market have, by and large, been minimised by legislation, the struggle to protect employment rights continues. McDonald's has been able to use its power to take advantage of weaknesses in national- and regional-level (European) regulation. Beyond its ability to invade the lives of large swathes of the world population through its increasing spending on advertising, it is also active in shaping national education systems for its own needs, despite considerable opposition from educational bodies and trade unions. We have also seen how, by taking the leadership of or establishing new employers' associations, McDonald's has been able to dominate or strongly influence collective bargaining agendas in some countries. In addition, the use of the franchise adds greatly to the inequality of the struggle. Franchises contribute significantly to McDonald's economic power, but at the same time conveniently 'absolve' McDonald's of any responsibility for the well-being of its employees in those restaurants, which constitute the majority of its operations. In this kind of contest, the trade unions cannot get anywhere near their opponent. The reach of McDonald's is so long that it can stay outside the ring by using its franchisees as a barrier to responsibility. Should the corporation actually be caught in the ring, the unions' hands are often tied through a combination of legal loopholes and the company's ability to simply buy off dissenting voices.

Of course, McDonald's represents a particular form of low-skilled and part-time work, but, as suggested by the growth in the wider service sector, it is this kind of work which is on the increase. It also presents unions with considerable problems because, unlike manufacturing industry, the new service industry employees have no tradition of union membership, may be less likely to define their interests collectively and are generally difficult to organise. Workers in high-skilled sectors are always likely to be in more demand and enjoy more protection from the worst excesses of the market. While it is argued here that the 'European model' is preferable when compared with that of the USA or most other countries, we do not suggest that it is beyond criticism. Despite more 'collectivist' approaches to labour market regulation, most European countries still share some of the contradictions found in the USA. In particular, European labour markets, just like those in the USA, depend on what Galbraith (1992) describes as the 'functional underclass', i.e. ethnic minorities who have often served as a kind of reserve army of unskilled, low wage and unorganised labour.

Nevertheless, despite these faults, Europe may be the last frontier on which the battle for decent labour standards can be defended. In nation-states such as Denmark, workers enjoy significant protection, and even mighty corporations such as McDonald's have had to give ground. Indeed, the irony is that in these countries McDonald's can still make profits in a system that treats workers in a reasonable fashion. Of course, it may be that because these countries are only small markets they have not felt the full weight of corporate disapproval. On the other hand, it could be that the powerful intervention of trade unions in these countries has forced McDonald's into more co-operative relations.

This point raises another issue of much concern to writers, such as Hutton (1996), who argue that above and beyond any moral democratic argument the European model has much to recommend it. Despite the 'considerable burdens' that 'collectivist' systems of industrial relations impose on employers in most mainland European countries (for example statutory works councils), Europe still has a fundamentally sound economy. Germany and France in particular have consistently enjoyed very high levels of productivity since the post-war period. Many of the detractors of the European model frequently make their claims on the basis of outdated liberal economic models, such as the OECD Labour Standards Index (see Chapter 1) and NAIRU.[2] NAIRU was developed at the end of the 1960s and has frequently played an important role in policy formation since that time. It has been used to calculate what is termed the 'structural rate of unemployment' and has often restricted the actions of governments in their use of demand management policies (Larsson, 1998). As Keegan (1999: 2) asks:

... is the old European economic model finished? Just ask Boeing of Seattle what it thinks of the way it is being outsold by European Airbus.

Indeed, research has shown that labour law, job security and workers' representation do not necessarily make labour markets work less effectively (Sadowski, 1995; Nickel, 1997; Commission on Co-determination, 1998; Larsson, 1998). Galbraith (1987) has long argued in his theory of 'social balance' that the classic economics framework was created at a time of mass poverty and was reborn in the 1970s, but it is a model that simply cannot deal with the richer and more complex society that exists today.

If Fukuyama (1992) was correct in his prophecy of *The End of History* then workers are likely to face a bleak future of continuing deregulation and the undermining of workers rights in a context of increasing social upheaval. Nevertheless, as both Karl Marx and Max Weber have wisely suggested to us in different ways, social life inevitably involves an element of contradiction and paradox because unexpected outcomes will often arise from our actions. The inherent instability of the capitalist system could lead to even more undesirable, and therefore potentially radical, destabilising outcomes than those suggested in this book. Just a few weeks into the new millennium, the champion of economic liberalism, the USA, achieved yet another startling statistic: although the US population represents less than 5% of the world's total, it has 25% of the world's prison population now sitting in its jails. In the meantime, McDonald's, as any number of other corporations, is likely to strive for yet more deregulation in its efforts to undermine collectivist ideals. Those commentators who rally to the cry of economic liberalism seem to want to turn the clock back to some 'golden age' of classic economics. Perhaps this is not so surprising; as the German philosopher G. W. F. Hegel pointed out a long time ago, 'History teaches us that people never learn anything from history'. The struggle outlined in this book focuses on workplace democracy, but it is a struggle that is symbolic of a deeper and more disturbing undercurrent in society and one that raises fundamental concerns about the fate of workers and the future regulation of modern civil society. Surely now is the time to regulate the multinationals more effectively, to rethink the mantra of free trade and unfettered markets and sing the praises of the collectivist ideals that are still in contention in Europe.

Appendix
Doing the research

The research began in September 1993 and set out to examine the activities of the McDonald's Corporation in Germany and the UK. This initial study was then extended 4 years later to examine the corporation's activities in thirteen European countries. These additional countries are Austria, Belgium, Denmark, Finland, France, The Netherlands, Ireland, Italy, Norway, Spain and Sweden. All in all, the study has spanned a period of just over 6 years. A variety of research methods were used in the study, including questionnaires and a period of observation while working in McDonald's restaurants in Germany and the UK. However, the bulk of the material has come from interviews. The interviews have included members of trade unions, of trade union federations, of international trade union organisations, of national and international employers' associations, of McDonald's senior management, of restaurant management, of franchise operators and a large number of employees, including works councillors and trade unions representatives in the restaurants.

Why undertake a comparative study?

There seems little doubt that the increasing internationalisation of business and the growth of multinational corporations and the growing importance of regional trade blocs such as the European Union require a better and more precise understanding of foreign institutions, cultures and business practices. Comparative studies allow us to be clearer about what is distinctive and intractable in international human resource management and international industrial relations, and hopefully provide us with a better understanding of the *realities* of management practices across national borders. This is important not only in terms of the pragmatic search for better management practices but also to understand the wider context of differing industrial relations systems in which management practices operate. Furthermore, we need to know much more about the implications of these practices for the lives of ordinary workers. This is something that, as yet, has received relatively little attention in many comparative studies. Multinational corporations are a natural focal point for these issues, increasingly operating beyond the reach of national governments yet affecting increasingly larger numbers of the world's population. Comparative studies may also allow us to understand other ways of seeking solutions to the problems in the political economy that confront broader society. It is generally accepted that policy-makers can learn a great deal from observing and understanding other national systems, but such static models cannot be understood in isolation – they need to be examined in terms of how they operate in practice. It is to be hoped that studies of this kind will go some way to help us unravel some of these issues.

Of course, comparative work of this kind is not a straightforward matter – it requires an understanding of the historical, political, sociological and economic contexts in which individuals, businesses and institutions operate. There are also many pitfalls in this kind of research, not only of a methodological but also of a practical nature. In practical terms, how do researchers deal with the problems of foreign languages, of customs and of arranging interview schedules and periods of observation? Furthermore, in methodological terms, simplistic interpretations of nation-states can lead to the danger of interpreting societies as 'wholes'. The danger of this approach is that although it allows us to understand differences between societies we do not see the differences *within* societies. The levels of analysis are therefore very important; neither the nation-state nor the employer alone can provide the appropriate level of analysis without oversimplifying the data. We also need to try to understand the actors' views of their roles within organisations, institutions and 'cultures'. The problems of comparative work are undoubtedly considerable but the rewards can also be great, providing powerful new insights into the realities of modern society.

Gaining access

Of course, obtaining access to undertake research is often problematic in many organisations and particularly where the subject matter may lead to some criticisms of the way in which organisations function. This means that in many cases of research into employment relations researchers will often want to ask awkward and unwelcome questions. Unsurprisingly, therefore, many organisations are unwilling to open their doors to researchers in this area and many more are deeply suspicious. Here, we have a classic paradox: if, as managers and as society, we want to learn about solving problems and about the pros and cons of institutional arrangements in different countries then we need to examine the reality of practices and not merely a doctored version of processes. Organisations are in many cases the gatekeepers to this world; if they are unwilling to allow us access then we will never uncover the reality of practices and outcomes.

Of course, the management in some organisations may be more suspicious than in others. McDonald's is well known for its tendency for secrecy. In fact, Reiter (1996) suggests that fast-food chains in particular are often wary about outsiders. This is not only because they are concerned about giving away 'secrets' to competitors but also because they are constantly worried about the 'danger' of trade union infiltration. Reiter's own attempts to gain access to McDonald's in Canada failed. Several requests were flatly refused; when she persisted, the Canadian McDonald's CEO wrote to her and her university chair of department informing them that she was to (Reiter, 1996: 78): '...cease and desist from all efforts to enter McDonald's'. Ultimately, Reiter had more luck with Burger King, who eventually gave their permission for her to work in one of their restaurants without pay.

How was access obtained in this study? Some access was secured at McDonald's UK before the study commenced. I had already undertaken some action research with McDonald's UK, examining the introduction of National Vocational Qualifications (NVQs) into McDonald's restaurants. There were additional links already established through other colleagues at the University who were piloting a post-graduate diploma for McDonald's managers. I was therefore already known to several members of the senior management at McDonald's UK. However, gaining access in other European countries was not so straightforward, and this would have been even more difficult if it was revealed to management that the research might involve some 'sensitive' issues. Germany was chosen as the first European country for examination partly because I am fluent in German and partly because, in terms of industrial relations research, Germany has often been seen as being at the opposite end of the spectrum to the UK. In this sense, it was considered that a comparison of the corporation's activities in the two countries would be likely to provide some interesting data.

The idea of a comparative study was floated with UK managers first; they gave their assent and provided some contact names and numbers at McDonald's in Germany. Access to managers, employees and franchises in the UK was generally very good, so it was not difficult to establish links with a large number of managers, franchise operators and employees at various levels in the organisation. The initial 'approval' from UK management turned out to be an important factor in the early stages of the project. Because of the sensitive nature of industrial relations research in this industry, it was decided to present the study as largely concentrating on employee profiles, job satisfaction, commitment, training and education matters. There are ethical issues associated with this decision. Should the researcher be explicit about the real intentions of the project and then be faced with the possibility of being refused access? In the end, it was decided that because of the company's well-known anti-union stance there would be no mention of works councils or unions in the introductory letter. Nevertheless, it appears that the research proposal was still treated with some caution. German management wrote to McDonald's UK asking them to confirm the author's identity and relationship with McDonald's UK.

After a delay of 2 months, the Personnel Director for McDonald's Germany agreed to an interview at the head office in Munich to discuss the proposed project in more detail. He agreed to distribute some questionnaires providing some of the questions were altered, e.g. I was not allowed to ask about the average number of hours worked by employees. The questionnaire was restricted to workers' profiles, past work experience and education and some questions about job satisfaction. While the questionnaires were limited, it was hoped that they might nevertheless provide some interesting material which would support data from other sources. In particular, it was hoped that the main thrust of the research would come from data based on qualitative interviews that would be far more wide ranging in scope. However, an initial request to interview regional and other head office management was refused. The personnel director stated:

> No, that's not possible and in any case you don't need to talk to them I know everything that they know.

Despite suggesting politely that this was not the point, permission was not forthcoming. Although the response was disappointing, it was not entirely unexpected. It was time to move on to plan 'B'. I asked whether it would be possible to work in some German restaurants for some weeks. This time the request was granted, and I requested that the work experience begin in the North of Germany because I had studied at university there, had worked there, knew the area quite well and had personal contacts there. It also seemed preferable to keep some distance from head office as it was hoped that the research would be less closely monitored. Indeed, this proved to be a very good decision; good relationships were struck up with several managers and franchise operators in the North of Germany, including some who had previously held senior posts in regional and headquarter offices. Over a period of weeks and months, a large number of interviews were carried out, including a large number with ordinary employees. Once access to the restaurants had been established, it was much easier to gain further access to additional data. For example, additional questionnaires were distributed, with some 200 questionnaires being returned from this part of the study.

Establishing and developing other research contacts

Important links were also established with the German trade union representing the fast-food sector, the NGG (Gewerkschaft Nahrung Genuss Gaststätten). The union proved to be an exceptional source for further interview contacts, particularly with other McDonald's workers and works councillors in a number of towns and cities across Germany. They also proved to be an excellent source of up-to-date information on a wide range of matters.

In 1997, it was decided to expand the research to include additional European countries; it was the European trade unions, their confederations and particularly the international trade union organisation the IUF that proved most helpful. I also travelled to Toronto for the IUF's World Congress in 1998 and had the opportunity to conduct additional interviews with trade union officials from several countries around the world, including officials from the USA and Canada. Over the period of the entire study, close to 200 in-depth face-to-face interviews were carried out covering a large number of countries. Additional data were also collected from other countries through the use of e-mail, telephone calls and other forms of correspondence. Overall, I owe a great deal to the European trade union movement and the many ordinary employees who took part in this study. Funding for the research was provided internally by the Nottingham Trent University; however, this was only available in small amounts, so several applications were made over time in order to acquire an adequate level of funding.

The problems associated with direct observation

Undertaking direct participation while working in both German and UK restaurants also provided a number of useful insights. Notes on observations were made informally during visits for interviews, either immediately after the visit or sometimes during the visit if the opportunity arose. Notes on observations that arose during interview visits were later appended to interview transcripts or compiled as a collection of field notes. I decided to work unpaid in restaurant kitchens in both countries. This did pose the limitation that I could not be a normal employee. On the one hand, this was a disadvantage in that it avoided what Jules-Rosette (1978) describes as the ideal of 'total immersion'. On the other hand, it did allow much more freedom of movement around the restaurants, allowing the possibility of talking informally to employees on their rest breaks and using the rooms in and around the manager's offices for interviews. Most of the unpaid work involved making burgers in the kitchen; this presented few opportunities for conversation because the work is normally carried out at a steady or fast pace when the restaurant is busy. Pollert (1981) also made a similar decision: she points out that if she had taken on the role of 'complete participant' then the advantages of experiencing for herself what it was like to carry out the job would have been heavily outweighed by the disadvantages. In other words, taking on a job under normal circumstances would have restricted her movement by having to abide by rules and losing the privileges of the outsider. Furthermore, as Reiter (1996) points out, making detailed field reports while working is difficult. Even in this 'unpaid' situation, once you had committed yourself to work a shift (or half a shift) it was not easy to leave the floor during busy periods.

This highlights the importance of trying to retain a marginal position throughout the fieldwork. Lofland (1971), for example, argues that the researcher can generate 'creative insight' from the marginal position of being at the same time an insider and outsider. It is not, however, easy to maintain this position because it involves a certain amount of insecurity and stress. Other researchers in quite different settings have also noted this difficulty (Wintrob, 1969; Wax, 1971; Johnson, 1975). The position of 'marginal native' (Freilich, 1970) is a common experience for many researchers. However,

Hammersley and Atkinson (1983) argue that these feelings are not to be avoided but are to be managed for what they are. They argue that if the researcher starts to feel at home then this is a danger signal.

Working hours in the kitchen were not the most difficult in this regard, but rest periods normally spent in the rest room brought home the marginality of the researcher's position. These periods were often accompanied by uncomfortable feelings. For example, the feeling that I did not belong and the awkwardness of relations with restaurant management because they were often uncertain as to how they should deal with this 'outsider'. On a practical level, observation notes could only realistically be made after work. McDonald's employee uniforms have no pockets and so it was often difficult to keep pen and paper to hand. Although the questionnaire and observation material were undoubtedly useful, by far the richest sources of data came from interviews.

Reflexivity and reactivity

All research is subject to potential error of one kind or another. The broadly interpretativist and naturalist positions argue that there is no way that a researcher can avoid having some effect on the data. Hammersley and Atkinson (1983) suggest that the positivist solution to this is by the standardisation of research procedures, whereas the naturalists try to surrender themselves to the cultures that they wish to study. Both assume, therefore, that it is possible to isolate a body of data, uncontaminated by the researcher. However, Hanson (1958) and Hammersley (1992) argue that attempts to find a neutral basis are pointless and that research in 'natural' settings does not guarantee validity but neither does research in 'artificial' surroundings automatically debar it from us. The researcher may strive to minimise his or her affects on the situation being examined, but the effects can nevertheless be significant regardless of the researcher's efforts. The danger is that any generalisation may be made invalid because the case under investigation may no longer be representative. As already indicated above, the researcher, therefore, needs to recognise the reflexive character of social research. Hammersley and Atkinson (1988: 15) argue that:

> ...we cannot avoid relying on 'common-sense' knowledge nor, often, can we avoid having an effect on the social phenomenon we study.

The roles of 'complete participation' and 'complete observer' may minimise the problem of reactivity because in neither case does the researcher *interact as a researcher*. However, they do not eradicate the reflexive nature of research. In any case, reactivity may be a useful source of 'data' itself; how people respond to the presence of a researcher may be as informative as how they react to other situations. Indeed, the following events detailed here are a good example.

Working in the kitchen provoked curiosity from most employees; they asked what I was doing, where I was from, was I working for the boss? Some treated me with suspicion. Most employees quickly grasped that I was not a 'normal' employee. A particularly good example of reactivity occurred one lunchtime with a change of shift in one of the German restaurants. A different floor manager or shift leader (*Schichtführer*) began his shift. He had the job of shouting orders to the kitchen, while I was busy dressing burgers. Not long into the shift, the manager clearly became irritated with my slowness in the kitchen and began pointedly to shout at me, saying that I should work faster because customers were waiting. This went on for some 20 minutes before another employee said something to him about my 'special' position. The shouting stopped and the manager began to nod and smile at me over the counter. During a lull in activity some time later, he made a point of coming over to me and was extremely apologetic: 'I'm so sorry about that I didn't know you were working for the boss'. As Hammersley and Atkinson (1988) point out, reactivity should not only be treated as a source of bias but should also be put to good use by the researcher. It was clear that in this role I would not be treated as a 'normal' employee. I, in effect, managed to 'negotiate' a new role for myself: that of interviewer and 'observer as participant' rather than 'participant as observer'. In effect, a different role was exploited in order to get access to another kind of data.

Some methodological issues

The term 'case study' has often been misinterpreted and taken as a partial synonym for 'qualitative research'. Furthermore, the simple dichotomy between 'qualitative' and 'quantitative' research is rather unhelpful. This has often given the impression that there are two alternative research paradigms. This distinction is neither helpful in understanding the research strategies used in much social science today nor of any value on a philosophical level. Hammersley (1992) suggests that recent epistemological debate is not a dialogue between these two positions; the arguments are much more complex than this.

Nevertheless, the concept of case study does confront us with questions about the number of cases to be chosen and how these are selected. Cases can range from micro to macro, from an individual to a national society or an international system. Hammersley and Atkinson (1988) argue that neither positivism nor naturalism provides an adequate framework for social research. Both neglect its fundamental reflexivity, i.e. the fact that we are part of the world we study. By including our own role within the research focus and systematically exploiting our participation in the world under study as researchers, we can develop and test theory without placing reliance on futile appeals to empiricism of either positivist or naturalist varieties. However, it is not intended to enter into theses debates here, the basic position taken in this study is one invoking a broadly realist epistemology. This view does not question that there is a reality to be found; this is in contradiction to the fully fledged post-modernist or 'idealist' position.

Archer (1988) argues that both the idealist and realist approaches have pitfalls and that we should take a position which falls between these two, i.e. that of internal realism. This position sees a 'reality' beyond the individual that also exists for the researcher, mediated through, as Watson (1994: 79) puts it, '...the social and cultural processes whereby human beings makes sense of the world'. Hammersley (1992) also argues for a similar approach to internal realism, which he describes as 'subtle realism'. This position shares with relativism the recognition that all knowledge is based on assumptions and purposes and is a human construction. But it also retains from realism the idea that research investigates independent knowable phenomena. In other words, we cannot see anything without some form of cultural and human mediation. It is therefore crucial that the reader knows as much as possible about the way in which the 'data' are collected and analysed, thus helping to reveal the role of the researcher in the final product. An idiographic rather than a nomothetic approach has been chosen because the research aims to identify the 'distinct character' of the units operating in divergent institutional and societal surroundings (Lammers and Hickson, 1979). However, I do regard the investigation as a gathering of unproblematic 'data'. I treat the accounts given by individuals, either orally or on paper, as giving insight into what is actually happening in the corporation in the different countries involved. Clearly, there are limitations, but it is hoped that the quality of analytical generalisation to be put forward in this case study will provide some convincing arguments.

Notes

1 Liberalism, collectivism and the multinational corporation

1 GATT, General Agreement on Tariffs and Trade; NAFTA, North American Free Trade Agreement.
2 Although this debate is prominent in Europe at the institutional level, it is also clear that the arguments are an important rallying point for academics, opposition parties and NGOs in any number of countries.
3 The distinction between political and economic liberalism is mirrored in the evolution of academic work articulating these two perspectives, e.g. see the work on political liberalism put forward by Rawls (1971).
4 'Think-tanks' include the Institute of Economic Affairs, the Centre for Policy Studies and the Adam Smith Institute and organisations such as the National Association for Freedom, Aims of Industry and the Society of Individualists. In addition, influential intellectual gatherings such as the Mont Pèlerin Society, founded by Hayek after the Second World War, were important in articulating and disseminating these ideas.
5 However, it should also be noted that in the USA Roosevelt's *New Deal* (Johnson, 1997) was also very much about the preservation of capital.
6 OECD, Organisation for Economic Co-operation and Development; a twenty-five-member club of industrialised nations.
7 The 'core standards' are (i) freedom of association and the effective recognition of the right to collective bargaining; (ii) the elimination of all forms of forced or compulsory labour; (iii) the effective abolition of child labour; and (iv) the elimination of discrimination in respect of employment and occupation (ILO, 1998: 7).
8 The term social dialogue has been used in a number of ways, but here we use the term to describe the relationship between management and labour (the social partners) and the European Commission. These social dialogues have their legal base in the 1993 revision of the Treaty on European Union and can occur at both the interprofessional and the sectoral European level (Keller and Sörries, 1999).
9 It not within the scope of this book to examine these issues further. However, they are dealt with in detail in a number of other texts, e.g. Waters (1995).

4 McDonald's at work

1 Although, for those who are interested, it should be clear from this analysis that the epistemological position taken here is that culture is something an organisation 'is' not 'has'.

5 'There's no place like home': the impact of trade unions and collective bargaining frameworks

1 Federal Minister of Labour (1949) Collective Agreements Act and Ministry of Social Affairs (1952) Minimum Working Conditions Act.

6 Co-determination? What the hell is that?!

1 Under some circumstances, there are situations in which participation can be found at the end of the continuum, where employees have total or almost total control over decisions. However, in practice, this is rare. Where this does exist, it is mostly confined to workers' co-operatives, the old Yugoslavian self-management system or that (and then only formally) introduced in Algeria and some other countries (Bean, 1994).
2 In this regard, it is interesting to note that the name given to the McDonald's European works council is the 'McDonald's European Communications Group'; see Chapter 8.
3 A more detailed analysis of these 'avoidance strategies' is available in Duve (1987) and Royle (1998, 1999a).
4 The issue of works council rights, *'das passive Betriebsratswahlrecht'*, is covered in paragraph 53 of the ArbVG. For non-EU citizens, this may be a particularly controversial issue in Austria, especially in view of the recent election success of Jörg Haider and his far-right Freedom Party with its hard line anti-immigrant stance (Frey and Hall, 1999).
5 In fact, Sweden did operate a system of works councils between 1946 and 1977, but they were never very strong and the unions withdrew from the agreement in the late 1970s (IDS, 1996).
6 The three main union confederations, Confederazione Generale Italiana del Lavoro (CGIL), Confederazione Italiana Sindacati dei Lavatori (CSIL) and Unione Italiana del Lavoro(UIL), have all signed the agreement.
7 Even German works councils appear to be vulnerable to a wide range of 'avoidance strategies': legal or illegal measures, regulatory loopholes, 'co-option' or 'capture', 'bypass', 'coercive comparison' and 'recruited acquiescence' (Royle, 1998).

7 For a few dollars more: comparing pay and conditions

1 These rates were increased in 2000 to £3.70 and £3.20 per hour respectively.
2 All figures are calculated on the basis of exchange rate figures provided by the *Financial Times* on 1 December 1999, with a rate of DM3.09 to £1.00. This method of comparison is only a 'rough guide' not only because comparing pay in this manner does not take into account a range of issues (such as taxation) but also because exchange rates are continually fluctuating, especially over the long term.
3 ZIHOGA: Zentrale und Internationale Management und Fachvermittlung für Hotel- und Gaststättenpersonal.
4 The Federal Employment Service (BfA) has its remit under the Employment Promotion Act and was established primarily for job placement, the planned promotion of employment, the implementation of job creation schemes and the administration of unemployment insurance. It is a self-governing body headed by a tripartite Administrative Council, which is made up of equal numbers of employee, employer and government representatives.

8 Where's the beef? The European Works Council

1 Trade unions have been attempting to establish transnational structures for co-operation based on voluntary agreements with employers since the 1960s, but these early attempts met with employer hostility. In the 1980s, a few largely state-owned French corporations established 'European information committees'; these were based on voluntary agreements between management and employee representatives from the various national subsidiaries (Rehfeldt, 1995). However, by the end of 1990, only nine employers had signed such agreements, and this number did not increase significantly until after 1994, when the EWC directive was finally adopted. Thirty-seven companies had signed agreements in 1994, and eighty signed in 1995 (Barrie and Milne, 1996; Rivest, 1996; Schulten, 1996). By May 2000 it was estimated that some 600 EWCs had been established; this still leaves some 800 multinationals which have yet to establish EWCs in accordance with the directive. Approximately 450 of the EWCs in place are voluntary agreements signed before the September 1996 deadline, 70–80% of which were established in the 12 months leading up to September 1996 (EIRR, 1997c; 2000a; Marginson *et al.*, 1998).

2 The other thirteen (excluding the UK) are Austria, Belgium, Denmark, Finland, France, Greece, Holland, Ireland, Italy, Norway, Portugal, Spain and Sweden.

9 Conclusion

1 As suggested in Chapter 1, there is not enough scope in this book to provide a proper analysis of 'globalisation' debates. It should not be confused with the concept of 'convergence', although it does relate to similar issues. The convergence thesis first put forward in the 1960s by Kerr *et al.* (1960) is rather simplistic and it is still used to describe an increasing similarity of certain kinds of behaviour across national borders. For example, it has often been used in this way to describe the 'Japanisation' of work practices. The problem with the concept of 'convergence' is that there is often confusion regarding different levels of analysis. As Baldry (1994) points out, it is one thing to suggest a convergence via increasing uniformity of legal and political processes and quite another to see a convergence through the advent of new technologies or changing markets. Differing interpretations of the globalisation concept tend to be much more sophisticated in their analysis, with the more convincing of these suggesting that 'globalisation' is a complex mixture of homogenising *and* differentiating trends (Robertson, 1990).

2 NAIRU, non-accelerating inflation rate of unemployment.

References

Abbott, B. (1993) 'Small firms and trade unions in services in 1990s', *Industrial Relations Journal*, 24, 4: 308–17.

Ackers, P., Marchington, M., Wilkinson, A., Goodman, J. (1992) 'The use of cycles? Explaining employee involvement in the 1990s', *Industrial Relations Journal*, 23: 268–83.

Ackers, P., Smith, C., Smith, P. (1996) 'Against all odds? Trade unions in the new workplace', in Ackers, P., Smith, C., Smith, P. (eds) *The New Workplace and Trade Unionism*, London: Routledge.

Adams, R.J. (1999) 'Why statutory union recognition is bad labour policy: the North American experience', *Industrial Relations Journal*, 30, 2: 96–100.

Advertising Age (1990) 'Adman of the decade: McDonald's Fred Turner: making all the right moves', *Advertising Age*, 1 January: 6.

Albrecht Schulz Sigle, Loose, Schmidt-Diemitz & Partners (1988) 'Cases and comment: Germany: are franchisees salaried employees?', *The Journal of International Franchising and Distribution Law*, March, 2: 149–50.

Algemeen Dagblad (1998) 'Medewerkers McDonald's ontevreden over naleving cao', *Algemeen Dagblad*, 24 May: 7.

Almond, P., Rubery, J. (1998) 'The gender impact of recent European trends in wage determination', *Work, Employment and Society*, Notes and Issue, 12: 675–93.

Anthony, P. (1994) *Managing Culture*, Buckingham: Open University Press.

Appleyard, B. (1994) 'Big Mac vs. small fries', *The Independent*, 4 July: 17.

Archer, S. (1988) 'Qualitative research and the epistemological problems of the management disciplines', in Pettigrew, A.M. (ed.) *Competitiveness and the Management Process*, Oxford: Blackwell.

Ardagh, J. (1987) *Germany and the Germans: An Anatomy of Society Today*, London: Hamish Hamilton.

Atkins, R. (2000) 'Returning power to the worker,' *Financial Times*, 13 July: 20.

Baldry, C. (1994) 'Convergence in Europe: a matter of perspective?', *Industrial Relations Journal*, 25: 96–109.

Barnett, A. (1996) 'British firms defying Social Chapter opt-out', *The Observer*, 4 August: 20.

Barrie, C., Milne, S. (1996) 'Firms opt in despite opt-out', *The Guardian*, 28 September: 2–3.

Bartlett, C.A., Ghoshall, S. (1989) *Managing Across Borders: The Transnational Solution*, London: Century Business.

Bean, R. (1994) *Comparative Industrial Relations*, London: Routledge.

Beaumont, P. (1993) *Human Resource Management: Key Concepts and Skills*, London: Sage.

Bell, D. (1962) *The End of Ideology*, New York: Collier.

Benders, J., Mol, B. (1998) 'How strong is convergence? McDonald's in the Netherlands', paper presented to the sixteenth International Labour Process Conference, University of Manchester, 7–9 April.

Benson, S.P. (1986) *Counter Cultures: Saleswomen, Managers, and Customers in American Department Stores 1890–1940*, Urbana: University of Illinois Press.

Big Mäc Nachrichten (1994) McDonald's Promotion GmbH, Munich, *Big Mäc Nachrichten*, January: 11.

Blundy, A. (1999) 'Russian workers accuse McDonald's of blocking union', *The Independent*, 23 June: 14.

Blyton, P., Turnbull P. (1994) *The Dynamics of Employee Relations*, London: Macmillan.

BNA [Bureau of National Affairs (USA)] (1985) *Retail/Services Labour Report*, Washington, DC, 10 June, 23: 1–31.

BNA [Bureau of National Affairs (USA)] (1991) *Bulletin to Management*, Washington, DC, 7 March: 66–71.

Bowley, G. (1998) 'German unions seek safety in numbers', *Financial Times*, 10 March: 3.

Braverman, H. (1974) *Labour and Monopoly Capital*, New York: Monthly Review Press.

Brittan, S. (1972) 'Why unemployment is still an enigma', *Financial Times*, 24 February.

Brown, K. (1999) 'Survey – world steel industry: facing up to the challenges, new products', *Financial Times*, 14 May: 3.

Brown, W., Marginson, P., Walsh, J. (1995) 'Management: pay determination and collective bargaining', in Edwards, P.K. (ed.) *Industrial Relations: Theory and Practice in Britain*, London: Blackwell.

Brulin, G. (1995) 'Sweden: joint councils under strong unionism', in Rogers, J., Streeck, W. (eds) *Works Councils: Consultation, Representation, and Co-operation in Industrial Relations*, London: University of Chicago Press.

Buffalo News (1998) 'Workers who led first strike against McDonald's fired', *Buffalo News*, 12 June : 8A.

Burawoy, M. (1979) *Manufacturing Consent: Changes in the Labour Process Under Monopoly Capitalism*, London: University of Chicago Press.

Burck, C.G. (1970) 'Franchising's troubled dream world', *Fortune*, March, 148–52.

Buschbeck-Bülow, B. (1989) 'Arbeits- und Sozial Recht: Betriebsverfassungsrechtliche Vertretung in Franchise-Systemen', *Betriebs-Berater*, 20 February: 352–4.

Chan, P.S., Justis, R.T. (1990) 'Franchise management in East Asia', *Academy of Management Executive*, May, 75–85.

Clarke, T. (1996) 'Mechanisms of corporate rule', in Mander, J., Goldsmith, E. (eds) *The Case Against the Global Economy*, San Francisco: Sierra Club Books.

Clegg, C., Nicholson, N., Ursell, G., Blyton, P., Wall, T. (1978) 'Managers' attitudes towards industrial democracy', *Industrial Relations Journal*, 9, 3: 4–17.

Cockett, R. (1995) *Thinking the Unthinkable: Think-Tanks and the Economic Counter-Revolution 1931–1983*, London: HarperCollins.

Cohon, G. (1999) *To Russia with Fries*, New York: McCland and Stewart.

Commission on Co-determination (1998) *The German Model of Co-determination and Corporate Governance*, Bertelsmann and Hans Böckler Foundations (eds), Gütersloh: Bertelsmann Foundation Publishers.

Cressey, P. (1993) 'Employee participation', in Gold, M. (ed.) *The Social Dimension: Employment Policy in the European Community*, London: Macmillan.

Davies, N. (1997) *Europe: A History*, London: Pimlico.

Delftse Courant (1998) 'Werknehmers McDonald's Klagen over naleving CAO', *Delftse Courant*, 24 May: 9.

Der Spiegel (1981) 'Land des Lächelns', *Der Spiegel*, 22: 72–5.

Der Spiegel (1996) 'Sozialer Konflikstoff der Zukunft', *Der Spiegel*, 18: 128–30.

Der Spiegel, (1997) 'Zehn Prozent Abschlag', *Der Spiegel*, 45: 138–9.

Der Spiegel (1998) 'McDonald's Selbst Gebacken', *Der Spiegel*, 18: 140.

De Vos, T. (1981) *U.S. Multinationals and Worker Participation in Management*, London: Aldwych.

Dex, S., Robson, P., Wilkinson, F. (1999) 'The characteristics of the low paid: a cross-national comparison', *Work, Employment and Society*, 13: 503–24.

Diller, J. (1999) 'A social conscience in the global marketplace? Labour dimensions of codes of conduct, social labelling and investor initiatives', *International Labour Review*, 138, 2: 99–129.

Disney, R., Gosling, A., Machin, S., McCrae, J. (1998) 'The dynamics of union membership in Britain: a study using the family and working lives survey', Employment Relations Research Series, 3, London: Department of Trade and Industry.

Dowling, P.J., Schuler, R.S., Welch, D.E. (1994) *International Dimensions of Human Resource Management*, California: Wadsworth.

Dunning, J. (1993) *Multi-national Enterprises in a Global Economy*, Wokingham: Addison-Wesley.

Dussel Peters, E. (1997) *La Economia de la Polarización*, Mexico: P.F.I. Editorial Jus.

Duve, F. (1987) *Unternehmermethoden gegen Betriebsratswahlen (Reportagen aus Grauzonen der Arbeitswelt)*, Hamburg: Rowohlt Taschenbuchverlag.

Eberwein, W., Tholen, J. (1990) *Managermentalität: Industrielle Unternehmungsleitung als Beruf und Politik*, Frankfurt: FAZ.

The Economist (1989a) 'Big Mac's counter attack', *The Economist*, 13 November: 71–2.

The Economist (1989b) 'Pushkin, coke and fries', *The Economist*, 18 November: 62.

The Economist (1990) 'Slow food', *The Economist*, 3 February: 84–5.

The Economist (1993a) 'Big Mac's counter attack', *The Economist*, 13 November: 71–2.

The Economist (1993b) 'Big MacCurrencies', *The Economist*, 17 April: 79.

The Economist (1996a) 'MacWorld', *The Economist*, 29 June: 77–8.

The Economist (1996b) 'Germany: is the model broken?', *The Economist*, 4 May: 21–3.

The Economist (1997) 'Management brief: Johannesburgers and fries', *The Economist*, 27 September: 107–8.

Edgecliffe-Johnson, A. (1999a) 'The Americas: McDonald's advances 12%', *Financial Times*, 23 April: 6.

Edgecliffe-Johnson, A. (1999b) 'McDonald's buys a slice of pizza market', *Financial Times*, 7 May: 31.

Edgecliffe-Johnson, A. (1999c) 'Burger with fries and videos to go: the fast-food war for American stomachs has moved on to new ground', *Financial Times*, 17 April: 7.

Edmunts, C. (1998) 'Wahlhilfe bei McDonald's: dieser Betriebsrat ist einfach gut', *Süddeutsche Zeitung*, 12 June, 132: 3.

Edwards, P.K. (1986) *Conflict at Work*, Oxford: Blackwell.

Edwards, P.K. (1990) 'The politics of conflict and consent: how the labour contract really works', *Journal of Economic Behaviour and Organisation*, 13: 41–61.

Edwards, P.K., Hall, M., Hyman, R., Marginson, P., Sisson, K., Waddington, J., Winchester, D. (1998) 'Great Britain: from partial collectivism to neo-Liberalism to where?', in Ferner, A., Hyman, R. (eds) *Changing Industrial Relations in Europe*, Oxford: Basil Blackwell.

Edwards, R. (1979) *Contested Terrain: The Transformation of the Workplace in the Twentieth Century*, New York: Basic Books.

EIRR (1992) 'Germany: minimum pay setting', *European Industrial Relations Review*, November, 226: 14–16.

EIRR (1997b) 'Renault closure sparks EU-wide controversy', *European Industrial Relations Review*, April, 278: 1.

EIRR (1997c) 'McDonald's serves up improved social relations', *European Industrial Relations Review*, April, 279: 19–21.

EIRR (1997d) 'EWCs state of play', *European Industrial Relations Review*, May, 280: 14–16.

EIRR (1997e) 'Commission consults on national-level information and consultation', *European Industrial Relations Review*, July, 282: 13–15.

EIRR (1997f) 'Extending the EWCs Directive to the UK', *European Industrial Relations Review*, November, 286: 21–22.

EIRR (1999a) 'Germany: collective bargaining in 1998', *European Industrial Relations Review*, June, 305: 17–21.

EIRR (1999b) 'Ireland: unions and employers agree compromise on union recognition', *European Industrial Relations Review*, May, 304: 27–30.

EIRR (2000a) 'European Works Councils Update', *European Industrial Relations Review*, 316: 20–22.

EIRR (2000b) 'Commission issues EWC report', *European Industrial Relations Review*, 317: 19–22.

Emerson, R. L. (1990) *The New Economics of Fast Food*, London: Van Nostrand Reinhold.

Emmott, B. (1993) 'Everybody's favourite monster', *The Economist*, 27, 3, supplement.

Escobar, M. (1995) 'Spain: works councils or unions', in Rogers, J., Streeck, W. (eds) *Works Councils: Consultation, Representation, and Co-operation in Industrial Relations*, London: University of Chicago Press.

Eurostat (1993) *Labour Force Survey Results*, Luxembourg: 3C Statistical Office of the European Community.

Evans, P., Lorange, P. (1989) 'The two logics behind human resource management', in Evans, P., Doz, Y., Laurent, A. (eds) *Human Resource Management in International Firms: Change, Globalization, Innovation*, London: Macmillan.

Featherstone, L. (1998) 'The burger international', *Left Business Observer*, 86, November.

Felstead, A. (1991) 'The social organisation of the franchise: a case of controlled self-employment', *Work, Employment and Society*, March, 5: 37–57.

Felstead, A. (1993) *The Corporate Paradox: Power and Control in the Business Franchise*, London: Routledge.

Ferner, A. (1994) 'Multinational companies and human resource management: an overview of research issues', *Human Resource Management Journal*, Spring, 4, 2: 79–102.

Ferner, A., Hyman, R. (1998) 'Introduction: towards European industrial relations?', in Ferner, A., Hyman, R. (eds) *Changing Industrial Relations in Europe*. Oxford: Basil Blackwell.

Festinger, L.A. (1962) *A Theory of Cognitive Dissonance*, London: Tavistock.

Financial Times (1999a) 'Protests in Italy and Greece: Kosovo update', *Financial Times*, 6 May: 2.

Financial Times (1999b) 'Bill Gates on business: speed gives life to digital nervous system', *Financial Times*, 18 March: 16.

Flecker, J., Schulten, T. (1999) 'The end of institutional stability: what future the German model?', *Economic and Industrial Democracy*, 20: 81–115.

Franchise World (1993) 'The key to the Golden Arches', *Franchise World*, September/October, 32–8.

Franchise World (1994) 'Voice for franchisees in £37 million marketing budget', *Franchise World*, January/February, 5.

Frantz, J. (1993) 'Friede, Freude, Fanta, Fritten', *Manager Magazin*, August: 76–81.

Freilich, M. (ed.) (1970) *Marginal Narratives: Anthropologists at Work*, New York: Harper & Row.

Frey, E., Hall, W. (1999) 'Big gain for right in Austrian elections', *Financial Times*, Monday 4 October: 9.

Friedmann, J. (1990) 'Being in the world: globalization and localization', in Featherstone, M. (ed.) *Global Culture: Nationalism, Globalization and Modernity*, London: Sage.

Friedman, S., Hurd, R.W., Oswald, R.A., Seeber, R.L. (eds) (1994) *Restoring the Promise of American Labour Law*, Ithaca, NY: ILR Press.

Fukuyama, F. (1992) *The End of History and the Last Man*, London: Free Press.

Fuller, L. and Smith, V. (1991) 'Consumers reports: management by customers in a changing economy', *Work, Employment and Society*, 15: 1–16.

Fürstenberg, F. (1991) 'Structure and strategy in industrial relations', *Bulletin of Comparative Labour Relations*, Special Issue, 21: 1–199.

Gabaglio, E. (ed.) (1998) *European Works Councils, the EC Directive: ETUC Analysis and Comments*, 2nd edn, Brussels: European Trade Union Confederation.

Gabriel, Y. (1988) *Working Lives in Catering*, London: Routledge and Kegan Paul.

Galbraith, J.K. (1987) *The Affluent Society*, Harmondsworth: Penguin.

Galbraith, J.K. (1992) *The Culture of Contentment*, Harmondsworth, Penguin.

Garson, B. (1988) *The Electronic Sweatshop: How Computers are Transforming the Office of the Future into the Factory of the Past*, New York: Simon and Schuster.

Giddens, A. (1990) *The Consequences of Modernity*, Cambridge: Polity Press.

Giddens, A. (1998) *The Third Way: the Renewal of Social Democracy*, Oxford: Blackwell.

Goetschy, J. (1998a) 'The ETUC and the construction of European unionism', in Gabaglio, E., Hoffman, R. (eds) *The ETUC in the Mirror of Industrial Relations Research*, Brussels: European Trade Union Institute.

Goetschy, J. (1998b) 'France: the limits of reform', in Ferner, A., Hyman, R. (eds) *Changing Industrial Relations in Europe*, Oxford: Basil Blackwell.

Gold, M., Hall, M. (1994) 'Statutory European Works Councils: the final countdown?', *Industrial Relations Journal*, 25, 3: 177–86.

Goldsmith, E. (1996) 'Global trade and the environment', in Mander, J., Goldsmith, E. (eds) *The Case Against the Global Economy*, San Francisco: Sierra Club Books.

Gorringe, T. (1999) *Fair Shares: Ethics and the Global Economy*, London: Thames and Hudson.

Gould, W. B. (1994) *Agenda for Reform: the Future of Employment Relationships and the Law*, Cambridge, MA: MIT Press.

Gouldner, A.W. (1964) *Patterns of Industrial Bureaucracy*, New York: Free Press.

Grahl, J., Teague, P. (1992) Integration theory and European labour markets, *British Journal of Industrial Relations*, 30: 515–28.

Gray, J. (1992) *The Moral Foundations of Market Institutions*, London.

Gregory, A., O'Reilly, J. (1996) 'Checking out and washing up', in Crompton, R., Gallie, D., Purcell, K. (eds) *Changing Forms of Employment: Organisations, Skills and Gender*, London: Routledge.

The Guardian (1999) 'Sleepless in Seattle', *The Guardian*, 27 November: 23.

Hall, M. (1992) 'Behind the European Works Council Directive: The European Commission's Legislative Strategy', *British Journal of Industrial Relations*, 30: 547–66.

Hall, M. (1994) 'Industrial relations and the social dimension of European integration: before and after Maastricht', in Hyman, R., Ferner, A. (eds) *New Frontiers in European Industrial Relations*, Oxford: Basil Blackwell.

Hammersley, M. (1992) *What's Wrong with Ethnography?*, London: Routledge.

Hammersley, M., Atkinson, P. (1983) *Ethnography: Principles in Practice*, London: Routledge.

Handelsblatt (1998) 'DIW kritisiert 620-DM-Pläne als Stückwerk', *Handelsblatt*, 1 December: 3.

Hanson, N.R. (1958) *Patterns of Discovery*, London: Cambridge University Press.

Hassel, A., Schulten, T. (1998) 'Globalization and the future of central collective bargaining: the example of the German metal industry', *Economy and Society*, 27: 486–522.

Hayek, F.A. (1944) *The Road to Serfdom*, London: Routledge.

Hege, A., Dufour, C. (1995) Decentralisation and legitimacy in employee representation: a Franco-German comparison', *European Journal of Industrial Relations*, 1: 83–99.

Henley, J. (1999) 'McDonald's campaign spawns French hero', *The Guardian*, 11 September: 14.

Hepple, B. (1999) 'A race to the top? International Investment Guidelines and Corporate Codes of Conduct', paper presented to the WG Hart Workshop: Legal Regulation of the Employment Relationship, Institute of Advanced Legal Studies, University of London, July.

Herzberg, F. (1966) *Work and the Nature of Man*, New York: Staples Press.

Heskett, J.L. Sasser, W.E., Hart, C.W.L. (1990) *Service Breakthroughs: Changing the Rules of the Game*, New York: Free Press.

Hirst, P., Thompson, G. (1996) *Globalisation in Question*, Oxford: Polity Press.

Hochschild, A.R. (1983) *The Managed Heart: Commercialisation of Human Feeling*, Berkeley: University of California Press.

Hofstede, G.H. (1980) *Culture's Consequences, International Differences in Work-Related Values*, California: Sage.

Holliday, R. (1995) *Investigating Small Firms: Nice Work?* London: Routledge.

Honig, N.E. and Dowling, D.C. (1994) 'How to handle employment issues in European deals', *Preventative Law Reporter*, Spring, 13, 1: 3–9.

Hughes, E.C. (1984) 'Work and self', in *The Sociological Eye*, New Jersey: Transaction Books.

Hutton, W. (1996) *The State We're In*, London: Vintage.

Hyman, R. (1988) 'Flexible specialisation: miracle or myth', in Hyman, R., Streeck, W. (eds) *Trade Unions, Technology and Industrial Democracy*, Oxford: Basil Blackwell.

Hyman, R. (1994) 'Introduction: economic restructuring, market liberalism and the future of national industrial relations systems', in Hyman, R., Ferner, A. (eds) *New Frontiers in European Industrial Relations*, Oxford: Basil Blackwell.

IDCH (International Directory of Company Histories) (1990) *Food Service and Retailers: McDonald's Corporation* London: St. James Press, pp. 646–8.

IDE (Industrial Democracy in Europe Group) (1981) *Industrial Democracy in Europe*, Oxford: Clarendon Press.

IDE (Industrial Democracy in Europe Group) (1993) *Industrial Democracy in Europe Revisited*, Oxford: Oxford University Press.

IDS (Income Data Services) (1996) *European Management Guides: Industrial Relations and Collective Bargaining*, London: Income Data Services, Institute of Personnel Development

IDS Employment Europe (1998) The Netherlands: works council reforms revealed, January, 433: 7.

IDS Focus (Income Data Services) (1997) 'Agenda 98', 84, December: 1–16.

ILO (International Labour Organisation) (1998) *ILO Declaration of Fundamental Principles and Rights at Work and its Follow-up*, Geneva: International Labour Organisation.

d'Iribarne, P. (1989) *La Logique de l'Honneur; Gestion des Entreprises et Traditons Nationales*, Paris: Editions du Seuil.

Jacobi, O., Keller, B., Müller-Jentsch, W. (1998) 'Germany facing new challenges', in Ferner, A., Hyman, R. (eds) *Changing Industrial Relations in Europe*, Oxford: Basil Blackwell.

James, N. (1989) 'Emotional Labour: skill and work in the social regulation of feeling', *Sociological Review*, 37: 15–42.

Johnson, J. (1975) *Doing Field Research*, New York: Free Press.

Johnson, P. (1997) *A History of the American People*, New York: HarperCollins.

Jules-Rosette, B. (1978) 'The veil of objectivity: prophecy, divination, and social enquiry', *American Anthropologist*, 30: 549–70.

Keegan, W. (1999) 'Grant us livery from free trade', *The Observer*, 5 December 1999.

Keller, B., Sörries, B. (1999) 'Sectoral social dialogues: new opportunities or more impasses?' *Industrial Relations Journal European Annual Review*, 3, 5: 77–98.

Kelly, J.E. (1998) *Rethinking Industrial Relations: Mobilization, Collectivism and Long Waves*, London: Routledge.

Kerr, C., Dunlop, J.T., Harbison, F., Myers, C.A. (1960) *Industrialism and Industrial Man*, Cambridge, MA: Harvard University Press.

Kochan, T.A., Weinstein, M. (1994) Recent developments in US industrial relations', *British Journal of Industrial Relations*, 32: 483–504.

Kochan, T.A., McKersie, R.B., Cappelli, P. (1984) 'Strategic choice and industrial relations theory', *Industrial Relations*, 23: 16–39.

Kotthoff, H. (1994) *Betriebsräte und Bürgerstatus, Wandel und Kontinuität betrieblicher Mitbestimmung*, München-Mehring: Rainer Hampp Verlag.

Kristof, D. (1992) 'Billions served (and that was without China)', *The New York Times*, 24 April: 6.

Kroc, R. (1977) *Grinding It Out: The Making of McDonald's*, Chicago: Contemporary Books.

Laabs, J.J. (1991) 'The Golden Arches provide golden opportunities', *Personnel Journal*, July: 52–7.

Labour Research (1994a) 'Do part-timers have equal rights', *Labour Research*, July: 8–10.

Labour Research (1994b) 'Europe's "flexi-mania"', *Labour Research*, July: 11–12.

Labour Research (1999a) 'New era for Euro Unions', *Labour Research*, September, 88, 9: 17–19.

Labour Research (1999b) *The Employment Relations Act 1999*, London: LRD Booklets.

Lammers, C.J., Hickson, D.J. (1979) 'Towards a comparative sociology of organisations', in Lammers, C.J., Hickson, D.J. (eds) *Organisations Alike and Unalike*, London: Routledge and Kegan Paul.

Landes, D.S. (1986) 'What do bosses really do?', *Journal of Economic History*, September, 66: 585–623.

Lane, C. (1989) *Management and Labour in Europe*, Aldershot: Edward Elgar.

Lane, C. (1994) 'Industrial order and the transformation of industrial relations: Britain, Germany and France Compared', in Hyman, R., Ferner, A. (eds) *New Frontiers in European Industrial Relations*, Oxford: Basil Blackwell.

Langenhuisen, R. (1995) 'McDonald's kauft sich von Betriebsräten frei', *Kölner Express*, 7 December: 36.

Larsson, A. (1998) 'The European employment strategy and the EMU: you must invest to save', *Economic and Industrial Democracy*, 19: 391–415.

Lawrence, P. (1996) *Management in the USA*, London: Sage.

Leidner, R. (1993) *Fast-food Fast Talk: Service Work and the Routinisation of Everyday Work*, Los Angeles: University of California Press.

Levinson, C. (1972) *International Trade Unionism*, London: George Allen & Unwin.

LFS (Labour Force Survey) (1996) *Labour Market Trends*, May: 215–25.

Libération (1994) 'A Lyon, ça ne se passe pas comme ça chez McDonald's', *Libération*, 6 July: 13.

Locke, R. (1995) 'The transformation of industrial relations? A cross-national review', in Wever, S., Turner, L. (eds) *The Political Economy of Industrial Relations*, Madison, WI: Industrial Relations Research Association Series.

Lofland, J. (1971) *Analyzing Social Settings: A Guide to Qualitative and Observational Analysis*, Belmont, CA: Wadsworth.

Love, J.F. (1995) *McDonald's Behind the Arches*, London: Bantam Press.

Lowery, C.M., Scott, C. (1996) 'Union organizing among hospitality workers', *Hospitality Research Journal*, 19, 4: 3–16.

LRD (Labour Research Department) (1995) *A Trade Unionist's Guide to European Works Councils*, London: Trades Union Congress (TUC).

LRD (Labour Research Department) (1998) *Working Time: a Trade Unionist's Guide to the New Regulations*, London: Labour Research Department Publications.

LRD (Labour Research Department) (1999) *The Employment Relations Act 1999: a Guide for Trade Unionists*, London: Labour Research Department Publications.

Lucas, R. (1996) 'Industrial relations in hotels and catering: neglect and paradox?', *British Journal of Industrial Relations*, 34: 267–86.

L'Unita (1998) 'Antisindicale: Il Pretore condanna McDonald's', *L'Unita*, 23 April: 6.

Luxenburg, S. (1985) *Roadside Empires: How the Chains Franchised America*, New York: Viking.

McGregor, D. (1960) *The Human Side of Enterprise*, New York: McGraw-Hill.

McLaughlin, A., Greenwood, J. (1995) 'The management of interest representation in the European Union', *Journal of Common Market Studies*, 33, March: 144–56.

McLaughlin, A., Jordan, G., Maloney, W. (1993) 'Corporate lobbying in the European Community', *Journal of Common Market Studies*, 31, June: 191–212.

Maguire, M. (1986) 'Recruitment as a means of control', in Purcell, J., Wood, S., Watson, A., Allen, S. (eds) *The Changing Experience of Employment: Restructuring and Recession*. London: Macmillan.

Maier, F. (1991) 'The regulation of part-time work: a comparative study of six EC countries', *Discussion Paper FSI 01-9*, Berlin: Wissenschaftszentrum für Sozialforschung.

Maitland, A. (1999) 'The value of virtue in a transparent world', *Financial Times*, 5 August: 14.

Marchington, M. (1995) 'Involvement and participation', in Storey, J. (ed.) *Human Resource Management: A Critical Text*, London: Routledge.

Marginson, P., Sisson, K. (1994) 'The structure of transnational capital in Europe: the emerging Euro-Company and its implications for industrial relations', in Hyman, R., Ferner, A. (eds) *New Frontiers in European Industrial Relations.* Oxford: Basil Blackwell.

Marginson, P., Sisson, K. (1998) 'European collective bargaining: a virtual prospect?', *Journal of Common Market Studies*, December, 36: 505–28.

Marginson, P., Edwards, P.K., Martin, R., Purcell, P.J., Sisson, K. (1988) 'Structure, strategy and choice', in Marginson, P., Edwards, P.K., Martin, R., Purcell, P.J., Sisson, K. (eds) *Beyond the Workplace: Managing the Industrial Relations in the Multi-Establishment Enterprise*, Oxford: Blackwell.

Marginson, P., Gilmar, M., Jacobi, O., Krieger, H. (1998) *Negotiating European Works Councils: An Analysis of Agreements under Article 13*, Luxembourg: European Foundation for Working and Living Conditions, Commission of the EU.

Marr, A. (1999) 'Friend or foe', *The Guardian*, 5 December: 28.

Martin, R. (1998) 'McDonald's Corporation Japan Ltd: company profile', *Nation's Restaurant News*, 32, 4, January: 112.

Martinez Lucio, M. (1998) 'Spain: regulating employment and social fragmentation', in Ferner, A., Hyman, R. (eds) *Changing Industrial Relations in Europe*, Oxford: Basil Blackwell.

Meek, V.L. (1988) 'Organisational culture: origins and weaknesses', *Organisation Studies*, 9: 453–73.

Mendelsohn, M. (1992) 'Franchise prospects in central and eastern Europe', *Franchise World*, Jan/Feb: 34–5.

Miller, D., Stirling, J. (1998) 'European Works Council Training: an opportunity missed?', *European Journal of Industrial Relations*, 4: 35–56.

Mintzberg, H. (1994) *The Rise and Fall of Strategic Planning*, Hemel Hempstead: Prentice-Hall.

Morgan, G. (1986) *Images of Organization*, London: Sage.

Morgan, O. (1999) 'Interference on the line', *The Observer*, 28 November: 4.

Mueller, F., Purcell, J. (1992) 'The Europeanization of manufacturing and the decentralisation of bargaining: multi-national management strategies in the European automobile industry', *International Journal of Human Resource Management*, May, 3: 15–34.

Müller-Jentsch, W. (1995) 'Germany: from collective voice to co-management', in Rogers, J., Streeck, W. (eds) *Works Councils: Consultation, Representation, and Co-operation in Industrial Relations*, London: University of Chicago Press.

Nader, R., Wallach, L. (1996) 'GATT, NAFTA, and the subversion of the democratic process', in Mander, J., Goldsmith, E. (eds) *The Case Against the Global Economy*, San Francisco: Sierra Club Books.

Nickel, S. (1997) 'Unemployment and labour market rigidities: Europe versus North America', *Journal of Economic Perspectives*, 11, 3: 55–74.

Northrup, H., Rowan, R.L. (1979) *Multinational Collective Bargaining Attempts*, Philadelphia: University of Pennsylvania.

O'Reilly, J., Bothfeld, S. (1998) 'For better or worse? Part-time work in Britain and West Germany. A comparison of the German socio-economic panel and the British household panel', Work, Employment and Society Conference, University of Cambridge, 14–16 September.

Ouimet, W.G. (1991) 'The impact of organizational hypermodernity on managers' psychic equilibrium', paper given at the tenth Colloquium of the European Group for Organizational Studies, July, Vienna.

Overell, S. (1996) 'Row follows PepsiCo works council deal', *Personnel Management*, 12 September: 6.

Pankert, A. (1993) 'Adjustment problems of trade unions in selected industrialised market economy countries', *International Journal of Comparative Labour Law and Industrial Relations*, 9: 3–14.

Parker, T. (1992) *Russian Voices*, London: Macmillan.

Pilger, J. (1998) *Hidden Agendas*, London.

Pollack, W. (1995) 'Der Arbeitsstrich von Frankfurter Großmarkt', *Welt am Sonntag*, 2 April: 44.

Pollert, A. (1981) *Girls, Wives, Factory Lives*, London: Macmillan.

Poole, M. (1986) *Towards a New Industrial Democracy: Workers Participation in Industry*, London: Routledge.

Poole, M., Mansfield, R. (1992) 'Managers' attitudes to human resource management: rhetoric and reality', in Blyton P., Turnbull P. (eds) *Reassessing Human Resource Management*, London: Sage.

Prais, S.J. (1981) *Productivity and Industrial Structure: A Statistical Study of Manufacturing Industry in Britain, Germany and the USA*, Cambridge: Cambridge University Press.

Prechel, H. (1994) 'Economic crisis and the centralization of control over the managerial process: corporate restructuring and neo-Fordist decision-making', *American Sociological Review*, October, 59: 723–45.

Quiney, M. (1994) *An Introduction to GMB Organisation in Hotel and Catering*, London: General Municipal and Boiler Makers Union.

Rainnie, A. (1989) *Industrial Relations in the Small Firm: Small Isn't Beautiful*, London: Routledge.

Ramirez, A. (1990) 'In the orchid room...Big Macs', *The New York Times*, 30 October: 1-5.

Ramsay, H. (1980) 'Phantom participation: patterns of power and conflict', *Industrial Relations Journal*, 11, 3: 46–59.

Ramsay, H. (1983) 'An international participation cycle: variations on a recurring theme', in Clegg, S. *et al.* (eds) *The State; Class and the Recession*, London: Routledge and Kegan Paul.

Ramsay, H. (1991) 'The community, the multinational, its workers and their charter: a modern tale of industrial democracy?' *Work, Employment and Society*, 5: 541–66.

Ramsay, H. (1997) 'Fool's gold? European works councils and workplace democracy', *Industrial Relations Journal*, 28, 4: 314–22.

Rawls, J. (1971) *A Theory of Justice*, New York: ILR Press.

Regalia, I. (1995) 'Italy: the costs and benefits of informality', in Rogers, J., Streeck, W. (eds) *Works Councils: Consultation, Representation, and Co-operation in Industrial Relations*, London: University of Chicago Press.

Regalia, I., Regini, M. (1998) 'Italy: the dual character of industrial relations', in Ferner, A., Hyman, R. (eds) *Changing Industrial Relations in Europe*, Oxford: Basil Blackwell.

Rehfeldt, U. (1995) 'Die Europäischen Betriebsräte – Bilanz der französischen Initiativen', in Lecher, W., Platzer, H.W. (eds) *Europäische Union – Europäische Arbeitsbeziehungen?*, Cologne: Bund-Verlag.

Reiter, E. (1996) *Making Fast Food: From the Frying Pan into the Fryer*, Montreal and Kingston: McGill-Queens University Press.

Ritzer, G. (1993) *The McDonaldization of Society*, California: Sage.

Rivest, C. (1996) 'Voluntary European Works Councils', *European Journal of Industrial Relations*, 2: 235–53.

Robb, D.J. (1998) 'NLRB gets union cards from Macedonia McDonald's workers', *The Plain Dealer*, 2 June: 1B.

Robb, D.J. (1999) 'McDonald's strikers settle beef', *The Plain Dealer*, 10 February: 1B.

Robertson, R. (1990) 'Mapping the global condition: globalization as the central concept', in Featherstone, M. (ed.) *Global Culture: Nationalism, Globalization and Modernity*, London: Sage.

Robertson, R. (1992) *Globalization*, London: Sage.

Rothwell, S. (1995) 'Human resource planning', in Storey, J. (ed.) *Human Resource Management: A Critical Text*, London: Routledge.

Royle, T. (1997) 'Globalisation, convergence and the McDonald's Corporation: industrial relations and the multinational enterprise in Germany and the UK, a comparative study'. Unpublished PhD Thesis, April, The Nottingham Trent University.

Royle, T. (1998) 'Avoidance strategies and the German system of co-determination', *The International Journal of Human Resource Management*, December, 9: 1026–47.

Royle, T. (1999a) 'The reluctant bargainers? McDonald's, unions and pay determination in Germany and the UK', *Industrial Relations Journal*, June, 30: 135–50.

Royle, T. (1999b) 'Where's the beef? McDonald's and the European Works Council', *European Journal of Industrial Relations*, November, 5: 327–47.

Royle, T. (1999c) 'Recruiting the acquiescent workforce: a comparative analysis of McDonald's in Germany and the UK', *Employee Relations*, November, 21: 540–55.

Royle, T. (2001) 'Workplace representation under threat? The McDonald's Corporation and the effectiveness of legislatively underpinned works councils in seven European Union countries', *Comparative Labor Law and Policy Journal*, January (forthcoming).

Rubin, P.H., (1978) 'The theory of the firm and the structure of the franchise contract', *Journal of Law and Economics*, 21: 223–35.

Sadowski, D., Backes-Gellner, U., Frick, B. (1995) 'Works Councils: barriers or boosts for the competitiveness of German firms?', *British Journal of Industrial Relations*, 33: 493–513.

Sage, A. (1994) 'France puts bite on Big Mac', *The Observer*, 10 July: 16.

Salamon, M. (1998) *Industrial Relations: Theory and Practice*, Hemel Hempstead: Prentice Hall.

Sathe, V. (1983) 'Implications of corporate culture: a managers' guide to action', *Organizational Dynamics*, Autumn: 5–23.

Sauga, M., Student, D., Weidenfeld, U. (1996) 'Längst auf dem Weg', *Wirtschaftswoche*, 20, 9 May: 16–18.

Schein, E.H. (1984) 'Coming to a new awareness of organisational culture', *Sloan Management Review*, Winter: 3–16.

Scheuer, S. (1998) 'Denmark: a less regulated model', in Ferner, A., Hyman, R. (eds) *Changing Industrial Relations in Europe*, Oxford: Basil Blackwell.

Schneider, S.C. (1988) 'National vs. corporate culture: implications for human resource management', *Human Resource Management*, 27, 8: 231–46.

Schuler, R., Jackson, S. (1987) 'Linking competitive strategies with human resource management practices', *Academy of Management Executive*, 1: 207–19.

Schulten, T. (1996) 'European Works Councils: prospects for a new system of European industrial relations', *European Journal of Industrial Relations*, 2: 303–24.

Shelton, J.P. (1967) 'Allocative efficiency vs X-efficiency: comment', *American Economic Review*, December, l.57, 5: 1252–8.

Sisson, K. (1993) 'In search of HRM', *British Journal of Industrial Relations*, 31: 201–10.

Sklair, L. (1995) *Sociology of the Global System, Social Change in Global Perspective*, Hemel Hempstead: Harvester Wheatsheaf.

Smircich, L. (1983) 'Concepts of culture and organisational analysis', *Administrative Science Quarterly*, 28: 339–58.

Sodan, H. (1998) 'Die Neuregelung der 620-DM-Jobs ist mit der Verfassung unvereinbar', *Handelsblatt*, 1 December: 1.

Sparrow, P., Schuler, R., Jackson, S. (1994) 'Convergence or divergence: human resource practices and policies for competitive advantage worldwide', *International Journal of Human Resource Management*, May, 5: 268–99.

Statistisches Bundesamt (1994) *Statistisches Bundesamt*, Bonn: Jahresbericht.

Stern (1999) 'Abgebraten bis die Kasse stimmt', *Stern*, 4 November, 45: 115–28.

Streeck, W. (1984) 'Co-determination: the fourth decade' in Wilpert B., Sorge A. *International Perspectives on Organisational Democracy*, Chichester: John Wiley.

Streeck, W. (1991) 'More uncertainties: German unions facing 1992', *Industrial Relations*, 30: 317–49.

Streeck, W. (1992) 'National diversity, regime competition and institutional deadlock: problems in forming a European industrial relations system', *Journal of Public Policy*, 12, 4: 301–30.

Streeck, W. (1994) 'European social policy after Maastricht: the social dialogue and subsidiarity', *Economic and Industrial Democracy*, 15: 151–77.

Streeck, W. (1995) 'Works councils in Western Europe: from consultation to participation', in Rogers, J., Streeck, W. (eds) *Works Councils: Consultation, Representation and Co-operation in Industrial Relations*, London: University of Chicago Press.

Streeck, W. (1997) 'German capitalism: does it exist? Can it survive?' *New Political Economy*, 4: 251–83.

Streeck, W., Vitols, S. (1995) Europe: between mandatory consultation and voluntary information', in Rogers, J., Streeck, W. (eds) *Works Councils: Consultation, Representation and Co-operation in Industrial Relations*, London: University of Chicago Press.

SVR (Sachverständigenrat) (1994) 'Sachverständigenrat zur Begutachtung der gesamtwirtschaftlichen Entwicklung, Jahresgutachten 1993/94', *Bundestagsdrucksache*, 11/8472, Bonn.

Taylor, I., Walton, P. (1971) 'Industrial sabotage: motives and meanings', in Cohen, S. (ed.) *Images of Deviance*, Harmondsworth: Penguin.

Tchobanian, R. (1995) 'France from conflict to social dialogue?', in Rogers, J., Streeck, W. (eds) *Works Councils: Consultation, Representation and Co-operation in Industrial Relations*, London: University of Chicago Press.

Teague, P. (1993) 'Co-ordination or decentralization? EC social policy and European industrial relations', in Lodge, J. (ed.) *The European Community and the Challenge of the Future*, London: Pinter.

Terry, M. (1994) 'Workplace unionism: redefining structures and objectives', in Hyman, R., Ferner, A. (eds) *New Frontiers in European Industrial Relations*, Oxford: Blackwell.

TICL (Transnational Information Centre London) (1987) *McDonald's: From Local Store to Transnational*, London: Calverts Press.

Towers, B. (1997) *The Representation Gap: Change and Reform in the British and American Workplace*, Oxford: Oxford University Press.

Towers, B. (1999a) *Developing Recognition and Representation in the UK: How Useful is the US model?* London: Institute of Employment Rights.

Towers, B. (1999b) 'Editorial: "...the most lightly regulated labour market..." the UK's third statutory recognition procedure', *Industrial Relations Journal*, June, 30, 2: 82–95.

Traxler, F. (1991) 'Gewerkschaften und Arbeitgeberverbände: Probleme der Verbandsbildung und Interessenvereinheitlichung', in Müller-Jentsch, W. (ed.) *Konfliktpartnerschaft*, München: Rainer-Hampp Verlag.

Traxler, F. (1998) 'Austria: still the country of corporatism', in Ferner, A., Hyman, R. (eds) *Changing Industrial Relations in Europe*, Oxford: Basil Blackwell.

Turnbull, P. (1988) 'The economic theory of trade union behaviour: a critique', *British Journal of Industrial Relations*, 26: 99–118.

UBS (Union Bank of Switzerland) (1997) *Prices and Earnings Around the Globe*, Zurich: Economic Research Department, Union Bank of Switzerland.

UNCTAD (United Nations Conference on Trade and Development) (1994) 'Transnational corporations, employment and the workplace', in *World Investment Report*, New York: UN.

Utchitelle, L. (1992) 'Coming soon: the all-Russian Big Mac', *International Herald Tribune*, 28 February: 7.

Vallely, P. (1995) 'The Big Mac', *The Independent*, 10 June: 18.

Van der Pijl, K. (1989) 'The international level' in Bottomore T., Brym R.J. *The Capitalist Class*, Hemel Hempstead: Harvester Wheatsheaf.

Van Maanen, J., Kunda, G. (1989) 'Real feelings: emotional expression and organisational culture', Cummings, L.L., Staw, B.M. (eds) *Research in Organisational Behaviour*, Greenwich, CT: JAI Press.

Vidal, J. (1997) *McLibel: Burger Culture on Trial*, London: Macmillan.

Vikhanski, O., Puffer, S. (1993) 'Management education and employee training at Moscow McDonald's', *European Management Journal*, March, 11: 102–7.

Visser, J. (1995) 'The Netherlands: from paternalism to representation', in Rogers, J., Streeck, W. (eds) *Works Councils: Consultation, Representation and Co-operation in Industrial Relations*, London: University of Chicago Press.

Visser, J. (1998a) 'European trade unions in the mid-1990s', in Towers, B., Terry, M. (eds) *Industrial Relations Journal: European Annual Review 1997*, Oxford: Blackwell.

Visser, J. (1998b) 'The Netherlands: the return of responsive corporatism', in Ferner, A., Hyman, R. (eds) *Changing Industrial Relations in Europe*, Oxford: Basil Blackwell.

Wall, T.D., Lischerson, J.A. (1977) *Worker Participation: A Critique of the Literature and Some Fresh Evidence*, Maidenhead: McGraw-Hill

Wallerstein, I. (1990) 'Culture as the ideological battleground of the modern world-system', in Featherstone, M. (ed.) *Global Culture*, London: Sage.

Walraff, G. (1985) *Ganz Unten*, London: Methuen & Co.

Waters, M. (1995) *Globalisation*, London: Routledge.

Watson, T.J. (1994) 'Managing, crafting and researching: words, skill and imagination in shaping management research', *British Journal of Management*, Special issue, June, 5: 77–87.

Wax, R. (1971) *Doing Fieldwork: Warnings and Advice*, Chicago: University of Chicago Press.

Weber, M. (1968) *Economy and Society*, New York: Bedminster Press.

Wever, K. (1997) 'Renegotiating the German model: labour management relations in the new Germany', in Turner, L. (ed.) *Negotiating the New Germany: Can Social Partnership Survive?* New York: Cornell University Press.

Wheeler, H.N., McClendon, J.A. (1998) 'Employment relations in the United States', in Bamber, G.J., Lansbury, R.D. (eds) *International and Comparative Employment Relations*, London: Sage.

Whitley, R.D. (1991) 'The societal construction of business systems in East Asia', *Organization Studies*, 12: 1–28.

Whitley, R., Kristensen, P.H. (eds) (1996) *The Changing European Firm: Limits to Convergence*, London: Sage.

Wildavsky, B. (1989) 'McJobs: inside America's largest youth training program', *Policy Review*, 49: 30–7.

Williamson, O.E. (1985) *The Economic Institutions of Capitalism*, New York: The Free Press.

Willmott H. (1993) 'Strength is ignorance; slavery is freedom: managing culture in modern organisations', *Journal of Management Studies*, 30: 515–52.

Wilson, G.K. (1990) 'Corporate political strategies', *British Journal of Political Science*, 20: 281–8.

Winfield, I. (1994) 'Toyota UK Ltd: model HRM practices?', *Employee Relations*, 16: 41–53.

Wintrob, R.M. (1969) 'An inward focus: a consideration of psychological stress in fieldwork', in Henry, F., Saberwal, S. (eds) *Stress and Response in Fieldwork*, New York: Holt, Rinehart and Winston.

Wright, E.O. (1976) *Class, Crisis and the State*, London: New Left Books.

Index